Web Services Business Strategies and Architectures

Kapil Apshankar

Henry Chang

Mike Clark

Eduardo B. Fernandez

Peter Fletcher

Whitney Hankison

J. Jeffrey Hanson

Romin Irani

Kunal Mittal

Judith M. Myerson

David O'Riordan

Dimple Sadhwani

Gunjan Samtani

Bilal Siddiqui

Jørgen Thelin

Mark Waterhouse

Chanoch Wiggers

Liang-Jie Zhang

Expert **Press**

Web Services Business Strategies and Architectures

© 2002 Expert Press

EXPERT

Published by Expert Press Ltd,
Arden House, 1102 Warwick Road, Acocks Green,
Birmingham, B27 6BH, UK
Printed in the United States
ISBN 1904284132

Trademark Acknowledgements

Expert Press has endeavored to provide trademark information about all the companies and products mentioned in this book by the appropriate use of capitals. However, Expert Press cannot guarantee the accuracy of this information.

Credits

Editors
Peter Fletcher
Mark Waterhouse

Contributing Authors
Kapil Apshankar
Mike Clark
Henry Chang
Eduardo B. Fernandez
Peter Fletcher
Whitney Hankison
J. Jeffrey Hanson
Romin Irani
Kunal Mittal
Judith M. Myerson
David O'Riordan
Dimple Sadhwani
Gunjan Samtani
Bilal Siddiqui
Jørgen Thelin
Mark Waterhouse
Chanoch Wiggers
Liang-Jie Zhang

Assistant Editors
Kristin Pålsson
James Hart
Dan Robotham

Principal Reviewer
Mark Horner

Technical Reviewers
Kapil Apshankar
Mike Clark
Romin Irani
Andrew Krowczk
Saurabh Nandu
Chanoch Wiggers

Production Coordinators
Rachel Taylor
Pip Wonson

Index
Bill Johncocks

Illustrations
Rachel Taylor
Pip Wonson

Production Assistant
Helen Pickering

Proof Reader
Agnes Wiggers

Cover
Dawn Chellingworth

The image used on the cover is a design for the Business Promotion Centre, Duisburg, Germany. Used with the permission of Foster and Partners Architects.

About the Authors

Kapil Apshankar

Kapil has three years experience in knowledge management, i18n, L10n, and manufacturing domains. He works as a team leader for a major software corporation in India. Currently he is working with Web Services in all their forms to devise ways and means to take this nascent technology to its limits.

His other interests include Linux, networking, and distributed computing. When not dabbling with his computer, he can be seen playing the harmonica or drawing pencil portraits. Kapil can be reached at kapilapshankar@yahoo.co.in.

Mike Clark

Mike is currently working solely on Research and Development around Web Services and ASP.NET technology. He is solely responsible for www.salcentral.com, the world's first Web Services brokerage along with www.webservicebuy.com, www.uddiregistrar.com and a suite of Web Services available at www.soapengine.com. All his spare time is taken up with his wife and two kids, though it's seldom enough to stop the feeling of guilt for the time spent "playing in the attic" as the kids call it.

You can contact Mike Clark at mikec@lucin.com.

Henry Chang

Dr. Henry Chang is a research manager of B2B service infrastructure in the IBM Watson Research Center. He has developed IBM's B2B extranet web portal. He is now leading research in the areas of web business services integration, business process solution management, and on-demand e-utility hosting infrastructure.

Eduardo B. Fernandez

Eduardo B. Fernandez (Eduardo Fernandez-Buglioni) is a professor in the Department of Computer Science and Engineering at Florida Atlantic University in Boca Raton, Florida. He has published numerous papers on authorization models, object-oriented analysis and design, and fault-tolerant systems. He has written three books on these subjects. He has lectured all over the world at both academic and industrial meetings. He has created and taught several graduate and undergraduate courses and industrial tutorials. His current interests include object-oriented design and Internet security. He holds a MS degree in Electrical Engineering from Purdue University and a Ph.D. in Computer Science from UCLA. He is a Senior Member of the IEEE, and a Member of ACM. He is an active consultant for industry, including assignments with IBM, Allied Signal, Motorola, Harris, Lucent, and others. More details can be found at http://www.cse.fau.edu/~ed.

Peter Fletcher

Peter Fletcher is Managing Editor of Web Services Architect
(http://www.webservicesarchitect.com/). Previously he developed web-based applications for
the publishing group Peer Information, including content management and e-commerce
systems. He holds a Masters degree in Cognitive Science.

Whitney Hankison

Whitney is a Systems Analyst with the County of Santa Barbara, California, USA. She has co-
authored *Professional Windows DNA*, and *Professional VB .NET 1st* and *2nd editions* with Wrox
Press. She can be reached at whankison@earthlink.net.

J. Jeffrey Hanson

Jeff Hanson has more than 18 years of experience in the software industry, including working
as Senior Engineer for the Windows OpenDoc port and Lead Architect for the Route 66
framework at Novell. He is currently Chief Architect for Zareus, Inc., which specializes in
providing Web Service frameworks and platforms for J2EE-based installations. Jeff has also
authored numerous articles.

Romin Irani

Romin Irani is a Senior Software Engineer at InSync Information Systems, Inc. in Fremont,
California. His primary job focus is on utilizing Web Services Technologies to help ease
Enterprise Application Integration (EAI). Prior to that, he was the team leader on a J2EE-
based eProcurement Marketplace. Romin has 7 years of professional experience with the last
4 years completely focused around J2EE. Romin has contributed several articles in the field of
Web Services and has been a co-author of the following books: *AXIS: The Next Generation of
Java SOAP, Professional Java Web Services* , and *Beginning JSP Web Development*, all published by
Wrox Press.

Kunal Mittal

Kunal Mittal (kunal@kunalmittal.com) is a Technical Architect at Infosys Ltd, Pune, India
specializing in Service Based Architectures using Java-based Web Services. Kunal would like
to thank Doron Sherman, CTO, Collaxa and Dave Shaffer, Principal Consultant, Collaxa for
their contributions to the case study presented in this paper (http://www.collaxa.com/).

Judith M. Myerson

Judith M. Myerson is a Systems Engineer/Architect with a Master's Degree in Engineering. A noted columnist and writer with over 150 articles/reports published, she is the editor of *Enterprise Systems Integration, 2nd Edition*, and the author of *The Complete Book of Middleware*, and articles in *New Directions in Internet Management* – all by Auerbach Publishers. In addition to Web Services, her area of interest covers enterprise-wide systems, databases, enabling technologies, application development, network management, distributed systems, component-based technologies, and project management among others. She can be reached at jmyerson@bellatlantic.net.

David O'Riordan

David O'Riordan (dave@bindsys.com) is co-founder and Chief Architect at Bind Systems (http://www.bindsys.com/) who provide business process software products based on Web Services standards. He has 15 years experience of designing enterprise software systems at companies such as Siemens and IONA Technologies. Before founding Bind Systems in 2000, he was the product architect of the Java CORBA product line at IONA Technologies.

Dimple Sadhwani

Dimple Sadhwani is Senior Software Engineer at Island ECN based in New York. She has many years of experience working for financial and telecommunication companies on large-scale trading systems, CRM applications, Internet/Intranet portals, and client/server applications. She is co-author of the book *B2B Integration – A practical guide to collaborative e-commerce*, Imperial College Press. She has also authored several articles in the field of Web Services. Her e-mail address is dsadhwani@island.com.

Gunjan Samtani

Gunjan Samtani is Divisional Vice President, Information Technology at UBS PaineWebber, one of the world's leading financial services firms. He has several years of experience in the management, design, architecture, and implementation of large-scale EAI and B2B integration projects. He is the primary author of *B2B Integration – A practical guide to collaborative e-commerce*, Imperial College Press. He has presented research papers at several national and international conferences and is the author of more than 100 articles and research publications in the field of finance and technology. His e-mail address is gsamtani@ubspw.com.

Bilal Siddiqui

Bilal Siddiqui is an Electronics Engineer, an XML consultant, and the co-founder of WaxSys, a company focused on simplifying e-Business. After graduating in Electronics Engineering from the University of Engineering and Technology, Lahore, in 1995, he began designing software solutions for industrial control systems. Later he turned to XML and used his experience programming in C++ to build Web- and WAP-based XML processing tools, server-side parsing solutions, and service applications. He is a technology evangelist and a frequently published technical author.

Jørgen Thelin

Jørgen Thelin is the Chief Architect at Cape Clear Software Inc. where he is responsible for the overall technical direction of the company's flagship CapeConnect Web Services Integration Platform product. Previously, he has worked on the development of a number of middleware products and major line-of-business software projects for blue-chip companies such as ICL, Reuters, J.P.Morgan, and BSkyB before joining Orbware to develop an enterprise server middleware product. He holds a Computing Science Honours degree from Stirling University, Scotland, and an MBA from Warwick Business School, England. He has been using the Java programming language since early 1996, and is a Sun Certified Java Programmer, Developer, and Architect.

Mark Waterhouse

Mark Waterhouse has been a technical editor for a little over two years. Having initially worked for Wrox Press, he moved to Tect where since September 2001 he has edited the Web Services Architect web site (http://www.webservicesarchitect.com/) and associated papers. Before working, Mark was a volunteer advisor for the Citizen's Advice Bureau, and has studied Philosophy (BA) and Cognitive Science (MSc).

Chanoch Wiggers

Chanoch is a Software Developer at Kiwi Media Design having left Wrox Press from his position as Editor. In addition to having been the architect of *Professional Java SOAP* and *Professional Java Web Services*, he has written for a number of articles and books published by Wrox Press and the Web Services Architect web site. You can contact him at chanochwiggers@hotmail.com.

Liang-Jie Zhang

Dr. Liang-Jie Zhang is a Research Staff Member at IBM's T.J. Watson Research Center, where he has been actively working on B2B integration using Web Services. He is the lead author of Business Explorer for Web Services (BE4WS). His other research interests include Web Services-oriented business process outsourcing technologies and broadband-media commerce. He chaired the special session on Web Services at IC2002.

Table of Contents

Table of Contents

Table of Contents

Web Services Business Strategies and Architectures

What is this book about? It's about Web Services, it's about business strategies, and it's about architectures. This collection of papers aims to shed light on the impact of Web Services on an organization and its functional processes. Consequently, we do not become embroiled in a technical discussion of programming implementation details, instead taking an architectural view of the subject. If you need to know what Web Services are in more general terms, without seeing actual implementations – why and how they might have a role to play in your business – then this is the book for you. It is therefore aimed as much at IT managers and business decision makers as it is at systems architects and lead developers with an eye for the bigger picture.

What Are Web Services?

Not too long ago, a few XML-based standards for passing information over the Internet were brought together and began to be touted as the Next Big Thing. In a way, they are, although Web Services have undoubtedly received more than their fair share of hype. So, what's all the fuss about? The basic premise behind Web Services is that a piece of code is made available to remote machines, using specific protocols, over the Internet. The Service part of Web Services relates to the idea of providing access to functionality without having to download or install the code, and the Web part refers to the means through which the functionality is accessed.

The three component standards of Web Services are the Simple Object Access Protocol (SOAP), Universal Description, Discovery and Integration (UDDI), and Web Services Description Language (WSDL.)

SOAP provides the first piece of the puzzle: a means for one piece of code to communicate with another piece of code. The important thing about SOAP is that it enables communication across all languages (from Java to Visual Basic, say), and doesn't come in different versions for connecting different pairs of languages. The same SOAP message should work as well between Java and Visual Basic as it does between C++ and Perl. This language independence means that a Web Service implemented in one language can be accessed by several languages through one interface.

UDDI describes a registry in which Web Services can be advertised. The initial idea was that the details of a required Web Service would be discovered dynamically, shortly before it was to be used. Although technically possible, this remains an unlikely situation for a number of reasons, including the speed of the discovery process, the need for trust, and the quality of the data in the UDDI registry. What is more likely to happen is that a potential subscriber to a Web Service would find details of interesting Web Services in the UDDI registry, and then contact the providers of those services in a more conventional way before attempting to use any service. Once a relationship has been established between the subscriber and the provider, business would continue as normal.

WSDL is the XML-based format in which a publisher describes their Web Service. An entry in a UDDI registry would point to a WSDL file, which would supply important details about the service. These details would include the name of the service, any parameters that must be passed to it, and what form the response will take.

Do They Mean Business?

So much for the technology behind Web Services, but what is the business perspective? Web Services can be pictured as a relationship between a service provider and a service consumer, or publisher and subscriber. The service provided can be either functionality (all manner of calculations), or data access (providing a regulated view of any repository of data). The provider and consumer could well be within the same company, since Web Services potentially enable a rapid application development solution to integration problems. Alternatively, Web Services could be used to integrate systems between trusted partner companies.

Web Services are a way to drive down costs by reducing data and functionality duplication within an organization. Rather than having three departments running three different packages to do the same job because they're all using different systems, the functionality can be centralized and accessed as Web Services, regardless of the platform each department uses for its own needs. Web Services are also a way to drive up income, by allowing an organization to market their previously purely internal functionality to a wider audience. If part of your system does a good job of providing a certain type of valuable information in a timely manner, it could be a candidate for exposure as a Web Service so that it can be marketed as a service to other companies.

What Web Services Are Not

It is worth briefly noting what Web Services are not, as there is a tendency among some sources to get carried away and not look at the limitations.

First and foremost, Web Services are not a magic solution to all your IT problems (neither will they do your laundry). There is often a tendency for people to think that a new technology will solve their problem, when in fact they don't have the problem clearly defined in the first place. Web Services may not be appropriate for your situation, either now due to lack of maturity, or in the future because the nature of the problem is such that it can't be solved by what is essentially remote procedure calling, over Internet protocols.

Web Services are not a strategy in their own right, neither will they make a bad business model any better, nor even provide the answer to fast-tracking new business relationships. Web Services are a tool, to be employed as part of an overall strategy – a new technology shouldn't make you change your business strategy just because a few magazines and commentators say so. Web Services shouldn't be employed because they're the hot new thing, but instead because they're the right choice for your existing strategy. If your strategy or business model isn't very good, there's little chance that using Web Services will make it better – they might, but it's not guaranteed. Regardless of how fast and easy it is to find potential service providers, trust and reliability are still prime concerns that Web Services have yet to solve convincingly.

Web Services are not free. This may come as a surprise to some, but implementing Web Services will be like implementing any new technology. There will be costs at the start, both in time and money, but they will be less than for many new technology projects. The maintenance costs, however, should be less than for a similar project undertaken with other technologies.

Web Services are not an automatic marketplace-building tool. Although they can make such building easier, work still needs to be done.

Web Services are not an operating system, and they do not exist in a vacuum. Web Services need to work with other systems, and they don't do this without some effort. The effort is relatively small, but it must still be made.

Why Web Services Are Important

As we've seen, Web Services are many things to different people, and because of these varied applications they are important in several ways. There are three areas in which Web Services can become important to an organization, as follows:

- ❑ Financial Imperatives.
- ❑ Strategic Imperatives.
- ❑ Structural Imperatives.

Financial Imperatives

The importance of money is something that is not lost on most people, although we all wish we had more to spare. Web Services have the potential to free up money within an organization, by driving down integration costs, reducing expensive functionality duplication, and providing new revenue streams from existing functionality or data. At least, that's what people say, but how accurate is this rosy picture of Web Services, and how far away is its realization?

As with all new technologies, people make bold claims about Web Services in an effort to get them adopted more quickly. The hope is that reality will be brought into line with the vision, so that the vision is proved right. This means that for the early adopters of Web Services the results may not be as dramatic as the vision would claim. As implementations of the technology catch up with the vision, so will the cost reductions. Even so, Web Services are being adopted by large organizations, such as French institutional and corporate bank CDC (Caisse des Depots et Consignations, http://www.caissedesdepots.fr/). According to an article on Line56.com (http://www.line56.com/articles/default.asp?ArticleID=3702), CDC are an advanced client of Mercator (http://www.mercator.com/) for integration using Web Services. The reasons behind the need for integration are common amongst growing organizations, namely several business units using different systems.

Web Services are also being adopted to provide new revenue. Lloyds TSB Commercial Finance (http://www.ltsbcf.co.uk/) have exposed their credit rating facilities as Web Services, another move reported by Line56.com (http://www.line56.com/articles/default.asp?NewsID=3360). This Web Service, which replaces the old manually requested version, is largely made possible through use of Microsoft's BizTalk Server. As well as improving the number of requests they can handle (only exceptions are dealt with manually), the service is a product in its own right, and is frequently used by other divisions of the company.

Strategic Imperatives

As well as improving the financial position of an organization by reducing costs and increasing revenue, Web Services can have a beneficial impact on strategy. Web Services could provide smaller organizations with an affordable means to access functionality or data in a form more readily useable by their internal systems. This means that, as the costs involved would be less than those of attempting to acquire the same functionality using proprietary means, it is more reasonable for an organization to incorporate the functionality into its own systems. The reduction in costs, both financial and time, allows the company to focus on other issues.

On the other side of the coin, organizations publishing Web Services have an increased range of services they can sell, to an increased range of potential customers. By exposing the information in a standard manner, there is no restriction on the customer to use a particular system, allowing the publisher to sell to smaller organizations. As well as being able to sell more functionality to more people, Web Services provides a cheaper and more efficient distribution channel, increasing the attractiveness of the proposition.

Finally, because Web Services make it easier to subscribe to functionality provided by external agencies, outsourcing that functionality and data management to expert companies becomes much more viable for the smaller business. Having externally provided functionality and data management further allows the organization to focus on strategy.

Structural Imperatives

Hand in hand with reshaping strategy is realigning structure, and the adoption of Web Services may increase the desirability – if not the necessity – of restructuring. For example, if we consolidate financial reporting to a head-office-based Web Service, this may well imply the need for a reorganization of the company's finance departments. Since this restructuring could mean a reduction in staff, the system would become more efficient by giving the same results with fewer resources. This streamlining of departments, by centralizing functionality without reducing its accessibility, means that an organization can become leaner and more flexible through increased access to functionality and data.

Using Web Services to provide functionality from a central location would also allow work to become less location-dependent. If the principal functionality a worker depends on to do their job is accessible over the Internet, then the work can be carried out wherever the Internet can be accessed from (almost anywhere, these days). Equally, it means that the work can be consolidated into fewer locations, further streamlining the organization.

How Web Services Do All This

Web Services, if viewed from a certain angle, can seem like the solution to all our integration, outsourcing, restructuring, and financial problems. As we've already seen, they're good but not that good, although they can provide many benefits. The key question, that the papers collected here aim to answer is how?

Ranging from business issues to the more technology-based papers, this collection is not intended to be read in sequential order, hence the papers are not numbered. Despite this, the earlier papers tend to be more business-oriented than the later ones, which focus on the more obviously technology-based aspects of Web Services.

We begin with a look at the all-important **Return on Investment** (ROI). Here, Gunjan Samtani and Dimple Sadhwani examine how Web Services will provide a substantial ROI for most companies. The focus is on how to work out what the ROI will be for your company if you plan to use Web Services.

Next up, Mike Clark takes us through the things we need to know about Web Services if we're thinking about **selling** them to other people. Equally, the information is useful if you're thinking about buying Web Services – pointers to what to look for in a company proposing Web Services.

The next three papers form a small trilogy with each one focused a different aspect of integration. Gunjan Samtani and Dimple Sadhwani take time to acquaint us with **Enterprise Application Integration** (EAI), **Business-to-Business Integration** (B2Bi), and **Integration Brokers**. In each instance, we examine how Web Services can make the task easier and cheaper. These three papers form the key to understanding how Web Services can improve the financial situation of a company, become strategically important, and allow structural freedom not previously available.

One of the other mainstays of enterprise computing is **Enterprise Resource Planning** (ERP). Kapil Apshankar discusses ERP and how Web Services can be used to streamline the processes involved, and looks at how some of the major ERP software vendors are moving towards Web Services-enabled applications.

Another important use for computers in the enterprise is the automation of logistics processes. Liang-Jie Zhang and Henry Chang present the outlines of an **E-Logistics Process Integration Framework**, explaining how Web Services can be used to increase speed and efficiency.

Another integration-based application for Web Services, specifically UDDI, is that of an **Electronic Marketplace**. Bilal Siddiqui takes us through using UDDI and WSDL to streamline the operations of an electronic marketplace beyond the benefits already provided by these portals.

It isn't just business in general that can benefit from Web Services, as Kunal Mittal shows with a look at Web Services and the **Real Estate** industry. Although aimed at a specific vertical industry, the lessons to be learned from this paper can easily be extrapolated to similar areas.

As a herald of things to come later in the collection, David O'Riordan looks at emerging **Business Process Standards** for Web Services. Without an efficient way of organizing workflow, important business processes could easily occur out of sequence. Fortunately, there are supporting proposed standards that will provide much-needed control of workflow if Web Services are to become serious candidates for application provision.

Web Services are an ideal candidate for helping to introduce new systems and processes, as is the case with **Straight Through Processing** (STP). Gunjan Samtani and Dimple Sadhwani examine the impact that STP promises to have on the financial services industry, focusing on how Web Services could be used to introduce this important concept.

Although the majority of Web Services discussed in the papers are influenced by two principal parties (the publisher and the subscriber), there is always room for a middleman. Mike Clark and Romin Irani look at the opportunities that Web Services provide for the existence of such **Intermediaries**, how they would work and make money, and a closer examination of a particular type, the Web Services **Broker**.

Web Services (in the guise of WSDL, UDDI, and SOAP) are not the only XML-based standards that can make electronic business easier. Romin Irani presents an **Introduction to ebXML**, which includes an exploration of how Web Services can be combined with ebXML (and vice versa).

The final third of the collection is more oriented towards explaining the technologies and architectures involved in Web Services. Judith M. Myerson kicks this section off with a look at the leading **Web Services Architectures**, encompassing offerings from the principal vendors and commentators.

Even though Web Services are touted as platform-and language-neutral, they still need to be implemented somewhere, which brings us to one of the largest sources of contention – **.NET or J2EE?** J. Jeffrey Hanson compares the two leading competitors' offerings for implementing and invoking Web Services, with additional material from Chanoch Wiggers.

In a similar vein is Gunjan Samtani and Dimple Sadhwani's **Application Frameworks**. Like the previous paper, the focus is split between .NET and J2EE, although the view is from a higher level.

As with all computing, **Security** is one of the key issues in Web Services. Eduardo B. Fernandez provides us with a round-up of the state of play in Web Services Security, looking at what vendors are offering, as well as the benefits of different security options, and the reasons for different types of security.

On a similar topic, Whitney Hankison explains how **Network Security** can be enforced to help keep our Web Services safe. Having Web Services encrypted as they pass information across the Internet is all very well, but if your network isn't secure it may not be worth all that much.

The final paper in the collection, from Jørgen Thelin, looks at the relationship between Web Services and **Remote References**. The paper looks at how the two technologies address similar problems of distributed computing, and how they might work together.

Resources

Throughout the book you will find URL's for further references. Due to the length of some of these, and for your convenience, we have collected them together in one place on the Internet: http://www.webservicesarchitect.com/book.asp.

Authors: Gunjan Samtani and Dimple Sadhwani

- Return on Investment

- Cost and Expenses

- Benefits

- ROI Model and Formula

- Risk Management

Return On Investment (ROI) and Web Services

In this paper, we have tried to keep a realistic, pragmatic, and balanced approach in determining the return on investment on Web Services. It is worth mentioning that, no matter how promising a new technology is, promoting and encouraging its usage through such articles and papers is not justified until there is a solid business case for its adoption. It is fundamentally important for us to warn about the pitfalls as and where we foresee them, leaving the final decision up to the readers who range from senior management (technical and business), through business analysts and systems architects, to project managers, and software developers.

Defining Return On Investment (ROI)

There are several definitions of return on investment as far as IT is concerned, and its meaning may vary from company to company. We will, though, try to keep it simple by taking a baseline definition that is applicable to all technologies and companies.

Return on investment (ROI) is a key financial metric of the value of business investments and expenditures. It is a ratio of net benefits over costs expressed as a percentage. This formula can be expressed as:

> **ROI = [(Monetary Benefits (Tangible and Intangible) – Cost of using Web Services Technology) / Cost of using Web Services Technology] x 100**

An Example of ROI Calculation

As an example, the IT group within a company determines that there is a 10 percent increase in the automation of software development following the implementation of Web Services for an organization's IT project. Other data from the IT group reveals that each one percent increase in the automation of software development is equal to increased annual revenue of $25,000. Furthermore, it is known that the Web Services implementation will cost $75,000. For this example the ROI is calculated as follows:

[($250,000 – $75,00) / 75,000] x 100 = 233%

That's $25,000 for each one percent increase, for a total of $250,000 for a ten percent increase. This means that for every $1 invested in the Web Services implementation, the organization realized a net benefit of $2.33 in the form of increased revenue from the automation of software development.

ROI Analysis

There are two fundamental methodologies through which companies can conduct ROI analysis of a new technology such as Web Services. They are **discounted cash flow analysis** and **payback period analysis**. Before we look at both these methods, let's discuss some of the fundamental concepts behind them.

Direct and Indirect Measures

Both the direct, cash flow-generating contributions of a new technology or project, as well as the indirect measures valued by management should be considered when calculating the ROI.

Discount Rate or Weighted Average Cost of Capital (WACC)

The discount rate, also known as the weighted average cost of capital (WACC), is the opportunity cost of capital, which is the expected rate of return that could be obtained from other projects of similar risk.

Net Present Value (NPV)

Net present value is the difference between the cost of an investment and the return on an investment measured in today's dollars. In other words, NPV calculations account for money's time-value by discounting the future cash flow of the investment at some rate that varies with the risk of the investment. The NPV calculation determines the present value of the return and compares it to the initial investment. We calculate the present value as in the following formula:

Present Value = [Net Cash flow for Year 1 / (1 + discount rate)]+ [Net Cash Flow for Year 2 / (1 + discount rate)] * 2 +……. + [Net Cash flow for Year N / (1 + discount rate)] * N

We calculate the net present value as follows:

> **NPV = Initial Investment + Present Value**

For example, if Web Services technology costs $200,000 and will save (or generate return) of $50,000 per year for five years, there is a $50,000 net return on the investment. The NPV of the investment, however, is actually less than $50,000 due to the time-value of money.

Internal Rate of Return (IRR)

If there is an investment that requires and produces a number of cash flows over time, the internal rate of return is defined to be the discount rate that makes the net present value of those cash flows equal to zero. In other words, the discount rate that makes the project have a zero NPV is the IRR.

The IRR method of analyzing investment in a new technology or using a technology in a project allows a company to consider the time value of money. IRR enables you to find the interest rate that is equivalent to the dollar returns that are expected from the technology or project under consideration. Once a company knows the rate, it can compare it to the rates that it could earn by investing money in other technologies or projects or investments.

Payback Period

ROI is just a percentage, so include the payback time to make it persuasive. For example, if a $100,000 investment in Web Services technology is generating $400,000 a year in profit, it pays for itself within three months. Costs divided by monthly benefits yield the number of months to payback.

Discounted Cash Flow Analysis

In the discounted cash flow ROI analysis methodology, the expected cash flows relating to investments for a new technology or IT-related project spanning several years are discounted using an appropriate rate to determine an NPV and/or IRR. If the NPV is positive, then the project's present value exceeds its required cash outlay, and the project should be undertaken. When a project has a positive NPV, the NPV decreases as the discount rate used increases. Similarly, if the IRR is greater than the cost of capital for the company, then the project should be undertaken.

Payback Period Analysis

In the payback period ROI analysis methodology, the period of time it takes for a new technology or IT-related project to yield enough returns to pay for the initial investment, or to break even, is considered.

ROI Analysis Becoming a Necessity

Return on investment for technology projects, both new and existing, is no longer a single-dimensional function of operational cost reduction. It has to account for multi-dimensional functions related to operational costs, changes in business activities, growth, efficiency, and productivity.

ROI analysis is gradually becoming a core requirement for the kick-off of any new project or use of new technology, as well as for measuring the success or failure of any existing project. A good ROI analysis can lead a new project or introduction of any technology to lower costs, improved business performance, and competitive advantage.

ROI and Web Services

Web Services offer a platform-neutral approach for integrating internal and external applications, so that it can be used to integrate diverse systems, in a way supported by industry-wide standards rather than proprietary standards. The ability of a company to have real-time access to business information spanning several companies, in-house departments, applications, platforms, and systems is one of the most important driving factors behind the adoption of Web Services.

"What will be the return on investment?" is probably the first question that any company would consider before investing any resources. Just because it is a hot technology and has everyone talking about it, is certainly not a good enough reason. How much companies will have to invest in implementing this solution and what the payoff will be – both near-term and long-term – are natural questions that need to be answered.

There is little doubt that the first Web Service is the hardest to implement. The cost and difficulty level in business process re-engineering and integration can be high, although both these issues are typically small, and fade away with the implementation of subsequent Web Services. Companies can, thereafter, enjoy the fruits of incremental cost reduction inherent in using XML-based standards and service-oriented architectures.

A company should calculate the implementation and ongoing costs associated with Web Services including software, hardware, system integration, and future production support expenses. These cost estimates should be carefully examined to determine the ROI for the proposed solution.

ROI Not Just About Technology

Whatever the underlying technology for which ROI is being calculated, there is always a set of business and personnel factors that have a great impact on it. We cannot stress enough the fact that technology alone will not produce the quantifiable results and benefits as projected in any ROI matrix or calculation. Several business factors, such as the speed of rollout and systems adoption rate, play a critical role in determining the final numbers.

Calculating ROI of Web Services

Now that we have discussed the fundamentals of ROI and Web Services, it is worth discussing in detail the formulae and matrix for actually calculating the ROI for Web Services.

How do you measure the ROI of Web Services? Well, there is a right way and a wrong way to measure ROI. The wrong way is to measure the time representatives save in reduced paper work, or in revenue the company saves by reducing the need for data entry. The right way is to measure the amount of reduction in operational and developmental costs. The ROI on Web Services comes from the increased operational efficiency and reduced costs that are achieved by streamlining and automating business processes, reduced application development cycle time, and increased reusablility of applications in the form of services.

Building an ROI Model

To build a ROI model for Web Services, we have to consider the cost savings from using a service-oriented architecture built on open standards and the way these services impact the IT and business units, leading to potential tangible (direct) and intangible (indirect) benefits. The classification of direct and indirect benefits comes from how readily cost savings and revenue can be attributed to the usage of Web Services. Direct benefits include reduced costs, increased revenues, and more efficient and effective systems development, while indirect benefits include innovation, new product developments, and capital expenditures.

It is worth mentioning, however, that some of the benefits of Web Services extend beyond the confines of the proposed model. It is important to remember that the correct application of this depends a lot on the estimation and validation of data, as it will not exist previously. Measuring ROI for Web Services presents a big obstacle irrespective of the model, because the new processes they bring are an important benefit; because these processes are new, existing measurement tools may miss those benefits. This argument is compounded by the fact that benefits from multi-year technology implementations are inherently difficult to measure. We think will this be the case with Web Services, where the implementations affect different applications, systems, and business functions and processes within a company.

Finally, let us warn the readers that there is no one or single ROI model/matrix that is capable and sophisticated enough to produce credible numbers for Web Services within companies of all sizes. The main reasons for the lack of such a matrix are:

- ❑ The technology is too new and there are not many large-scale implementations that provide reasonable numbers and statistics.

- ❑ Such small Web Services implementations as are taking place are not standard within companies and each implementation is in a way unique. Uniqueness within each company, of course, will apply to each technology, but it is more an issue for Web Services, as the user base is relatively small.

- ❑ There is a lack of information, knowledge, and understanding about how Web Services really impact the business processes.

❑ The development tools and servers for Web Services are still evolving. It is thus too early in the life cycle of this technology to make any kind of prediction about a reliable ROI, as a lot would depend on whether companies would be able to use existing assets (such as integration brokers, application servers, and databases) for Web Services.

Factors to be Included in ROI Calculation

In this section, we will list the different factors that have to be considered while calculating ROI for Web Services. The relevance and importance of each of these factors will vary greatly from company to company, application to application, and implementation to implementation. If all these factors are considered together, however, you can get a pretty decent result from the ROI model used for Web Services. The factors we will look at are:

❑ Costs and expenses.

❑ Technical benefits.

❑ Business benefits.

Costs and Expenses

Here we examine the principal costs to be weighed in the ROI calculation.

1. Hardware Requirements

Find out the difference in hardware requirements in developing an application based on Web Services and your current architecture. Hardware costs make a large portion of the overall project cost. Explore whether using Web Services will allow you to reduce the new hardware required and squeeze the most value out of the existing and new hardware, by including the following parameters for the development, quality assurance, and production environments:

❑ Number of servers required.

❑ Configuration of the servers required.

❑ Estimated percentage increase or decrease in the performance of the existing hardware through the usage of Web Services-oriented architecture.

❑ Estimated cost reduction or increment.

Other parameters, such as man-hour savings for the administration of reduced hardware, or increase in man-hour expenses due to increased hardware requirements, should also be considered.

2. Software Requirements

It is critical to determine the Web Services solution that meets your Web Services usage goals. Software costs will probably be one of the biggest expenses. This expense, however, can be significantly lowered if existing assets in the form of application servers and integration brokers are used for Web Services as well. Determine the following:

- ❏ The support for Web Services by your existing application servers and integration brokers, and whether other software is needed to support your Web Services strategy.

- ❏ The cost of upgrading your current software.

- ❏ The cost of bringing in new software.

- ❏ Any associated additional operational costs.

3. Training Requirements

Training your IT staff on Web Services technology is going to be a big investment. In tough economic times, all companies like to cut on this cost as much as possible. It should be realized, however, that the incorrect usage and implementation of a new technology, due to lack of proper training, might turn out to be more expensive in the long run. Account for the following in your ROI calculation:

- ❏ The total cost of training developers, architects, project managers, and system and network administrators on Web Services technology and supporting tools and servers.

4. Network Bandwidth Requirements

The use of XML-based standards in Web Services implies that the data is exchanged using XML messages. XML messages can be very large (in some cases five to ten times the size of their corresponding EDI and SWIFT messages) making it much slower than EDI and SWIFT. Such a large flow of data over the intranet or Internet uses up a lot of network bandwidth and slows down the whole process. Thus, there may be a need to overhaul both the internal and external network bandwidth for using Web Services. So, calculate the investment for the following:

- ❏ Estimate the load that Web Services put on your network bandwidth.

- ❏ Calculate the investment that will be required to meet the additional network bandwidth requirement.

- ❏ Determine the maintenance and ongoing operational expenses for the same.

5. Monitoring Tools

Using Web Services, especially external services, requires trust. You cannot afford not to monitor the performance of Web Services, because if they slow down (or worse, break) your applications, you would want to know immediately. There will be a need for your company to invest in monitoring tools that can check the quality, design time, and, most importantly, run-time performance and health of your Web Services, and application as a whole. This is most true in a business-to-business situation, where service-level agreements have to be adhered to. It is likely that monitoring and administrative tools will be provided by the Web Services solution, but if they are not you will need to determine the following:

- ❏ The investment that will be required to buy and maintain additional monitoring tools.

6. Operational Costs and Vendor Consulting

In any software project there will be several operational tasks, processes, and associated expenses, and Web Services-based projects are no different. Furthermore, there may be a need to bring in external vendors or consultants at different points or throughout the software development cycle. Account for the following in your ROI calculation for Web Services:

- ❑ Web Services-related software products installation, administration, and configuration expenses.
- ❑ Estimate the cost of external vendors or consultants throughout the project.

Technical Benefits

Here we look at the principal technical benefits to be considered for the ROI calculation.

7. Software Development Automation

We are a long way short of the point where applications will purely be orchestrations of Web Services. Nevertheless we should still find out if the use of Web Services within a given project would help you to achieve software development automation. This automation may well expand to other projects as well; a Web Service developed for one project might be usable as a plug-and-play architecture for other projects. Analyze how much your company will save in the development life cycles, using the following parameters:

- ❑ Estimated number of applications/systems that can reuse Web Services.
- ❑ Total saving software development in terms of man-hour effort through the usage of Web Services.
- ❑ Estimated saving in terms of productivity.

8. Streamlining of Middleware Technology

There is no question that, once Web Services technology matures, it will help in streamlining the now widely diverse middleware technology existing within companies of all sizes. We envision that this factor would probably be one of, if not the easiest to measure as a part of the ROI calculation on using Web Services. Use the following parameters:

- ❑ Estimate the reduction in hardware expenses.
- ❑ Repeat the same calculation for software-related expenses.
- ❑ Finally, do the same calculation for personnel-related expenses resulting out of streamlined middleware technology.

9 Usage of Standards-Based Integration

Every company – irrespective of size or sector – builds and maintains several proprietary interfaces to integrate internal and external systems. The addition of each new system to the puzzle results in a Cartesian product of new interfaces to be built, tested, and deployed. A change in any underlying system requires a coordinated change in all the interfaces, making the whole process very complex, tedious, time-consuming, and expensive. Measure the following parameters:

❑ Estimate the total number of proprietary interfaces that you will avoid building, deploying, and maintaining if you use Web Services.

❑ Determine the savings in terms of man-hours, hardware, and software through the use of standards-based interfaces.

10. Integration with Applications and Business Process Management

XML-based Web Services are an ideal technology for integrating diverse applications and systems as they allow applications to communicate across the Internet in a platform- and language-independent fashion. Furthermore, Web Services help in the clear separation of business process logic and the participating business services, thereby making the development, execution, and management of these services much easier. Measure the following parameters:

❑ Estimate the total savings resulting through using a platform-neutral application integration technology.

❑ Determine the savings in terms of automating and orchestrating business processes as Web Services.

11. End of Duplication of Software Code Leading To Reusability

In any organization, it is easy to find duplication of groups within the IT department. There is often little interaction between these groups, leading to the development and maintenance of duplicate code and applications. The existence of these silos significantly increases the operational costs of the IT department. Although technologies such as CORBA, DCOM, and J2EE Connector Architecture do try to bridge the gap between the disparate systems within a company, they fall short of giving the ability to expose the systems in a standard consistent way. This does not mean that Web Services will eliminate the technologies mentioned above. In fact, Web Services will work hand-in-hand with existing technologies in helping companies eliminate the duplication of groups and systems. Measure the following parameters as part of the whole ROI calculation:

❑ Estimate the total number of groups and the systems they manage that are working in silos.

❑ Analyze how many of these systems and applications are redundant and overlap each other.

❑ Calculate the savings (hardware-, software,- and personnel-related) that would result from eliminating the redundancy.

❑ Calculate the savings (hardware- software-, and personnel-related) that would result if the remaining useful systems can be exposed in a standard way. Keep in mind that the information of all the exposed interfaces can be published to a central repository, so that all the groups within the IT department can find and use them.

Business Benefits

Here we examine the business benefits to be taken account of in calculating the ROI for Web Services.

12. End-User Productivity

There is no direct formula for calculating increase or decrease in end-user productivity. Try instead to measure factors such as the reduction in the amount of human intervention required by building applications using Web Services, the overall improvements in response time, and the availability and usability of Web Services-based applications when they are deployed to the end-users. Use the following parameters:

- ❑ Estimate the number of end users using the applications in consideration.
- ❑ Determine the percentage productivity increase in their performance.
- ❑ Extrapolate that to the total cost savings through the usage of user-oriented Web Services.

13. Participation in Dynamic Business

One of the promises of Web Services technology is the ability it provides to participate in dynamic business relationships. Since the discovery, binding, invocation, and communication of Web Services are standards-based, companies can conduct business in a real-time mode rather than the traditional static mode. To measure the increase in profitability due to dynamic business participation, you will have to record and sample the data for some days – even weeks – before a reasonably correct forecast can be reached. Use the following parameters:

- ❑ Estimate the number of new business relationships.
- ❑ Determine the percentage increase in your business revenues due to new, dynamic business relationships resulting from using Web Services.

14. Collaborative Business Activities

Collaborative commerce, also known as c-commerce, allows Internet-enabled companies to share intellectual capital and exploit the core competencies of their trading partners. It promises to deliver significant increases in corporate innovation, productivity, and profitability, as well as create new opportunities for dynamic B2B collaboration over the Internet. Collaborative commerce is enabled by B2B integration which leads to shared databases, open tracking systems, enhanced inter-enterprise visibility and cooperation, streamlined business processes, new cost efficiencies, and an expanded customer base for every collaborative partner. All this results in a competitive advantage that traditional business models simply cannot duplicate. Web Services have the ability to bring reality to the vision of collaborative commerce. Measure the following parameters as part of the whole ROI calculation:

- Quantitatively calculate the cost efficiency resulting through Web Services-enabled collaborative commerce.

- Measure the cost savings as a result of increased inter-enterprise visibility in the whole supply chain.

- Finally, project the revenue and expenses incurred in new product development through collaboration among companies of the same sector using Web Services-enabled technology.

15. Better and Cheaper Customer Service

Web Services can play a major role in customizing a range of product packages suited for each customer's specifications and making it cheaper and faster to deliver. This can be achieved by assembling Web Services targeted for each product, and bundling them together. Of course the assumption here is that there will be servers and tools available that will make this orchestration of Web Services possible. Measure the following benefits of faster customer service:

- The increased revenue generated through targeting the marketing of products and services for each customer.

- Measure the cost savings as a result of automated customer services done using Web Services technology.

16. Other Benefits

There may be other direct and indirect benefits for the usage of Web Services, such as faster time to market, increased process efficiency, and increased efficiency through business process automation. These also have to be accounted for in your ROI calculation.

ROI and Risk Management

No ROI analysis is complete without considering the risks associated with the underlying project and technology, and managing those risks with the goal of mitigating them. It is worth stressing that risk management is not merely a simple step-by-step process that can be performed effortlessly. Furthermore, companies can choose to stick to mature and proven technologies with known risks, but in doing so lose out on the high rewards and returns that might be associated with the new technology. Lastly, if every investment could be precisely quantified in terms of its return, the business wouldn't be taking enough risk, and competitors would gain the upper hand in innovation and value creation for their business partners, customers, and employees.

Companies must constrain risk associated with Web Services by implementing disciplined project management and by testing extensively and at regular intervals. Risk management issues should be outlined in your Web Services strategy and should be applied to the pilot project.

Let's briefly discuss the risks associated with Web Services technology, as they should be considered in any ROI model:

17. New Technology

Web Services technology and the tools and servers supporting it are still new and evolving. In their current state, Web Services can be utilized only for non-transactional, call-and-response type scenarios. This limitation restricts the amount of business value that companies can immediately derive through Web Services.

18. Standards not Matured or Finalized

The standards supporting Web Services technology such as UDDI, WSDL, and WSFL are still evolving and have not yet matured. There is no guarantee that if you implement a Web Service today, using the current standards, you will not have to modify it later when the standards change.

19. Web Services Development Tools and Servers

Practically every major player in the server software industry is providing initial support for Web Services. This support, though, may not be sufficient to build, deploy, and execute mission-critical Web Services. It is worth mentioning that the quality of service offered by application servers and integration broker platforms will rely and depend as much on Web Services standards and protocols as it will on the maturity, scalability, and integrity of the application server itself.

20. Quality of External Web Services

The quality of Web Services, such as availability, performance, and security aspects, will be critical to identify as potential risks while using external Web Services for B2Bi.

21. Security

Security is one of the primary factors that will determine the adoption of Web Services for all applications, by companies of all sizes, in all sectors. It also poses the greatest risk for this technology, and secured interoperability holds the key to the success of Web Services in the long run. The key security requirements for using Web Services are authentication, authorization, data protection, and non-repudiation. Be alert to potential security loopholes in Web Services since they are vulnerable to a wide array of security threats like denial-of-service attacks and spoofing. Any implementation of Web Services technology should not begin until the security risks are considered in respect of the security policy and existing solutions within the company.

Applying the ROI Formula

Now that we have discussed all the costs and expenses along with the technical and business benefits and risks of Web Services, it is time to apply the numbers to the ROI formula for Web Services. As presented earlier in the paper, you can either choose the discount cash flow analysis or payback period analysis.

We will arrive at the numbers through a series of simple steps:

1. Calculate the total cost of Web Services implementation. Sum up all the expenses that we listed from point 1 through 6.

2. Determine the total savings resulting through the technical benefits listed for the usage of Web Services by going through points 7 to 11.

3. Determine the increase in productivity, efficiency, and revenues through the business benefits of using Web Services. For this, traverse through points 12 to 16.

4. Quantify the risks associated with the introduction and usage of Web Services by going through points 17 to 21.

The last step is to categorize the results from Step 1 through 4 under the following headings:

❑ Project costs including capital expenses, implementation labor, management and support, operations and contract expenses (**A**).

❑ Project benefits including net tangible benefits (**B**).

❑ Project risks quantified as potential expenses (**C**).

Using the formula from earlier in the paper, we apply the figures as follows:

ROI for Web Services = (B − A − C)/ (A+C) * 100

The desired result for using Web Services will be if you get the following:

❑ Increased Revenue.

❑ Decreased Cost.

❑ Improved Efficiency.

❑ Higher Profitability.

❑ Shorter Payback Period.

❑ Higher IRR.

❑ Less Risk.

This scenario will make a business case for Web Services. It may be the case, however, that not all the factors listed above prove favorable. In this case, you will have to weigh all the options and make a decision based on the short and long-term goals.

Not the Only Model

Before we conclude this paper, we should mention that this is not the only model that can or should be used to calculate and measure ROI. Each company or organization may use a different model to measure ROI, such as using a method that begins by identifying the desired economic results of Web Services strategy and then focuses on creating the activities necessary to achieve those results. Use the model that best fits your organization. Finally, be sure that ROI should account for phased implementation of Web Services technology.

Conclusion

Web Services run through industry-standard protocols and offer the potential of eliminating the need for proprietary hardware, software, and network protocols. Companies will be able to lower their investment costs greatly in terms of increased ROI by implementing Web Services.

There is no fixed model for calculating the ROI of Web Services as of now, and the ROI in each company would greatly depend on how the technology is actually employed in solving software and business processes-related tasks. Any model used for calculating ROI should take into account the risks associated with the usage of Web Services.

Author: Mike Clark

- Web Services Benefit Development

- Examination of Web Services

- Threats to Web Services

- Web Services Companies

Selling Web Services

The term "Web Services" though applicable to any service offered on the Internet such as hosting, development, credit card checking, etc., has been adopted to describe a new phenomenon of computer-to-computer interaction using XML, and standard internet protocols such as HTTP. Normally, running an application on a remote computer system is difficult and time consuming because of the various operating systems and developers that you need to contend with. During the last two years, however, many leading vendors have agreed upon a standard that allows one computer system to run applications on a second by passing simple text messages between the two:

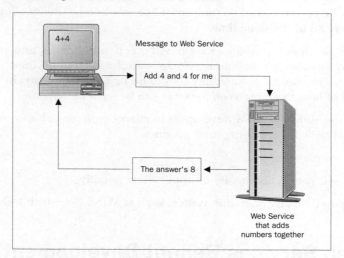

The previous example to add two numbers together explains in simple terms what happens when an application runs a Web Service. Obviously, a Web Service could perform far more complicated processing than this. For example you could send a message to debit your bank account and credit the bank account of your supplier.

This simple messaging standard (known within the industry as SOAP, Simple Object Access Protocol) has been largely brought into the spotlight through the efforts of major industry players such as Microsoft, IBM, SAP, and HP. These companies have taken up the commitment to integrate Web Services technology within new product launches for 2002/3. This has led us today to the edge of a startling new industry.

What's So Special About Web Services?

There's no doubt that interesting technical ideas come up in all software development fields; every day some bright spark admits to reinventing the Internet. So why Web Services? It's easiest to explain using the following points:

- ❑ Large corporations, many of which are usually in competition with each other, are adopting Web Services. For example IBM, Microsoft, BEA, Oracle, HP, and Sun. This becomes even more astonishing when you realize that historically this is the first time that large portions of the industry have so wholeheartedly adopted a new technology **all at the same time**.

- ❑ The Web Services technologies are based on open standards, and are therefore not owned by anyone. A cross-industry team of technical and business experts decide on what they should do and how they should do it. There is no royalty to pay: the standard of how to define Web Services can be used by anyone.

- ❑ It offers the ability to allow developers to charge someone else for using their functionality, without buying their product.

- ❑ It's very simple to use.

- ❑ You can sell your functionality or application globally.

- ❑ It can be used on any operating system, such as Windows, Macintosh, Unix, Linux, etc.

How do Web Services Benefit Development?

This new application of technology means that a computer programmer or a software development team will be able to take an application and allow customers to run it from any part of the world but without the customer having to download any software. They simply buy access to a Web Service and then call it from within their own application, therefore extending their own functionality, but at a fraction of the cost it would have taken them to develop it themselves.

Point by Point Examination of Web Services

Some examples of potential consumer Web Services:

- ❏ Name and address database.
- ❏ SMS text messenger (sending messages to a mobile phone).
- ❏ Fax on Demand.
- ❏ Stock price results.
- ❏ Cross-organization document retrieval (getting your statement electronically, say).
- ❏ Cross-organization ordering (sending a request to order stationery, say).
- ❏ Text translation.

Two potential uses of Web Services:

- ❏ When walking home you need to send a fax to someone confirming an order. Your WAP phone sends a message to the 'Fax on Demand' Web Service with any text you type on your phone.

- ❏ Employed by a large banking organization, you want to make accounts information available to customers and salespersons. You create your own Web Service that allows users to retrieve (password protected) account balances. You then get a dedicated web site team to incorporate it within your web site for general customer enquiries. You also get another development team to create an interface for your ICL mainframe call center, and yet another to develop an interface for WAP phones, all feeding off the **same** Web Service.

Customer advantages include:

- ❏ The time it takes to develop an application is immediately reduced.
  Note: This is certainly correct when developers' knowledge is sufficient to quickly grasp and create a link to a Web Service. In certain areas, though, such as ASP.NET, because it is such a new environment, the reduction in application development time will be preceded by many days spent on research, development, and getting the best out of this environment.

- ❏ No need to download any specialist software to run Web Services.
  Note: Correct, but you will need to have a toolkit or some software that understands and is able to traffic SOAP messages between your operating system and the Web Service.

- ❏ You can simply try the Web Service and then instantly buy the Web Service.
  Note: Currently there are only two brokerages that are able to perform this function: http://www.webservicebuy.com/ *and* http://www.serviceforge.com/.

- ❏ Web Services are easy to incorporate seamlessly within an existing application.

- ❏ You can use the same Web Service on any computer system you use, WAP, Windows, Unix, Linux, Mac, etc.

Customer disadvantages include:

- There may be hundreds of similar Web Services to choose from, making it difficult to make a decision.
  Note: This part of the industry is being rectified by specialist directories and Web Services brokerages becoming available. These brokerages (see http://www.salcentral.com/, http://www.webservicebuy.com/, http://www.allesta.com/, http://www.xmethods.com/*) give you additional information about your Web Service or Web Services provider to enable you to make an informed decision.*

- There is an inherent latency in running Web Services over the Internet.
  Note: This is true, but then as one of the methods of transferring SOAP requests is the TCP/IP protocol, it's also true to say that other commonly used methods such as COM would also have this same latency; in reality it's no slower than other methods.

- You must create a client application to use a Web Service.

Advantages to Web Services developers:

- Once developed there is no lead-time till marketing your Web Service.
  Note: This means that because you can put the Web Service on the Internet and make it immediately available to customers you can effectively develop it one day and sell it the next.

- A worldwide audience can use the service.

- Bugs can be fixed instantly and for all users.
  Note: Something that we'll all be pleased about is the ability to fix bugs, and since the code is running on your server, the fix will be instantly available to all your customers. One word of caution, however, is that errors can be introduced just as easily and quickly.

- The service can be used by any computer system.

- You do not need to be concerned about installing the application on different computers.

- You can combine with other companies to produce a series of Web Services together.
  Note: Partnerships with other like-minded developers or teams could allow large products to be created at a fraction of the conventional cost. These products might then be marketed globally.

Disadvantages to Web Services developers:

- You still need to market your functionality.
  Note: There's no getting away from it, marketing still needs to be done. Now, however, you also have other potential avenues. As before, you now have the option of approaching specialist Web Services brokerages that will market and sell the product, taking either a monthly administration fee or a percentage of sales.

- You may create a Web Service that already has significant competition.
  Note: An example of this would be anonymous e-mail. It is undoubtedly the most prolific Web Service around already and by the end of 2002 it is likely that at least 50 e-mail Web Services will be available.

❑   The SOAP standard is still developing.
Note: No significant changes are expected. As this is seen as a definitive standard for decades, however, it is not realistic to think that some changes won't occur as the experts work toward perfecting its definition.

❑   SOAP Toolkits have their work cut out in becoming compliant.
Note: Even though the SOAP standard is defined in some depth, because of the intrinsic versatility of XML there is a lot of scope for misinterpretation. Also, because of the size of the definition, many vendors are still having problems becoming fully SOAP-compliant.

Threats to Web Services' Rise to Power

As well as giving you insight into the current Web Services industry, we will also discuss the flip side of the coin: some of the potential pitfalls that may delay Web Services, or stop it in its tracks.

ASP or Not ASP?

Web Services publishers are not the first to charge for service-based technology. The Application Service Provider (ASP) market, for instance, has supplied and charged for functionality available over the Internet for years. Their failure at technical standardization, however, is a definite disadvantage, but they also have a distinct and not so obvious advantage: **a clearly defined business model**:

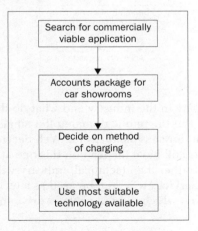

All development starts with a requirement for a revenue stream: for instance, 'accounts package for car showrooms'. The business model defines a method of charging. These admittedly simplified stages define the basic structure an ASP uses to create a commercially viable application.

It is not until both these stages are completed that the most suitable technology is found and used. The choice of technology is based on requirements of speed and any other peculiarities that have emerged in the first two stages of the business model.

The result is that ASPs end up with a well-defined charging mechanism, clearly outlined client interface and application, and a potentially profitable product before development has commenced. Web Services E-Business, however, **does not have a defined business model**:

In the case of Web Services, the ASP business model has been turned around. By defining the technology first, the technology is what seems to be driving the search for products to develop. This structure has obvious similarities with the unsuccessful dotcom strategy. Much of the dotcom discourse went along these lines:

Entrepreneur: 'I think my dotcom will succeed.'
Interviewer: 'What are you selling?'
Entrepreneur: 'I haven't decided yet.'

There is an inherent risk that the Web Services industry is falling into the same patterns of error. This direction of endeavor will, undoubtedly, change within the next few years, as developers become more familiar with this new technology, and many new and interesting products emerge. By then, though, the damage may have already been done.

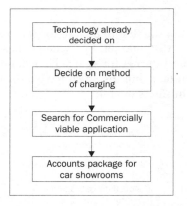

So what's the latest state of play in the industry and what do the signs tell us? Well currently most (if not all) Web Services in the public domain offer small amounts of functionality. Even now many are on the lookout for suitable ideas for Web Services to develop, therefore it leads me to believe that developers still have the lead on this one at the moment. Soon we should expect that the commercial (rather than technical) industry will start to champion this emerging technology. Web Services will then be used as a technological layer that is helpful for developing the solution but which did not actually drive the creation of the original idea for the project.

Let Them Be Free

Because of the low costs in producing and publishing them, the majority of Web Services are currently available free of charge. It should be noted, however, that these Web Services offer little in the way of functionality. In the infancy of an industry, this is not a bad thing: it simply helps promote a new technology and the companies producing its services.

As the Web Services industry matures over the coming years, organizations will stop gaining benefits from press activity and start to consider the possibilities of making money out of actual sales. The step from a market of free Web Services to one where they cost money is significant.

In fact, by the time we reach this stage in the development of Web Services, there may already be thousands of free Web Services on the market. They won't just come from single developers, but from large teams, attempting to make inroads into the Web Services market. The dotcom industry went wrong in a similar phase of its development, when the fundamentals of building a viable business model were often ignored. The current movement towards a market of free Web Services, therefore, follows a dangerous precedent set by numerous dotcom failures.

Web Services providers need to introduce pay-to-use Web Services over the next few months. This is not enough, however, as they also need to state immediately that they intend to charge for services. Microsoft has already made this statement when producing Passport/My Services. It is currently offered free of charge, but under the proviso that it may become a chargeable product in the future.

Customer Trust

To use a Web Service, your customer must be sure that it is reliable and available 100% of the time. This can be difficult to prove to a customer, especially when, for example, you're storing the names and addresses of visitors to their Web sites.

Imagine the problems that could occur if, for instance, a company produced a widely adopted Web Service to manage visitors to a Web site. Then one day their system was not as fail-safe as it first appeared and their Web Service suffered a fault. Effectively this one action could take down thousands of Web sites and stop people logging on and using their services.

Trust in Web Services is possibly one of the greatest inhibitors to a global Web Service industry. We expect that, as the industry progresses, companies will emerge dedicating their efforts to sifting and sorting research information on Web Services and Web Service providers. This research information will form the backbone of what will be commonly known as a Who's Who of Web Services – a list of individuals, companies, and products that are considered viable and commercially trustworthy.

In addition, because of the ease with which you can change Web Services, developers must have a definite line of communication with all their customers: any change they make must be advertised to their customers, almost on a minute-by-minute basis.

To ease this process you could also use the services of a body that acts as an intermediary to your changing Web Services definition. This organization simply watches a Web Service on your behalf and then e-mails any customers once your Web Service changes. Two Web sites performing this task are http://www.webservicewatch.com/ (SMS text and e-mail notification) and http://www.allesta.com/ (e-mail notification).

Dependent on Microsoft's New Software (a.k.a. .NET)

It's always exciting when an industry pretty much agrees that a new technology is the right direction to go. Some of the giants of the industry have taken the plunge and adopted the SOAP technology. In this type of industry, however, developers' conception of a particular product or idea can move mountains.

For example, the Microsoft .NET wave that's currently washing ashore is asking for six million VB developers to adopt this technology. This won't happen overnight, and while many will take up the challenge immediately, many will be looking for alternatives because of the steepness of the learning curve implicit in the migration to .NET, and the fact that there needs to be an incentive (potential future work programming VB.NET). So what if a bright spark comes along with a .NET look-alike, an application that allows you to create Web Services using existing technologies, such as Visual Basic 6? If widely accepted it would certainly slow down the growth potential in Visual Studio .NET (Microsoft's integrated .NET development environment).

Charging Mechanism

At the moment the Web Services industry has largely neglected to look for a method of charging for using Web Services, and is in this respect not dissimilar from the dotcom industry over the last few years. There are, however, two distinct methods of charging for a Web Service:

❑ **Creating your own charging mechanism**
   This scenario requires the Web Service developer to create their own charging mechanism to accept payments and validate users. The commitment from the developer is significant.

❑ **Using a brokerages' charging mechanism**
   This scenario requires the developer to use the services of a Web Services brokerage. This new term refers to a company that allows your customers to buy access to a Web Service and also for you to validate whether a user is allowed to use your Web Service.

Each of the above scenarios has its own advantages and disadvantages. Firstly, developing your own Web Services payment and validation method diversifies the intensity of the development itself, when developers could be concentrating on actual functionality. Using a brokerage, however, has an intrinsic cost implication, and you give away a portion of your revenue. The current thoughts on brokerages are that they will only charge small "per click" values, or even a simple monthly fee. A brokerage may not in fact support your preferred charging mechanism, in which case a developer should either change brokerage or collaborate with it to have a new mechanism successfully implemented.

As of this writing, there are currently only two brokerages that support charging for Web Services: http://www.grandcentral.com/, which offers a suite of services for integrating and charging for Web Services; and http://www.webservicebuy.com/, which offers an easy-to-implement authorization function, and allows for the charging of customers by credit card.

We can get some ideas about how to charge for Web Services from other industries. A good example is the telephone call industry. The rate cards that are used for 'phone calls work well for Web Services calls. They allow charging for calls on a sliding scale depending on the number of calls purchased.

To complete this section I have outlined below some of the charging schemes that are currently under consideration:

Scheme	How it works
Charge per call (Prepaid)	A customer buys a set number of calls to one of our Web Services. Every time this customer calls our Web Service, the call is registered. When the customer runs out of calls (or shortly before), they are automatically notified and asked to buy more.
Charge per month (Subscription)	A customer pays for unlimited use over a period of time. They pay to have access to a Web Service for a particular period of time: one month, three months, six months, or one year. Once that period ends, we either notify the customer and ask them to confirm that they wish to extend their subscription or, depending on the arrangement, automatically charge their account for another period of time.
One-off charge (Prepaid)	The customer makes a one-off payment for unlimited use of our Web Service for the lifetime of that Web Service. The lifetime might only be a few months: for instance, with the case of a news-feed for a specific Olympic games.
No charge (Freeware)	Our Web Service is free for a specific period. This could be for the lifetime of the Web Service or for a shorter trial period.

We don't have to use only one of the above charging methods for our Web Service. We could combine any of the above methods to make alternative payment schemes. For instance, we could start with the 'no charge' method for a trial period before using the 'charge per call' method.

It's Just Another Standard; I'll Wait for the Next One?

New technology is a little like a bus – there will be another one round in a minute – so how do we know if and when Web Services has really taken off? Consider the tactic employed by a stock market broker in the 1920's: "count the smoking chimneys". If enough steel works are busy, then the industry is booming.

Though a little basic, it's definitely worth considering who else is making the commitment towards Web Services. Microsoft for example has reportedly spent upwards of $5 billion in marketing and developing its .NET platform. Here's a shortlist of who's doing what:

Vendor	Product
Apache	Produced ApacheSOAP, an open-source SOAP Web Services server. Working on Apache Axis, the third generation of Apache SOAP.
Microsoft	ASP.NET, the Web Service development tool, has rolled out first quarter 2002. Fully Web Services orientated, replacement over the next 5 years for Visual Basic (reportedly 6 million user base). Suite of servers that are Web Services orientated.
IBM	Produced a SOAP Web Services server through the Alphaworks program. IBM is also a very ardent supporter of Web Services – belonging to many of the Web Services specification bodies. IBM also provides a platform for Web Services based on the WebSphere server.
Sun	Sun controls the Java platform including its various APIs. Through its iPlanet product Sun hopes to provide a platform for Web Services. This company is also a member of the Liberty Alliance – a rival to Passport offering single sign-on authentication.
Oracle	Oracle has long been working at selling itself as a complete platform provider for enterprises. Its main contribution in this field is therefore in business system integration (ERP, CRM).
Borland	Producing support for Web Services under Linux. Producing support for Web Services under Delphi 6 (reportedly a four million user base).
Apple	Apple has added SOAP support to its new Mac OS X operating system for AppleScript to enable communication across your network so you can send AppleScript events from one Mac OS X system to another.

What Type of Companies Will Form Around Web Services?

With the onset of Web Services there are a multitude of different **types** of companies that will attempt to make commercial ventures into the Web Services market. Below is a list of some of the new industry roles that are emerging.

Web Services Development

A company that develops Web Services on behalf of others then sells access to those Web Services. This requires that the Web Service developer (team) has a suitable charging mechanism in place; look out for proof of reliability.

Asking questions about fail-safe backup measures may also see holes appearing in a company's use of Web Services. If they are transporting secure information also look for what security measures (encrypting data) they are using.

If their entire income is meant to be from others buying access to their Web Service, you must also evaluate the market that they've produced the Web Service for. An example would be a Web Service for SMS text messaging; the mobile phone industry, although saturated with phones, is also enjoying a substantial increase in SMS text messages being sent between phones.

Revenue Stream: Revenue from charging for use of a Web Service by monthly fee or number of times used, as well as Consultancy income.

Hosting of Web Services

A company that hosts Web Services on behalf of other developers. This is definitely a different method than simply hosting a web site, which most of us are used to. Web Services must be situated on a computer system that is accessible 24/7.

Specialist hosting companies will have a significant movement from web site hosting to ASP.NET hosting. Also a hosting company will usually be targeted around one platform, for example Linux, Microsoft, etc. Therefore look for a proven track record in hosting of other kinds; this will quite often serve as an excellent stepping stone to the specialist Web Service hosting.

Revenue Stream: Hosting companies will get their revenue from monthly payments from developers to host a Web Service. Also from storing data and code off-site away from the Web Service developer.

Testing Labs

Companies that test Web Services for a fixed or monthly charge. Because Web Services are now accessible globally, as a developer you could create a Web Service but let someone else test it for you just before it went commercially live. This allows you to get a stamp of approval for your Web Service based on certain factors, such as speed, reliability, and ability to work with all major development tools. Look for an accreditation scheme, one that gives a Web Service developer some added advantage to using this Web Services tester.

Revenue Stream: Testing labs will charge a fee for testing Web Services, and also charge a fee for regularly testing a Web Service.

Web Services Brokerages

Companies that buy and sell access to Web Services. Though a lot more difficult to get right, this service also offers one of the largest investment opportunities. For example, a Web Services developer asks a brokerage to sell their Web Service. Then a customer goes to the brokerage to look for a desired Web Service. Once one is found, the customer purchases calls to that Web Service using a special username and password, and the brokerage gets a commission.

Revenue Stream: From a percentage cut from the overall turnover of the Web Service (say, 20-40% of all revenues).

Web Services Toolkit Developers

Each operating system needs a small application to help it understand and operate with SOAP messages. There are already probably 20 such toolkits available on the market, many of which are free. This type of toolkit development can allow a company to become an industry leader in a niche area of development. When evaluating what area you would like to invest in, you'll need some significant technical expertise or help to make sure that you have an excellent chargeable product in a market which is saturated with free SOAP toolkits.

Revenue Stream: Selling application tools and specialist servers for developing Web Services.

Conclusion

So where do you go from here? It is essential that you consider and understand the commitment that many companies are making worldwide in Web Services. The market is completely open at the moment and an organization with the right backing could create a lead that would be difficult for others to attack later. If you're considering Web Services, it's certainly perfect timing to get into this exciting market. Don't consider Web Services as a method of making a quick buck, though; you should be prepared to wait for at least 12 to 24 months until massive products such as ASP.NET have taken hold in the industry. By that time with the right direction I would expect the pioneers of this industry to be well placed for the emergence of what many believe will be a global market economy.

Based on the activities of most key vendors, Web Services are definitely here to stay, and in 12 months' time will be top of the agenda for most companies and institutions. I hope, though, that we have now given you as a developer or decision maker the opportunity to see what the future may hold for this technology, and as such allow you to use this information to make some informed and extremely profitable decisions over the next few months.

Authors: Gunjan Samtani and Dimple Sadhwani

- EAI fundamentals

- Patterns for EAI

- Differences between EAI and Web Services

- Architectural pre-requisites

- ROI for Web Services

Enterprise Application Integration (EAI) and Web Services

An average Fortune 500 company may have 50 or more internal business applications deployed on different platforms, and sometimes even on different versions of the same technology. Not all large enterprises exist as one autonomous whole, often they have evolved from merger and acquisition, and house a diverse range of smaller enterprises with varying dynamics and technology infrastructures that need to be managed in concert with business priorities orchestrated by a head office. The information technology environment in such companies is extremely dynamic as they adopt, at different rates, the latest and the best-of-breed solutions provided by different vendors. The solution from each vendor may have different hardware, platform, and database requirements, which results in the implementation of multiple physically separate systems.

As companies move in the direction of collaborative business-to-business e-commerce, they will first have to look inward to their own internal systems, applications, and processes. Several business processes span multiple internal applications. These applications must be able to communicate dynamically in real-time before a company can effectively "e-communicate" with the outside world.

Enterprise Application Integration (EAI)

Most companies have an environment of disparate legacy systems, applications, processes, and data sources, which typically interact by a maze of interconnections that are poorly documented and expensive to maintain. Additional problems arise from management practices embedded in corporate culture, and market consolidation in the digital age, where mergers and acquisitions of companies can increase the complexity of system integration exponentially.

The segmentation of information systems was exacerbated with the introduction of commercial off-the-shelf applications such as enterprise resource planning (ERP), customer relationship management (CRM), supply chain management (SCM), and portals. Early on, these systems were designed as self-contained "black-boxes" with little or no means for accessing internal data or processes. Although many of these applications now provide better access to their underlying data and business logic, integrating them with other systems in the enterprise is still a challenge.

Each node in the following diagram maintains its own data, which may be shared among the nodes. Sharing of this data has been typically accomplished using data transfer methods including batch processes and data import/export jobs. Since the data of one node is not available in real-time to other nodes, the latter cannot analyze and make decisions while a transaction is being processed, or immediately after the transaction has been processed at the former:

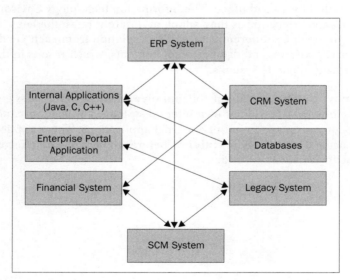

What is EAI?

As the need to meet increasing customer and business partner expectations for real-time information exchange continued to rise, companies were forced to link their disparate systems to improve productivity, efficiency, and, ultimately, customer satisfaction. The need for IT systems to communicate within an organization led to the evolution of **Enterprise Application Integration (EAI)**. EAI is the process of creating an integrated infrastructure for linking disparate systems, applications, and data sources across the corporate enterprise. The very origin of EAI solutions can be linked to the need for providing a full duplex, bi-directional solution to share seamlessly and exchange data between ERP, CRM, SCM, databases, data warehouses, and other important internal systems within the company.

The following diagram illustrates how EAI can tidy up the connections between disparate parts of a system:

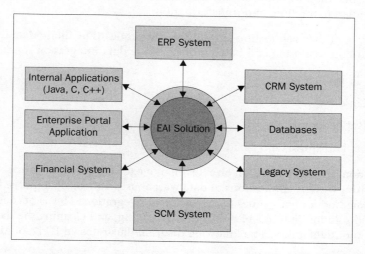

EAI is not an out-of-the-box solution; rather it is an ongoing process of creating a flexible, standardized enterprise infrastructure that allows new IT-based applications and business processes to be easily and efficiently deployed. The new infrastructure allows applications throughout an enterprise to seamlessly communicate with one another in realtime.

Types of EAI

EAI solutions can take on many forms and exist at many levels. The appropriate level of EAI can depend on many factors including company size, company industry, integration/project complexity, and budget.

There are four types of middleware solutions to EAI:

❑   Data-oriented Integration.

- ❑ Function or Method Integration.
- ❑ User Interface Integration.
- ❑ Business Process Integration.

Data-oriented Integration

Data-oriented integration occurs at the database and data source level within an organization. The integration is achieved by migrating data from one data source to another. Data integration is the most prevalent form of EAI in existence today. One of the biggest problems with data integration, however, is that the business logic usually exists only within the primary system, limiting real-time transactional capabilities.

Data-oriented integration can be either real time (such as synchronous replication, stored procedures, virtual data warehouses) or non-real time (such as asynchronous replication, batch transfer, scheduled extraction, and transformation).

There are a bevy of data replication and middleware tools to facilitate data transfer between data sources in both real-time and batch modes. Some data integration methods include:

- ❑ Batch Transfer.
- ❑ Data Union.
- ❑ Data Replication.
- ❑ Extract, Transform, and Load (ETL) Solution.

The ETL solution, which is based on an ETL engine extracting, transforming, cleansing, and loading data from various applications to data warehouses and/or data marts, has now become the preferred method for companies to achieve data integration. This is because it is a much more advanced solution in terms of transforming, routing, and cleaning the data as compared to data replication or data union. The following diagram illustrates an ETL solution process:

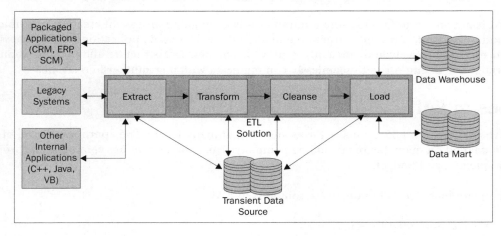

Function or Method Integration

Function or method integration involves the direct and rigid application-to-application (A2A) integration of cross-platform applications over a network. It can range from custom code (COBOL, C++, Java), through application programming interfaces (APIs), and remote procedure calls (RPCs), to distributed middleware such as TP monitors, distributed objects, common object request broker architecture (CORBA), Java remote method invocation (RMI), message-oriented middleware (MOM), DCOM, and Web Services.

The following diagram illustrates how function or method integration fits in between the systems to be integrated:

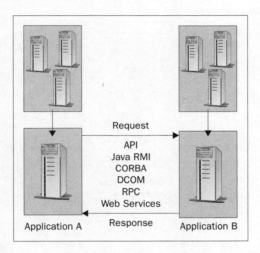

Function or method-oriented integration is primarily synchronous in nature: it's based on request/reply interactions between the client (requesting program) and the server (responding program).

User Interface Integration (Refacing)

Refacing is the process of replacing the terminal screens of legacy systems and the graphical interfaces of PCs with one standardized interface, typically browser-based. Generally, the functionality of terminal screen applications can be mapped on a one-to-one basis with a browser-based graphical user interface. The new presentation layer is integrated with the existing business logic of the legacy systems or packaged applications such as ERP, CRM, and SCM.

Enterprise business portals may also be considered a sophisticated refacing solution. A business portal consolidates the presentation of multiple applications into one customizable browser-based interface. The portal framework acts as a middleware solution in this type of EAI.

Business Process Integration

While data integration has proved a popular form of EAI, it can present problems from a security, data integrity, and business process perspective. The vast majority of data within an organization is accessed and maintained through business logic. The business logic applies and enforces the required business rules, processes, and security for the underlying data.

Business process integration occurs at the business process level, which spans multiple applications. It is often characterized by the use of advanced middleware such as message brokers, which standardize and control the flow of information through a bus or hub-and-spoke framework. The following diagram illustrates applications being integrated by being combined in one business process:

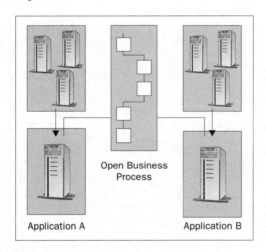

Open Business Process

Application A   Application B

Service-Oriented Architecture (SOA)

For true dynamic integration, software resources such as applications, objects, and programs should be loosely coupled. These resources should make their presence known to the world and provide public interfaces, which describe their actions. The communication between these resources and the applications using them should occur based on open standards. Using these resources, which can be personalized for each user, future applications could be built dynamically in a fraction of the time that it takes today to build applications using conventional mechanisms.

This is where SOA comes into the picture. It provides a framework and architecture for seamlessly interconnecting applications and software components. It gives the ability to invoke remote business services and install them as local components in a different application, all without writing a single line of low-level code.

Components and Operations of SOA

There are three components of service-oriented architecture. They are:

❑ **Service Provider** – This component is responsible for creating and publishing the interfaces of services, providing the actual implementation of these services, and responding to any requests for use. Any company or business can be a service provider.

❑ **Service Broker** – This component registers and categorizes public services published by various service providers and offers services such as search. Service brokers act like a repository or yellow pages for services. Companies that want to use services can search these yellow pages to find one matching their needs. Currently several companies including IBM and Microsoft are acting as service brokers. Companies can also develop and maintain internal repositories, so a service broker can be an internally hosted component. In fact, having a Service Broker within an enterprise is one of the key points of a Web Services integration mechanism within the enterprise.

❑ **Service Requestor** – This component is the actual user of the services. Service requestors discover services by searching the repository maintained by the service brokers and then invoke these services by communicating with the actual service providers. In the case of Web Services, the invocation could take place over the Internet, or locally over the intranet, in which case the requesting company would also be the service provider.

The three most basic operations through which the SOA participants interact are:

❑ **Publishing** – This operation allows the service provider to publish its services and interface requirements with a service broker. WSDL (Web Services Description Language) is an XML-based language used to perform the operation of describing interfaces of Web Services.

❑ **Finding** – This operation allows a service requestor to locate, search, and discover the services, published via a service broker, that are offered in a particular classification or by a specific service provider. Finding is enabled by the UDDI (Universal Description, Discovery and Integration) framework.

❑ **Binding** – This operation enables a service requestor to actually bind and use a service provided by a service provider. Binding is enabled by SOAP-based XML messages.

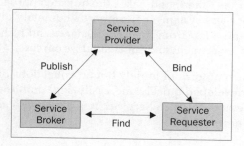

Web Services

Web Services, built on SOA, are a stack of emerging standards that describe service-oriented, component-based application architectures. They provide a distributed computing technology for revealing the business services of applications on the Internet or intranet using open and standards-based XML protocols and formats. The use of standard XML protocols makes Web Services platform-, language-, and vendor-independent, and an ideal candidate for use in EAI solutions.

Web Services eliminate the interoperability issues of existing solutions, such as CORBA and DCOM, by leveraging open Internet standards – Web Services Description Language (WSDL – to describe), Universal Description, Discovery and Integration (UDDI – to advertise and syndicate), Simple Object Access Protocol (SOAP – to communicate) and Web Services Flow Language (WSFL – to define work flows). Take a look at the World Wide Web Consortium (W3C) web site for details on how the adoption of these languages is progressing, at http://www.w3c.org/.

Thus, a Web Service is an interface that describes a collection of business operations that are network accessible through standardized XML messaging and that can be:

□ Described using WSDL.

□ Published using UDDI.

□ Found using UDDI.

□ Bound using SOAP (or HTTP GET/POST).

□ Invoked using SOAP (or HTTP GET/POST).

□ Composed with other services into new services using WSFL.

EAI and Web Services

Web Services are not EAI in and of themselves. Rather, Web Services are just another technology that enables EAI, and can significantly change the traditional point-to-point approach.

Using Web Services that loosely integrate applications, a company achieves just a subsection or a part of EAI. EAI, on the other hand, takes the holistic approach of tightly integrating and connecting all applications and systems that support a company's business. EAI takes years of continued commitment and effort from different business and technical units within the company, as well as high investment and substantial resources.

Web Services, in their current form of loosely bound collections of services, are more of an *ad hoc* solution that can be developed quickly and easily, and published, discovered, and bound dynamically. In this generation of Web Services, it is possible to achieve only function-level integration between applications.

They are not transactional in nature and provide basic "request/response" functionality. The next generation of Web Services, however, are likely to be functionally and technologically advanced, offering user interface encapsulation, transactions, service context, and security. They will be able to package an application and embed it into another application.

Web Services will give the independent groups within the IT department of a company an effective way for managing their systems and applications. Using Web Services, all applications will expose their methods using the same standard, exchange the data using the same standard, and use the same connection protocols. This will address the fundamental problems of multiple data standards and communication protocols associated with EAI today.

Salient Differences between Traditional EAI Solutions and Web Services

Some of these differences take into account the future enhancements proposed in Web Services.

A few essential differences between traditional EAI solutions and Web Services are as follows:

- ❑ **Simplicity**: There is no doubt that Web Services are much simpler to design, develop, maintain, and use as compared to a typical EAI solution which may involve distributed technology such as DCOM and CORBA. Once the framework of developing and using Web Services is ready, it will be relatively easy to automate new business processes spanning across multiple applications.

- ❑ **Basis in open standards**: Unlike proprietary EAI solutions, Web Services are based on open standards such as UDDI, SOAP, and HTTP, which is probably the single most important factor that would lead to the wide adoption of Web Services. The fact that they are built on existing and ubiquitous protocols eliminates the need for companies to invest in supporting new network protocols.

- ❑ **Flexible integration**: Since EAI solutions may require point-to-point integration, changes made at one end have to be propagated to the other end, making them very rigid and time-consuming in nature. Web Services-based integration is quite flexible, as it is built on loose coupling between the application publishing the services and the application using those services.

- ❑ **Reduced investment**: EAI solutions, such as message brokers, are very expensive to implement. They require a substantial initial investment. Web Services, in the future, may accomplish many of the same goals more cheaply and faster. Web Services can be deployed with decreased cost and effort.

- ❑ **Broader scope**: EAI solutions, such as message brokers, in integrating applications, treat them as single entities, whereas Web Services allow companies to break down big applications into small independent logical units and build wrappers around them. For example, a company can write wrappers for different business components of an ERP application such as order management: purchase order acceptance, status of order, order confirmation, accounts receivable, and accounts payable.

- **Increased efficiency**: As Web Services allow applications to be broken down into smaller logical components, integration is easier as it is done on a granular basis. This makes Web Services solutions for EAI much more efficient than traditional EAI solutions.
- **Dynamic rather than static**: Web Services provide a dynamic approach to integration by offering dynamic interfaces, whereas traditional EAI solutions are rather static in nature.

Example of Web Services for EAI

The following diagram shows an example of using Web Services within an organization. In this example, the portal application running within an application server aggregates information from multiple internal applications, providing a single point of entry into business processes spread across those applications. The portal application gets information about Web Services offered by internal applications using a private UDDI registry and invokes these services over the intranet. Binding information for frequently used Web Services can be cached by the application, to avoid the resource-intensive and time-consuming dynamic binding. In this example, the Web Services loosely integrate portal with CRM and ERP applications.

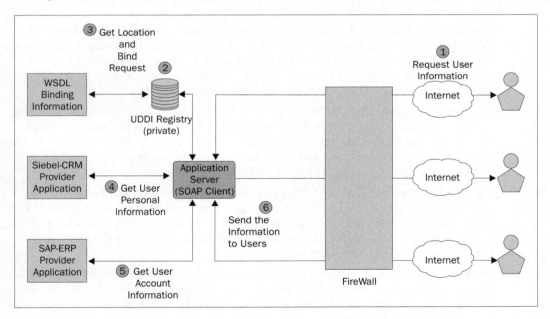

The sequence of steps is as follows:

1. After logging on to the company portal, users request personal and account-related information.

2. The application supporting the portal framework gets information about Web Services made available by the CRM and ERP applications by performing a look-up in the private UDDI registry.

3. The location and WSDL binding information of Web Services is sent to the application server.

4. The application invokes the Web Service published by the CRM application and retrieves the personal information, such as name, social security number, mailing address, and e-mail of the user. The communication is based on SOAP.

5. The application invokes the Web Service published by the ERP application and retrieves the account information, such as account number, balance, and transaction history of the user. The communication is based on SOAP.

6. The information is then formatted and sent to the user.

Essential Features of a Web Services Framework

A Web Services framework for EAI has to provide an integrated development environment and platform for easily building and deploying Web Services and service components. There are a few essential features that Web Services solution vendors will have to incorporate in order to successfully support Web Services, without which their use and adoption within companies is not possible. These features are as follows:

❑ Easy and secured connectivity to private and public UDDI, or any other repository.

❑ Effective audit mechanism through which the access and usage of Web Services can be closely monitored.

❑ Efficient security safeguards such as policy management and authentication, for the access and usage of Web Services.

❑ Easy development, deployment, publishing, finding, and dynamic binding for Web Services interfaces.

❑ A stable environment for rapid development of Web Services-based applications.

❑ Workflow Management and Personalization.

The following diagram illustrates these features:

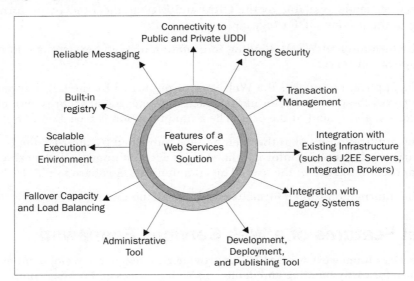

Convergence of EAI Solutions and Web Services

The current EAI solutions that predominately focus on integrating applications will have to be changed significantly, as legacy applications, databases, new in-house applications, and packaged applications in the future will expose their functions, business methods, and data as services using technologies such as XML, SOAP, and UDDI. Thus, the EAI solutions will have to provide a broad support for service integration rather than application integration.

Web Services will play a role – major and/or minor – in all types of EAI (internal applications and data integration patterns) discussed earlier in this paper.

Data-oriented Integration

With all the leading relational databases such as Sybase, DB2, Oracle, SQL Server already providing direct support for data transfer in an XML format (so there is no need for an intermediary application to pull the data from the data source and then format it in XML), Web Services will be crucial in real-time data-oriented integration. Web Services will help solve one of the most challenging tasks of data-oriented integration – reducing the discrepancies that exist in different data sources. Since XML documents are verbose and do make the process a lot slower, however, there is no doubt that the choice of using Web Services should be based on the nature and volume of data.

Business Process-oriented Integration

Some may consider that most of the features of a Web Services solution, as seen in the following diagram, are the same as an EAI integration broker solution, which typically enables business process-oriented integration. This is very true. There will be a huge convergence of these two, until Web Services becomes just another feature of an EAI integration broker solution. It makes absolutely no sense to reinvent the wheel by developing features such as messaging platform and transaction management services.

Already several leading EAI integration broker solution companies such as Tibco, BEA, IBM, and webMethods have announced support for Web Services in their products.

As depicted in the following diagram, support for Web Services will be just another feature of integration brokers:

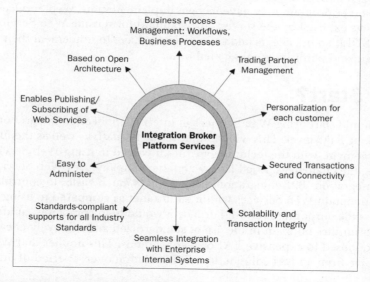

Function-or Method-oriented Integration

Adoption of Web Services by the leading software vendors for all packaged applications such as ERP, CRM, and SCM will largely determine how quickly and how widely companies start using Web Services for function-or method-oriented integration. All major vendors of packaged applications such as SAP, PeopleSoft, and Siebel have already announced their support for Web Services.

Key Differences Between Web Services and RPC/API-level Integration

As we mentioned in the previous section, Web Services offer a function-level integration solution for EAI. In most companies today, RPCs (remote procedure calls) and APIs (application programming interfaces) are used for this type of integration. So, what is different about Web Services?

51

RPCs and APIs typically require an agreement between the client (invoking program) and the server (implementation program) on the use of language, parameters, return types, translation mechanisms, etc. Web Services are based on XML – the new lingua franca for e-business, which standardizes the data formats, making the client and server independent of each other.

RPCs and APIs offer a static solution for function-level integration, even if they use XML for client/server communication. Web Services offer a dynamic approach to integration, where the services can be discovered, bound to, and used dynamically. This is primarily enabled because Web Services are found using a defined standard – UDDI.

RPCs and APIs can use any proprietary protocol, but Web Services are built and used over existing, universal protocols such as HTTP and SMTP.

RPCs and APIs do not offer servers a standard way of exposing their public methods to clients. Each server program may have its own implementation. Web Services, on the other hand, are always exposed by the servers in a standard form using Web Services Definition Language (WSDL). So the clients and servers do not have to implement their own proprietary format for using and publishing public methods.

Where to Start?

Companies should start using Web Services in internal application integration projects at the function, API, or RPC level. This will familiarise the IT staff, as well as the functional and general management, with the technology issues involved in using Web Services: very helpful in overcoming the challenges posed later when the company uses Web Services for external application integration (B2B integration) projects. It is much easier to control, manage, find, execute, and maintain Web Services within an intranet as compared to using them over the Internet across the corporate firewall. Further, it would help companies in identifying the business opportunities inherent in the use of standardized and relatively cheap Web Services solutions, as opposed to expensive EAI broker solutions. This implies that Web Services will gradually evolve from an EAI solution to a B2Bi solution over a period of time.

Taking Advantage of Existing Assets

It would be utterly naïve of companies to scrap the existing EAI infrastructure and blindly march towards deploying Web Services to replace it. Companies cannot abandon the EAI middleware frameworks, which provide full transactional services, in favor of Web Services, which don't (as yet). Instead, they should use Web Services to exploit the existing infrastructure.

Using Web Services, companies will also be able to use the resources they have invested in implementing any .NET and/or J2EE projects. Web Services technology works hand-in-hand with .NET and J2EE technologies, rather than as a competing technology. For instance, J2EE connectors give developers an interface for accessing legacy transactions and data, whereas Web Services provide a uniform, standards-based technique for exposing application functionality over the Internet or the corporate intranet.

Build an Internal Repository for Web Services

Early on in their adoption of Web Services, companies should make an effort to develop an **internal centralized service repository** for publishing information that internal applications can use to find information about published Web Services. If each group and department starts maintaining their own repository, over time there will be several repositories within the company, making the publishing, discovering, and using of Web Services a painful and a time-consuming process.

ROI on Using Web Services for EAI

"What will be the return on investment?" is probably the first question that any corporation would consider before investing any resources in Web Services. The fact that it is a hot technology and has everyone talking about it is certainly not a good enough reason. So, how much will companies have to invest in implementing this solution and what will be the payoff, both near-term and long-term?

There is little doubt that the first Web Service is the hardest to implement. The cost and difficulty level in business process re-engineering and integration is high. Both these features, however, fade away with the implementation of subsequent Web Services. Companies can, thereafter, enjoy the fruits of incremental cost reduction inherent in using XML-based standards-and-service oriented architectures.

A company should calculate the implementation and ongoing costs associated with Web Services including software, hardware, system integration, and future production support expenses. These cost estimates should be carefully examined to determine the ROI for the proposed solution.

Having said that, if a company does go through the process of Web Service enabling its internal applications, then the progression from internal applications to exposing them to be a part of a B2B integration process will be smoother and cheaper.

Bottom Line

Web Services, by themselves, are not the nirvana for EAI. An EAI platform within a Fortune 500 company would still comprise multiple solutions which together would offer both non-real-time and real-time integration, support for managing semantic transformations, business process integration, and application integration based on open standards and proprietary formats.

Conclusion

Web Services offer a platform-neutral approach for integrating applications, so that they can be used to integrate diverse systems, in a way supported by standards rather than proprietary systems. The ability of an enterprise to have access to real-time information spanning multiple departments, applications, platforms, and systems is one of the most important driving factors behind the adoption of Web Services. Companies should first start using Web Services for their internal integration projects for business processes that are non-transactional in nature, before they venture to use Web Services in B2B integration projects.

Companies will be able to lower their investment cost in implementing a Web Services solution by building it on top of their existing assets. If a company has invested millions of dollars to put its EAI infrastructure in place, it makes absolutely no sense to abandon it and just embrace Web Services.

Future EAI solutions will be significantly different from the existing ones, as they will be focused more on integrating services and less on integrating each individual application. They will include an integrated development environment and framework for easily building and deploying Web Services and service components.

Authors: Gunjan Samtani and Dimple Sadhwani

- B2Bi fundamentals

- Patterns for B2Bi

- Web Services in B2Bi

- Limitations of Web Services for B2Bi

- Web Services Networks or Intermediaries

Business To Business Integration (B2Bi) and Web Services

B2B integration is the enabling technology for most current business strategies such as collaborative e-commerce, collaborative networks, supply chain management (SCM), and customer relationship management (CRM) across multiple channels of delivery including wireless devices and the Internet.

What Is B2B Integration (B2Bi)?

B2B integration or B2Bi is about the secured coordination of information among businesses and their information systems. It promises to dramatically transform the way business is conducted between partners, suppliers, and customers or buyers. All companies (large, medium, small, or new) can experience increased growth and success through tightly integrated partnerships.

Companies from across a variety of industries are embracing B2Bi and realizing the enormous competitive advantage it provides, through faster time to market, reduced cycle times, and increased customer service. Through integration of business and technical processes, companies are able to strengthen relationships with partners and customers, achieve seamless integration inside and outside the enterprise, gain real-time views of customer accounts, increase operational efficiencies, and reduce costs. The following diagram illustrates the range of different sized companies that are embracing B2Bi:

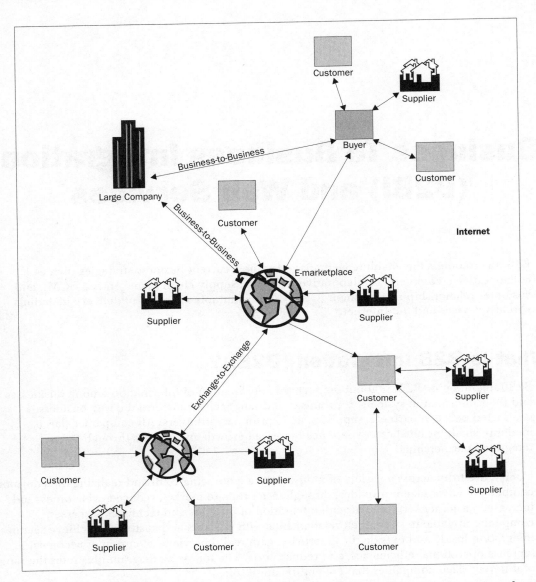

The market for B2Bi is huge. According to a report published in the post dot-com crash era from the International Data Corporation group, by 2005 B2B e-commerce will be of the order of 4.7 trillion US Dollars. B2B integration is expected to yield productivity gains of over a trillion USD by 2010.

An Intimidating Task

B2Bi is easier said than done – it is indeed a daunting effort. Integration is a big challenge, especially for global corporations that have hundreds or even thousands of trading partners. Managing the integration of so many business processes can turn out to be a time-consuming, complex, and expensive task. With the advent of new technologies, the potential for disparity further increases, and makes the exchange of electronic information even more complicated.

Essential Features of a B2B Integration Solution

Without the right selection of B2Bi solution(s) that meet your business and technical requirements, any integration implementation will be doomed. Before a company selects any B2Bi solution, it has to consider the following:

- ❑ Can the solution evolve with the company, with the industry, and with the IT industry?

- ❑ Does it offer comprehensive functionality with the flexibility to support third-party software vendors, and connect existing and new systems in a common framework?

- ❑ Does it work within scalable environments to accommodate customer and trading partner systems as well?

- ❑ Does it support open standards?

So, what are the key features that a company should look for before investing in any B2Bi software solution?

Firstly, the integration solution should be able to enable any transaction, any time – end-to-end and partner-to-partner. What this essentially means is that a B2Bi solution should be able to link a company automatically in real time to buyers, sellers, e-marketplaces, and collaborative networks. It should be able to fully automate real-time exchange of data between disparate applications using any integration pattern(s).

Secondly, the solution should be able to conduct all transactions securely, maintain audit logs, etc. This includes transactions for catalog management, order management, supply chain management, financial, and logistics.

Thirdly, the solution should support diverse sets of file formats, protocols, and security standards. A company should be able to make a single connection to its B2B integrator and let it take care of the complex behind-the-scenes work necessary to bridge quickly and painlessly the electronic protocol gap between its partners, vendors, and customers.

Fourthly, the solution should be based on open standards that allow a company and its partners to send transactions using any combination of applications and file formats, telecommunication pathways, communication protocols and B2B protocols, and XML standards such as RosettaNet, ebXML, OAG, Biztalk, OBI, etc. The solution should also provide support for Web Services.

Lastly, the solution should be scalable, that is, companies should be able to scale it horizontally and vertically. Further, it should offer robust load-balancing features, critical to the success of large applications.

A few leading B2Bi solutions include: IBM MQSeries Integrator; Extricity; BEA eLink; webMethods B2B Enterprise; Mercator Enterprise Broker, WebBroker, CommerceBroker; NEON eBusiness Integration Servers; SeeBeyond e*Exchange eBusiness Integration Suite; Tibco ActiveEnterprise, ActivePortal, ActiveExchange; Vitria BusinessWare; CrossWorlds Software; and Microsoft BizTalk Server.

Conventional B2Bi Patterns

There are several integration patterns that a company can use to achieve B2Bi. The choice of which integration pattern to choose depends on the agreement with the trading partners, existing infrastructure, and integration goals, such as the level of synchronization and degree of autonomy desired.

Companies can achieve B2Bi using one or more of the following integration patterns.

Portal-Oriented Integration

Portal-oriented integration is a quick way for small to medium-sized companies to provide data access to customers and trading partners through a Web-based interface. The following diagram illustrates how portal-oriented integration provides one place for several customers to gain access to the fruits of integration:

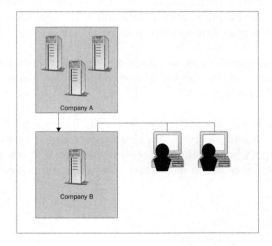

Data-Oriented Integration

Data-oriented integration provides data access interface abstraction. It always involves data sharing and can result in communication between an application and a data source or two data sources. It can be schedule-or event-driven, depending on the type of integration pattern used, such as synchronous replication or asynchronous replication, data warehouses or virtual data warehouses. The following diagram illustrates how data oriented integration links applications through shared data sources:

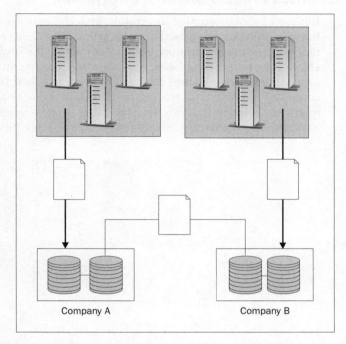

Application-Oriented Integration

Application-oriented integration involves API or RPC communication between application components, which may or may not involve data. Since cross-organization applications have to be integrated directly in this pattern, the participating companies have to work very closely to develop the applications jointly. Companies have less autonomy in this integration pattern, thus making it the least suitable for most B2Bi implementations. This type of integration, however, is synchronous in nature: the data is shared on a real-time basis. The following diagram illustrates how application-oriented integration brings several disparate applications together into one place:

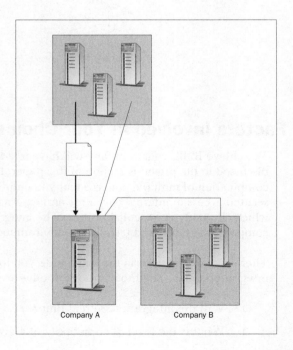

Business Process-Oriented Integration

Business process-oriented integration provides process interface abstraction that maintains the integrity of business rules. This integration type is increasingly being used by companies as it not only aims at integration, but also at making the business processes of a company more efficient by eliminating latency. Moreover, this integration type gives companies complete autonomy in terms of how they want to conduct their business, as long as they are able to communicate with their trading partners based on certain predetermined standards. The following diagram illustrates how business process-oriented integration brings several applications together by linking them into the same business process:

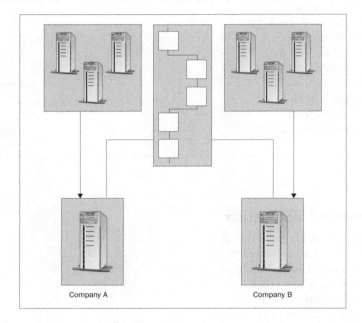

Factors Involved in Your Choice of Integration Pattern

To achieve B2Bi, your company will have to adopt one or more of the integration patterns discussed in the previous section of this paper. Irrespective of the integration pattern or a combination of multiple patterns that you employ for B2Bi, the final goal is to achieve real-time, secured access to internal corporate and external (suppliers, partners, and customers) data, which allows dynamic collaboration. The integration strategy should be in line with your company's business and technology environments, and short-term and long-term business goals.

There are several criteria that can guide you to determine which approach best suits your integration goals. The most important ones are:

❑   Will the integration be real-time?

❑   What is the level of complexity of a given solution?

❏ What is the degree of synchronization achieved in the integration?

❏ Is the solution robust and scalable enough to handle your integration needs?

❏ Is the solution flexible enough to adapt to your company's business processes?

❏ What is the level of autonomy or independence that your company will have in implementing the solution?

❏ How closely will the participating companies have to work in order to achieve integration based on the solution?

The following diagram shows the level of synchronization achieved in using different modes of integration:

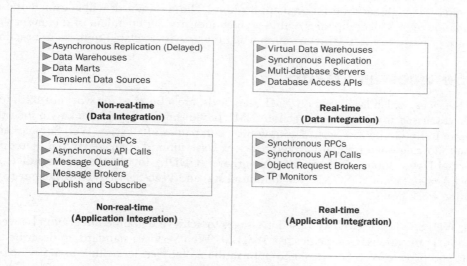

B2Bi involves forming formal agreements among the trading partners to decide various factors involved in integration such as level of integration, pattern of integration, scope of integration, data formats, and XML standards. These agreements are dynamic in nature and are continuously changing with the business environment and needs.

The Role of Extensible Markup Language (XML) in B2Bi

XML has become the *lingua franca* of the B2B e-business revolution. It has created a mechanism to publish, share, and exchange data using open standards over the Internet. There is little doubt that in the future XML will be used in each and every B2B application.

XML is not, however, an integration solution in itself – it is just a data definition language. Without global XML standards there can be no seamless business among companies spread out all over the world. These standards are a common set of industry-specific definitions representing business processes.

For XML messages to be interpreted by all companies participating in B2Bi they need to agree on a common XML-based B2B standard, which will define the document formats, allowable information, and process descriptions. These standards are like a common currency for conducting business. If companies use the same currency to do business then there is no need to convert one currency into another, based on today's conversion rate. In a similar way, communication based on these standards will be accepted and understood by every other company that is using the same standards.

The need for industry-wide B2B e-commerce standards in vertical industries is becoming increasingly critical and obvious. Several organizations have been working to define these market-segment-specific definitions. Standards such as RosettaNet, CIDX, and OASIS are making it possible for companies to share information with one another without having to completely re-engineer their internal applications. These standards will automate the flow of information across all companies within a given industry, independent of the underlying software or hardware infrastructure supporting the activities related to these transactions.

Web Services and B2Bi

Web Services, which are based on XML standards, are a boon to the world of B2B, for the reason discussed in the previous section. XML-based standards hold the key to the success of dynamic B2Bi and its widespread adoption by companies of all sizes. Web Services are based on the following open standards: Web Services Description Language (WSDL – to describe), Universal Description, Discovery and Integration (UDDI – to advertise and syndicate), Simple Object Access Protocol (SOAP – to communicate) and Web Services Flow Language (WSFL – to define work flows).

Thus, Web Services use SOAP-based messages to achieve dynamic integration between two disparate applications. Companies use WSDL, a Web Services standard, to describe their public and private Web Services, and publish their Web Services either to a private or public repository and directory using UDDI.

Essential Features of B2B Applications and Web Services

Let's discuss how Web Services fit in with some of the essential traits of B2B applications.

Distributed Transaction Management

It is very tough to maintain distributed transaction control even within disparate systems and applications within an enterprise. B2B transactions may be spread over disparate systems and applications across different enterprises, making them several times more difficult to maintain and control.

In their current state, Web Services are not transactional in nature and provide basic "request/response" functionality.

Security

B2Bi requires two levels of security. Firstly, B2Bi necessitates opening up corporate firewalls to enable cross-boundary communication between enterprises. Thus, whatever mode of integration is used, companies have to secure their internal network against malicious attacks through these open ports.

Secondly, the data transmitted over dedicated leased lines, such as EDI, Internet, or any other mode, has to be secured. The data may contain classified information, such as corporate information and business transaction information, and thus cannot be left unguarded.

In their current state, Web Services lack broad support and facilities for security. Thus, Web Services-based B2Bi architecture may potentially have big security loopholes.

Dynamic Approach

For companies to participate in true dynamic business with other companies, integration between the systems of the two companies has to happen in real time. Further, this integration is only possible if B2Bi is done using open standards over the Internet.

Web Services do provide a dynamic approach to integration by offering dynamic interfaces. Web Services are based on open standards such as UDDI, SOAP, and HTTP, and this is probably the single most important factor that would lead to the wide adoption of Web Services for B2Bi.

Integration Mode

The integration mode or pattern is the most important element of B2B integration. Is the B2Bi data-, business process-, application-, function-, or portal-oriented? The answer to this question determines a lot of answers involved in the modalities and technology used for B2Bi. Typically in B2B integration, companies involved take a joint decision based on the technology available in-house, budgets, and level of synchronization needed to support business functionalities.

In this generation of Web Services, it is possible to achieve only function-level integration between applications (for details on the difference between function-level integration using API or RPC and Web Services, please refer to our paper "*Enterprise Application Integration and Web Services*").

The next generation of Web Services, however, will be functionally and technologically advanced, offering user interface encapsulation and security. They will be able to package an application and embed it into another application.

Example of Web Services for B2Bi

The following diagram shows an example of using Web Services in a B2Bi scenario. In this example, the corporate procurement application running within an application server requests quotes from multiple vendors. The procurement application of the buyer gets information about Web Services offered by suppliers using a private UDDI registry and invokes these services over the Internet to get quotes for a specific item.

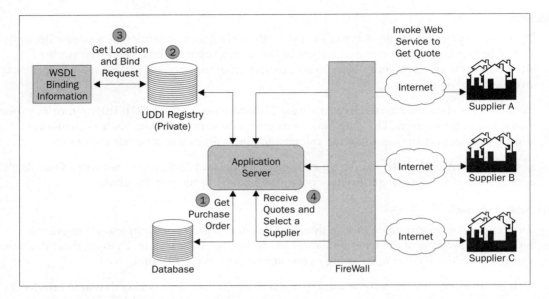

The sequence of steps is as follows:

1. The buyer's procurement application, running within an application server, has to generate a purchase order for a specific item.

2. The procurement application gets information about Web Services from different suppliers for that specific item by performaning a look-up in the private UDDI registry.

3. The location of and WSDL binding information for the Web Services is sent to the procurement application.

4. The application invokes the Web Services published by the suppliers to get quotes for that item. The communication is based on SOAP over the Internet.

5. The application receives quotes from different suppliers. The communication is based on SOAP over the Internet.

6. The information is then analyzed, leading to the creation of the purchase order.

Web Services Networks

The use of Web Services for B2Bi will be enabled through the emergence of trusted managers known as Web Services Networks. Web Services Networks will be built on open Internet standards including Web Services. They will take on the responsibility for managing the security, trading partner agreements, guaranteed messaging, audit trails, fault tolerance, load balancing, transaction management, versioning, publishing, finding, and deploying Web Services.

They will help in overcoming the biggest hurdle of using third-party Web Services for B2Bi – the inherent unreliability of unqualified sources. Grand Central Network and Flamenco Networks are examples of such Web Services Networks.

It is worth mentioning, though, that over time there will be too many such networks, and companies will have to make diligent choices about joining them. Most of these networks will meet the same fate as several e-marketplaces, which sprang up all over and gradually started disappearing.

An Example of B2Bi Enabled Through a Web Services Network

We will expand on our example of B2Bi and Web Services presented earlier in the paper. In this example, the buyer's procurement application utilizes SOAP-based communication, across the firewall and over the Internet, with the Web Services Network. The buyer's application is the Web Services client, which makes a request for quotes for a specific item. The Web Services Network maintains information about public Web Services offered for requesting quotes by different vendors. It invokes the Web Services of these vendors and gets information about the quotes and passes it on to the buyer's application.

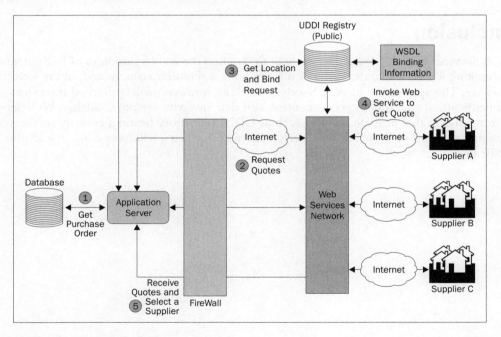

The sequence of steps is as follows:

1. The procurement application of the buyer, running within an application server, has to generate a purchase order for a specific item.

2. The procurement application passes on the request to the Web Services Network using SOAP-based messages.

3. The Web Services Network application looks up a public UDDI registry to get information about Web Services from different suppliers. The location of and WSDL binding information for Web Services is sent to the Web Services Network application.

4. The Web Services Network application invokes the Web Services published by the suppliers to get quotes for that item. The communication is based on SOAP over the Internet.

5. The Web Services Network application passes on the quote information from different suppliers to the buyer's procurement application. The communication is based on SOAP over the Internet.

6. The information is then analyzed, leading to the creation of the purchase order.

Conclusion

Web Services certainly have the potential to redefine the whole paradigm of B2B integration by making it truly dynamic, easily implemented in a modular fashion, and, in the longer run, cheaper. The application of Web Services for B2Bi, however, will be limited if services for authentication, encryption, access control, and data integrity are not available. Web Services intermediaries that provide services such as UDDI repository hosting, security services, quality assurance of Web Services, performance checks, etc., will have a big role to play in the B2Bi space.

Authors: Gunjan Samtani and Dimple Sadhwani

- Integration Broker Fundamentals

- Integration Broker Architectures

- Integration Broker Services

- Integration Brokers and Web Services

- ROI for Web Services Integration Brokers

Integration Brokers and Web Services

An integration broker, built primarily on messaging middleware, provides an end-to-end integration platform addressing the critical business components required to completely automate business processes across the extended enterprise, including the trading partners. It provides wide-ranging, pre-built application adapters and bi-directional connectivity to multiple applications, including packaged and mainframe applications.

An integration broker extracts data from the source node at the right time, transforms the data, converts the schema, and routes the data to the target node. Here, the node can be an application, a program, or a person – as defined in the business process workflow. Communication between applications and an integration broker occurs mostly in the form of messages. An integration broker also provides a repository for archiving, searching, and retrieving these messages.

An integration broker does not replace traditional middleware as MOM, RPC, and distributed TP monitors. It is rather built on top of existing middleware technology, most often on messaging middleware. Therefore, in this paper we will focus on integration brokers built on messaging middleware, also known as message brokers.

Examples of integration broker solutions include: IBM MQSeries Integrator; Extricity; BEA eLink; webMethods B2B Enterprise; Mercator Enterprise Broker, WebBroker, CommerceBroker; NEON eBusiness Integration Servers; SeeBeyond e*Exchange eBusiness Integration Suite; Tibco ActiveEnterprise, ActivePortal, ActiveExchange; Vitria BusinessWare; CrossWorlds Software; and Microsoft BizTalk Server.

Integration Brokers Enable a Best-of-Breed (BOB) Approach

A typical medium-to large-sized company needs multiple applications that collectively support its entire business operation. No single software vendor can provide all these applications with elaborate functionalities for each industry.

Integration brokers enable enterprises to select solutions from different software vendors that provide greater domain expertise and functional support. They provide this flexibility in selection by virtue of providing bidirectional adapters for a wide range of applications, thereby enabling their integration. Integration brokers integrate these diverse applications by sending, receiving, transforming, and routing messages in a secure way, possibly based on open standards such as XML.

With the use of an integration broker, for example, a company could implement Clarify CRM, PeopleSoft Human Resources, Ariba e-Procurement, Oracle Financial, i2 SCM, and SAP Utilities.

Architecture of Integration Brokers

Integration brokers are based on one of two distinct fundamental physical architectures: hub-and-spoke and message bus. Another derived architecture, known as multi-hub, connects several integration brokers, each of which is based on hub-and-spoke or message bus architecture.

Let's have a closer look at these architectures:

Hub-and-Spoke Architecture

In a hub-and-spoke architecture, there is a central server (hub) to which all internal and external applications (spokes) are connected. The central server is actually the integration broker that provides all the integration services. The addition of any new application is extremely simple in this architecture: it only needs to be plugged into the hub. From there on, it can communicate with any other application also connected with the hub (via the broker). Administration of the integration broker is fairly simple in this architecture, as everything is managed centrally.

The centralized nature of this architecture, however, is also its biggest drawback. If, for instance, connectivity to the integration broker is down due to network errors, then the entire system would come to a standstill. No application, internal or external, will be able to communicate with another. To avoid such situations, this architecture requires a clustered solution in which multiple instances of integration brokers run on different physical machines. For example, ERP (Enterprise Resource Planning) systems from one company, SCM (Supply Chain Management) systems from another, a CRM (Customer Relationship Management) package from a third, and a mainframe legacy system can all be linked with an integration broker:

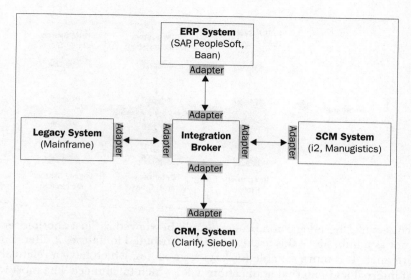

Note that for bidirectional connectivity, we need to install adapters at each end of the connection, as shown in the preceeding diagram. This architecture is suitable for small to medium-sized enterprises, which have relatively fewer internal and external applications with which to integrate. The most widely used integration brokers based on this architecture are from webMethods, CrossWorlds, and Vitria.

Message Bus Architecture

In a message bus architecture, the message bus forms the backbone communication link to which all applications are connected. Every message that flows between applications travels via the bus to the integration broker, which transforms, translates, and routes the message to the receiving application.

The addition of new applications is also simple in this architecture. The integration broker suite would provide either a prepackaged adapter for the application or APIs to build an adapter. After the new application is connected to the bus, it can communicate with all the applications that are connected to the bus. It is not reasonably possible for an integration broker solution to have pre-built adapters for all kinds of applications and thus it should provide the flexibility of building custom adapters.

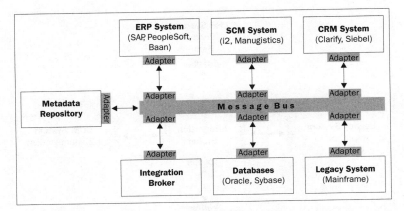

In this architecture, the integration broker should be viewed as "just another service on the bus" and not as a hub. Since this architecture is distributed in nature, it offers better scalability and performance. It is more suitable for large companies, which have a relatively large number of internal and external applications with which to connect. The most widely used integration brokers based on this architecture are from Tibco and SeeBeyond.

Multi-Hub Architecture

A multi-hub architecture is characterized by the presence of multiple integration brokers, each one of which has many applications connected to it. This configuration links together all the different integration brokers. The connectivity of the brokers is transparent to the underlying applications. Through their respective connection with an integration broker, they are integrated with all the other applications linked to different brokers in the system.

This architecture is very useful as a scalable solution, where multiple instances of the same integration broker can be deployed on different physical machines. More such instances can be added if the number of applications to be integrated increases, or the current solution is slow due to overload.

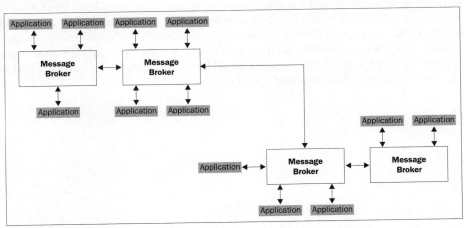

Services of Integration Brokers

The points mentioned below are generic and are not written for any specific integration broker solution. Thus, at several places you will find statements such as "an integration broker should..." It is worth mentioning that companies should evaluate their integration broker solutions based on these points.

Integration brokers provide the following essential services:

Enable All Types of Integration

The first and foremost feature of any integration broker is to enable all types of integration needs within an organization, and in an extended organization through translating, routing, and tracking of all types of data. They have to enable A2A (application-to-application), B2B (business-to-business), and B2C (business-to-consumer) integration, thereby eliminating the need for an individual software solution for each type of integration. There may be a few exceptions and qualifications on enabling all types of integration needs, which will primarily depend on the actual integration broker solution used by the company. Each broker has its own features and services.

For small to medium-sized organizations that do not have the resources to implement advanced B2B systems, integration brokers should provide functionality for rapidly developing B2B portals to enable Web-based participation in business processes.

Interoperability

Integration brokers should provide seamless interoperability with existing applications irrespective of the programming language (such as Java, C, C++, and COBOL) in which they were developed, or the platform (such as Windows, Unix, and mainframe) they run on. This is typically achieved using adapter and messaging technology based on open standards such as XML and SOAP.

Open Architecture

Integration brokers should provide open, non-invasive, and scalable architectures that support all the leading distributed computing architectures such as COM+, CORBA, and J2EE. The following diagram illustrate the advantages of an integration broker platform, and the services it offers:

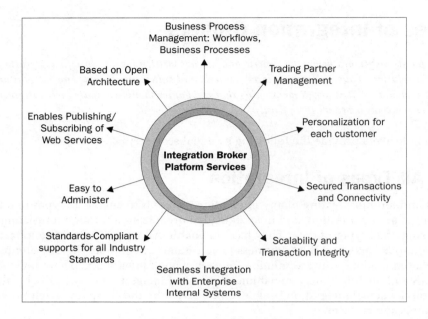

Support for All Communication Protocols

Integration brokers should provide support for all the data transmission protocols for B2B application integration. Some of the most commonly used communication protocols include FTP, HTTP, HTTPS, EDI, e-mail (POP, SMTP), WAP, SNA, and TCP/IP.

As depicted in the following diagram, in a typical B2B scenario a company can exchange data with other companies through multiple channels.

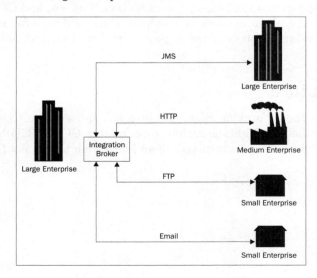

Directory Services

As seen in the multi-hub architecture figure, a real-world implementation is completely distributed in nature, with multiple instances of integration brokers connecting several applications and middleware resources.

The directory service of an integration broker is like a yellow pages that maintains an index of all source and target applications along with their location, communication protocol, and use. It provides a single point of entry, also known as a gateway, along with search facilities for all the applications and resources connected by the broker(s).

Trading Partner Management and Personalization

Integration brokers should provide a meta data repository, which can store the definition, preferences, and technical specifications (such as communication protocol, XML/EDI standard, delivery channel, and security requirements) unique to each trading partner relationship. Storing all this information would greatly speed up conducting business and would enable companies to offer personalized services to each customer, supplier, and distributor.

Security

Integration brokers should provide a complete security solution using encryption, PKI, digital authentication, digital certificates SSL, and S/MIME encryption. They should also maintain a transaction audit trail through which data privacy, data integrity, and transaction non-repudiation (non-repudiation of origin and non-repudiation of receipt) can be ensured.

Scalability

Integration brokers should provide a scalable platform that can support a company's business today and for years to come. They should be optimized for multi-processor systems and enable load balancing and failover solutions through a clustered architecture.

Transactional Integrity

An integration broker must provide transactional integrity (event-based processing, exception handling and built-in recovery) at every step, activity, and node for each transaction and business process that flows through it.

Typically, a business transaction is composed of several logical units of work, and each unit of work must complete successfully in order for the transaction to be committed. If even one unit of work fails, the whole transaction fails and all completed units of work have to be rolled back (reversed).

Since a business transaction may involve updating multiple databases it may take a long time to complete. If a database being updated by an application through messages is unavailable, the integration broker should store the message and make it available to the application when the database is up again.

Web Services

Web Services expose applications supporting business operations, encapsulating business logic, and accessing business data over the network or Internet using interfaces that can be invoked. Their main advantage is that companies can use Web Services interfaces for process management, logic transformation, and integration of legacy and packaged applications, instead of writing non standards-based custom code for each application.

Web Services can potentially be used for two distinct domains – enterprise application integration (EAI) and business-to-business integration (B2Bi). EAI is the process of creating an integrated infrastructure for linking disparate systems, applications, and data sources within the corporate enterprise. B2Bi is the process of secured coordination of information among businesses and their information systems, enabling cross-enterprise business applications such as collaborative e-commerce, collaborative networks, supply chain management (SCM), and customer relationship management (CRM) across multiple channels of delivery including wireless devices and the Internet.

Will Web Services Become Just Another Service of Integration Brokers?

Yes, undoubtedly. Integration brokers should provide the ability to create, test, deploy, publish, and manage Web Services and subscribe to a business partner's Web Services as an out-of-the-box solution. This would enable the enterprises to convert quickly the existing applications into Web Services. They would include an integrated development environment and framework for easily building and deploying Web Services and service components. This should include:

❑ **Support for SOAP** – An integration broker should be able to generate and exchange Web Services request and response SOAP-based messages.

❑ **Support for Web Services Standards** – An integration broker should provide complete support for Web Services standards including SOAP (as above), UDDI, WSDL, and XML.

❑ **Security** – An integration broker should be able to exchange Web Services request and response XML messages (based on SOAP) in a secured manner over multiple Internet protocols such as HTTP, HTTPS, FTP, and SMTP. It should provide easy and secured connectivity to private and public UDDI, or any other repository. Further, an integration broker should provide efficient security safeguards such as policy management and authentication, for the access and usage of Web Services.

- **Transactional Integrity** – Transactional integrity is one of the single most important factors that would determine the winners among the integration broker solutions that offer Web Services support.

- **Auditing** – An integration broker should provide an effective audit mechanism through which the access and usage of Web Services can be closely monitored.

- **Monitoring** – An integration broker should provide a monitoring solution to keep track of the current health of the Web Services network.

- **Development** – An integration broker should support easy development, deployment, publishing, finding, and dynamic binding for Web Services interfaces. It should provide a stable environment for rapid development of Web Services-based applications.

- **UDDI Connectivity** – An integration broker should provide easy connectivity to internal (private) and external (public) UDDI registries. Based on the registry type, there may be a need of an adapter or multiple adapters.

- **Workflow Management** – Workflow management through which usage of Web Services in a business process can be defined is one of the key requirements of an integration broker.

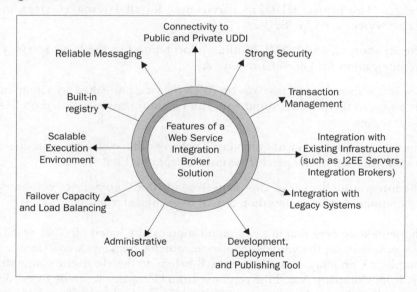

Easy Connectivity with Third-Party Web Services Solution

Integration broker vendors may decide to use a third-party Web Services solution, instead of developing their own. In this case, the third-party solution would be a very lightweight application server that would implement support for Web Services protocols.

The support for other protocols, such as DCOM, COM, COM+, and CORBA would continue to be provided by the integration broker. In order for this to work, the integration between integration broker solution and third-party Web Services solution has to be seamless, easy, secured, and robust, most likely using adapters.

An Example of Integration Brokers and Web Services

Here we will take an example of using integration brokers and Web Services in both an enterprise application integration (EAI) and a business-to-business integration (B2Bi) scenario.

In this example, the integration broker of Company A invokes the Web Service (Product Shipment Status) of Company B over the Internet, receives the response from the integration broker of Company B, and invokes Web Services published by SCM and ERP systems in-house to update the product shipment status information.

The sequence of steps is as follows:

Integration Broker and Web Service for B2Bi

1. Company A's integration broker gets information about Company B's Web Service (Product Shipment Status) by performing a look-up in the private UDDI registry. This private UDDI registry is used for all external services, in this case, Web Services used for B2Bi.

2. The location of, and WSDL binding information for, the Web Services is sent to the integration broker of Company A.

3. The integration broker invokes the Web Service published by Company B to get the status of the product shipment. The communication is based on SOAP over the Internet.

4. The integration broker of company B receives the Web Service request and gets the information of the product shipment from its ERP system.

5. The integration broker of Company B sends the Web Service response. Again, the communication is based on SOAP over the Internet.

It is worth mentioning here that this communication can be based on XML standards defined for business processes for the vertical industry to which Company A and Company B belong. As an example, if Company A and Company B belong to the electronic components industry, the request from Company A and the response from Company B can be based on RosettaNet's PIP. Other such examples of B2B XML standards include ebXML and cXML.

Integration Broker and Web Service for EAI

6. On receiving the response, Company A's integration broker gets information about the ERP and SCM packages' Web Service (Product Shipment Status) by performing a look-up in the private UDDI registry. This private UDDI registry is used for internal services, in this case Web Services used for EAI.

7. The location of and WSDL binding information for the Web Services published by the SCM and ERP systems is sent to the integration broker of Company A.

8. The integration broker invokes the Web Service and updates the product shipment information in both SCM and ERP packages.

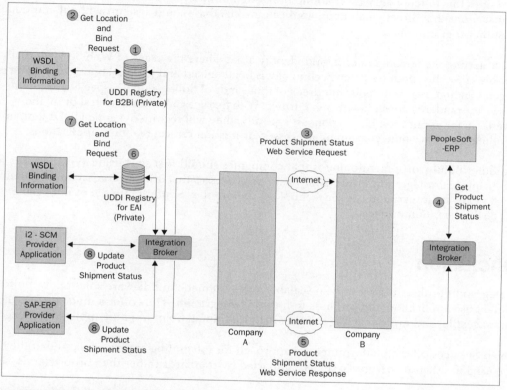

UDDI Registry for EAI and B2Bi

A point worth mentioning in this example is that we used two different UDDI registries – one for maintaining information on internal Web Services used for EAI, and the second for external Web Services. It is important for companies not to mix information about Web Services used for two separate domains – EAI and B2Bi.

Existing Integration Broker Infrastructure and Web Services

If a company has invested millions of dollars to put its integration broker infrastructure in place, it makes absolutely no sense to abandon it and just embrace some other Web Services solution. Several integration broker vendors, such as TIBCO, Sybase/Neon, Vitria, webMethods, SeeBeyond, and Mercator are already providing support for Web Services in their products. Companies can now use the same integration broker technology to launch Web Services initiatives.

The addition of Web Services support to the existing integration broker solution would allow companies to easily integrate internal and external applications. This would be based on services that define and implement business flows and processes with internal groups within an organization, and external trading partners, customers, and suppliers. Companies will be able to achieve faster and more efficient results, and a higher ROI, if the integration broker provides this functionality by enabling the design of internal and external business process transactions that directly call upon applications, databases, and systems without additional custom programming.

As a starting point, companies should identify areas where the usage of Web Services really makes sense. Just because a new technology is being talked and written about everywhere is not a good enough reason to pour hundreds of thousands of dollars into it, especially when the Web Services standards are still evolving. Further, Web Services are not the fastest of solutions available for application integration, as, typically, they will require dynamic UDDI look-up and binding which are time consuming processes for mission-critical real-time applications.

Another point worth mentioning is that companies should first start using Web Services for their internal integration projects for business processes that are non-transactional in nature using existing integration broker technology, before they venture into the use of Web Services in B2B integration projects.

Conclusion

Integration brokers offer a proven scalable and systematic middleware solution for both enterprise application and business-to-business integration. They offer a much neater, more manageable, and more scalable solution than traditional point-to-point application integration.

Web Services offer a platform-neutral approach for integrating applications, so that they can be used to integrate diverse systems, supported by standards rather than proprietary systems.

Leading integration broker solutions have already started supporting Web Services as one of their services. Companies will be able to lower their investment cost in implementing Web Services solutions by building on top of their existing assets.

Author: Kapil Apshankar

- ERP Business Drivers

- ERP Methodology

- Web Services and ERP Issues

- Comparison

- Economics

ERP and Web Services
The Third Wave

Introduction

Every major technology goes through a series of revolutions or "waves" with each wave building upon the generation before it. ERP is no exception. The first wave of ERP was the onset of computers in manufacturing. This was followed by a wave where specialized ERP applications began to emerge. Web Service-based ERP solutions constitute what can be appropriately termed as the Third Wave in Enterprise Resource Planning. This paper looks at what such solutions have to offer and who the major players in the foray are. We also take a look at solution architectures for the two immediate application areas of such solutions.

Enterprise Resource Planning is a generic term for the broad set of activities facilitated by multi-module application software that helps businesses manage their important facets. ERP also includes application modules for the finance and human resources aspects of a business. Typically, an ERP system uses or is integrated with a relational database system at the back end.

ERP annihilates the old standalone computer systems in finance, HR, manufacturing, and the warehouse, and replaces them with a single unified software program divided into modules that roughly approximate the old standalone systems. All the departments still get their own systems, except now the software is linked together so that someone in finance can look into the warehouse system to see if an order has been shipped. Most ERP vendors ensure that software is flexible enough to install some modules without buying the whole package. Many companies, for example, will just install an ERP finance or HR module and leave the rest of the modules for a sunny day.

This is what the installation manuals, product brochures, and marketing campaigns claim. In the field, however, it's often not as rosy as it looks. There are many things that go into deciding the fate of an ERP application – planning, foresight, business requirements, and change management. ERP applications are notorious for configuration issues, which can make or mar their fate. What Web Services provide is that they minimize risk and investment, and allow organizations some amount of flexibility in terms of cross-vendor integration.

ERP is both a product and a methodology for delivering a product. As a methodology, it manifests in the planning and consultation that goes behind implementing it as a product-based solution.

The Business Drivers Behind ERP

No solution would be embraced by the industry unless it is economically promising. Businesses accept ERP because it carries in its wake the promise to alleviate hitherto unsolved chronic problems. But to be objective there are many public cases that have gone through the courts in America in particular where the promise turned into an unhappy and financially costly experience. We may not want to play down the difficulties faced by the companies and the ERP supplier companies; the task can be massive and highly complex and can span years – so financial and productivity gains may be subject to a dynamic set of contingencies. It is further suggested that this is why many companies stick with only one or two modules. The following points are the key business drivers:

1. **Integrate financial information:** ERP creates a single version of internal information that cannot be questioned or doubted because everyone uses the same system.

2. **Integrate customer order information:** ERP facilitates a single point of view of customer information in the enterprise.

3. **Standardize and speed up manufacturing processes:** Often multiple business units across a company make the same widget using different processes and methodologies. Standardizing these processes and using a single, integrated computer system can save time, increase productivity, and reduce payroll expenditure.

4. **Reduce inventory**: ERP helps the manufacturing process flow more smoothly, and it improves the visibility of the order fulfillment process inside the company. Ideally we also need supply chain software in this scenario, but ERP is paramount because it facilitates the services just in time. There are specialized solutions emerging in this field that complement each other. Take for example i2 (http://www.i2.com/); i2 solutions combine planning and decision making with the execution phases of value chain management. The solutions they provide can be seen as a specialization of the SCM part of ERP, although sometimes they are direct competitors with the big ERP vendors.

5. **Standardize HR information**: Especially in companies with multiple business units, HR may not have a unified, simple, and all-pervasive method for tracking employee information, benefits, and services. ERP can fix that. This results in improved employee satisfaction and helps clear communication lines.

The Journey So Far

The concept of ERP is not new. It has existed since the dawn of civilization as Neolithic merchants sought to increase their business efficiency by using certain rules of thumb, passed down from the previous generation and refined by experience. Traders following the Silk Route always returned back home just in time for summer when they knew demand would be high for their products and inventory could be kept at a minimum. This could be looked upon as ERP in its most rudimentary form. Times have changed, and along with them the terminologies; the basic guiding principles however remain the same.

After the advent of the computer and the information age, the paradigm changed. We now look at ERP to automate the business processes, the computing paradigm replacing the "human brain" paradigm.

Knowing the history and evolution of ERP is essential to understanding its current application and its future developments. The following graph depicts the genesis of ERP by era:

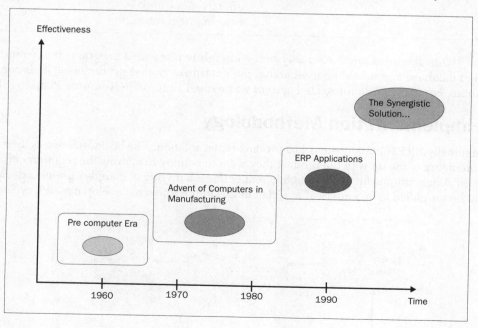

The following table looks at the advantages and focus of each of the eras through which ERP has progressed.

Decade	Era	Focus	Disadvantages
1960s	Pre-computer era	Inventory Control	Reorder Point System
1970s	Advent of computers in manufacturing	Materials Requirements Planning (MRP)	Open loops, no feedbacks
1980s	Advent of computers in manufacturing	MRP II – an improved version of MRP with some closed loops.	Duplication
1990s	ERP Applications	Integrated software. Just in Time and Available To Promise philosophies.	Duplication
2000s	Web Services	Synergy, effectiveness, and ease of integration	None?

In the 1990s, the need to develop a system with tightly integrated programs that would use a unified database and would be used across the enterprise gained prominence. This common-database, company-wide integrated system was named Enterprise Resource Planning (ERP).

ERP Implementation Methodology

Traditionally ERP is implemented as a product-based solution. The businesses assess their requirements, come up with the product they want to employ to address the requirements, and then go about customizing it. Although in reality this is a myriad of complex business decisions, it could be simplified to an empirical waterfall model in the software development life cycle:

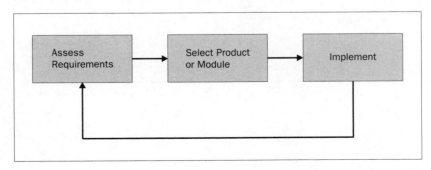

There are three commonly used ways of installing ERP.

1. **The Big Bang:** This is the most ambitious and difficult approach to ERP implementation. In this methodology, companies cast off all their legacy systems at once and install a single ERP system across the organization. Though this method dominated early ERP implementations, few companies dare to attempt it anymore because it calls for the entire company to mobilize and change at once. More often than not organizations have failed miserably using this approach.

2. **Franchising:** This approach suits large or diverse companies that do not share many common processes across business units. Independent ERP systems are installed in each unit, while linking common processes, such as finance management, across the enterprise. This has emerged as the most common way of implementing ERP. In this methodology, we would witness legacy applications being replaced one at a time, as requirements evolve.

3. **Try and Buy:** ERP dictates the process design in this method, where the focus is on just a few key processes, such as those contained in an ERP system's financial module. The try and buy approach is generally for smaller companies expecting to grow into ERP. The goal here is to get ERP up and running quickly and to avoid the re-engineering and tailoring issues in favor of the ERP system's out-of-the-box processes. The payback from this approach is not very high, but the experience gained is invaluable. Most use it as an infrastructure to support more meticulous installation efforts down the road.

Why ERP and Web Services?

A Web Service is any software component that makes itself available over the Internet or intranet and uses a standardized XML messaging system. Beyond this basic definition, a Web Service also has two additional and desirable properties. First, a Web Service has a public interface, defined in a common XML grammar. Web Services also facilitate a relatively simple and extremely powerful publishing mechanism through UDDI.

In the context of ERP, Web Services offer a two-fold advantage: ease of integration, and reduction in costs through the hosted application model.

Ease of Integration

Ease of integration is a major source of expenditure across enterprises. To put the importance of integration into perspective, it would be worth looking at benchmarking figures from the Meta Group. Global 2000 companies rely on an average of 49 enterprise applications, and they spend up to 33% of the IT budget just to get them to talk to one another.

ERP is complex and not intended for public consumption. It assumes that the only people handling order information will be employees who are highly trained and comfortable with the system.

Now, however, clients and outsourcing vendors are demanding access to the same information employees get through the ERP system – things like order status, inventory levels, and invoice reconciliation – except they want to get all this information simply, without all the ERP software. This is where Web Services come to the rescue, wherein seamless URL calls make it possible to expose just the appropriate amount of material to the authenticated users at the right time.

Integration is an age-old problem for IT. According to the IDC Digital Planet 2000 Report, there has been a tremendous expenditure during the last 10 years: $18 trillion in IT investment, and still there are integration problems. Indeed the more information that is produced, the more complex the issues of integration become. It is not so much a case of high volumes of data, but more a diversity of systems and architectures that don't communicate as well as a company would like. The fundamental questions are what needs to be shared or accessed, by whom, and how the end users or systems are geographically located.

Over time, different approaches have emerged – data adapters, message brokering and other types of middleware, and other approaches. These different technologies have collectively become known as Enterprise Application Integration (EAI). EAI is the process whereby a company integrates their disparate legacy systems and databases, often with recent systems additions.

With the availability of Web Services we can achieve integration with a superior quality of service on parameters of reliability, security, manageability, routing, discovery, testing, and effectiveness. Web Services basically use object-oriented technology to "wrap" data and programming elements in Web Service methods to be accessed by different applications. The client application need not be Web-based: a windows application can be a client and host the Web Service functionality. The typical example is a price lookup request by a customer. Using Web Services and Simple Object Access Protocol (SOAP), the browser can check out prices at different SOAP-based sites and then deliver a price comparison to the customer. The system provides the service behind the scenes by invoking different behavior and information from the various target systems.

There is one basic difference between Web Services and EAI: Web Services provide an open means of dealing with integration, where EAI has traditionally been driven by one or two vendors or is product-specific. A software bridge of sorts may exist to connect a PeopleSoft human resources package to SAP's R/3 system, but that same EAI bridge won't work for other human-resources packages trying to connect to SAP. It is worth remembering that Web Services is still primarily an interfacing architecture. Today's integration software companies, however, offer integration solutions that easily enable a company to replace any application through a hub and spoke system, and a standard adapter (for standard applications) or a tool to create an adapter, without changing any code.

On the other hand, SOAP, for one, is a standard backed by the World Wide Web Consortium. Also, where Web Services are meant from the get-go to be used in a distributed fashion, that's not always the case with EAI technologies.

Reduction in Costs Through the Hosted Application Model

The deployment of a traditional ERP system can involve considerable business process analysis, employee retraining, and new work procedures. A franchising strategy to adopt Web Services for ERP implementation or enhancement takes advantage of the investment made in the legacy ERP applications and gives them a new lease of life.

Web Services permit proprietary applications to communicate over the Web. The goal of chief vendors is to create "wrappers" to access a high-level tool that turns Java or any other proprietary program into a Web Service. Proprietary ERP applications and Web Services can talk to each other by using such high-level tools – HP's E-Speak toolsets; IBM's Dynamic e-business (infrastructure and software); and Sun's ONE (Forte technology and iPlanet's ECXpert) – all of which assist data flow and communications between vastly diverse applications.

ERP provides for integrated, multicomponent application software performing multiple business functions. It involves the use of packaged software instead of client-written custom software. It must be noted here that some ERP packages are customizable by the client: for example SAP has permissible client customization zones and naming conventions to identify client-developed functionality, so that when a new version of SAP is released the customization is preserved. There are of course areas that a client is not authorized to customize. Clients use SAP's language ABAP for this purpose.

ERP vendors are finding ways for different enterprises involved in the same supply chain to integrate their systems with the marketplace. This is actually a classic example of ERP using the already established concept of e-commerce. Let's take an example here; say six people need to communicate and they all speak different languages. One solution is to require each person to learn the other five languages. A better solution would be for all six people to learn one common language. RosettaNet aspires to solve this problem with PIPs (Partner Interface Processes). Companies that need to collaborate work with RosettaNet to form the language for their respective market. This mutually understandable dialog is documented in a PIP. This process ensures that enterprises name APIs for each other, decide on ways to find applications on the network, and come to an agreement on how data is exchanged between applications.

How Do Web Services Make ERP Easier?

The enterprise may still require an ERP application for its internal systems to function efficiently together. Web Services allow the enterprise to acquire the information needed to respond effectively, even in situations where tightly coupled application design isn't necessary.

By developing an integrated Internet information solution, ERP systems companies make public information that was never before accessible from the enterprise. Markets created in this way are by definition more efficient, because they permit companies to concentrate their efforts on customer service and profits. As this new technology gains business-wide support, more vendors will venture into product support for these Web Services. It would not be out of place to see an example here.

Hewitt Associates (FBR Research Brief, "Web Services 101 – A Glimpse Into The Next Software Computing Platform") is a consulting firm that provides outsourced human resources capabilities. The company has already started providing online 401k, pension, and health management services to over 250 organizations and their 12 million employees – a daunting task for any IT department.

Traditional ERP vendors had a hard time building the links between the Web and their software. Most of them are now presenting solutions helpful for bridging the gaps.

The number and functionality of available Web Services is starting to increase (for some idea of the range of services now available, see http://www.4arrow.com/), and ERP and accounting systems vendors are beginning to tackle the integration problem by introducing what are called Web Service **broker hubs**. A broker hub offers a portal to provide a user interface for consumers so that they can find, evaluate, subscribe to, cancel, manage, or monitor Web Services. Users of a specific accounting or ERP application can visit their software vendor's service broker hub to complement their accounting suite. The services brokered through these hubs can integrate fully with the back-end applications so that data such as banking, shipment, or credit information is not just delivered to a user's web browser but is sent to the local ERP database so users can view it within the ERP application.

An increasing number of accounting and ERP vendors are delivering Web Service broker hubs. SAP and Oracle offer them for users of mySAP and Oracle E-Business Suite. Intuit and Peachtree offer them for use with QuickBooks and Peachtree Complete Accounting, and Navision is one of the few ERP vendors that will offer a Web Service broker hub to users of midtier accounting software.

Web Service broker hubs offer a new way to customize an ERP application without any local code modifications, because they integrate the application with Web Services. This saves companies from relying on overstretched IT resources or expensive consultants for deployment and maintenance of the software. The service provider takes care of delivering the service, and its clients can subscribe for as long as they are interested in it, or use it on demand. This is a terrific and powerful application of Web Services. This really simplifies maintainability, efficiency of use, and productivity. Just imagine the improvements if the mission-critical and problematic elements of a system can be a Web Service supplied by the software house. It is very much akin to having the most technically sensitive parts of your system housed by the experts under 24/7 monitoring.

I expect most ERP vendors to offer a Web Service broker hub within the next few years and every ERP application to become a fusion that is neither a product nor a service, but both.

Current Scenario

Major enterprise application software vendors have already embraced the Web Services architecture. Oracle, SAP, and PeopleSoft are on the forefront on this aspect, with many of them already having graduated to the Web Services way of life. SAP and PeopleSoft are pursuing Web Services to help facilitate application integration.

SAP has fully embraced UDDI, becoming a global UDDI operator and aiming to build on UDDI for service integration and publish global services within the UDDI Business Registry. SAP plans to allow services built around its mySAP.com e-business platform to be published on UDDI. In addition, SAP customers will be able to use UDDI to find and integrate external services. SAP has already registered itself with UDDI and started to publish its global services offerings. SAP's Web Services push will begin in earnest after it puts Java on a par with its own ABAP programming language.

Key components of this new strategy will come with version upgrades to SAP's Web Application Server, which will allow application components to be provided as Web Services. By the end of 2002 there should be direct ties between SAP's proprietary realm and the world of Java programming in Version 6.3 of SAP's Application Server. Both virtual engines will run in the same kernel environment. This coexistence will allow users to switch easily between Java- and SAP-centric applications and Web Services.

PeopleSoft has just overhauled its offerings to a 100% Internet architecture giving it the edge to transform the business around a new set of integrated applications and promising rapid return on investment (ROI). PeopleSoft will add more Web Services support next year by enhancing its toolkits so they understand how to interrogate SOAP and UDDI message definitions.

Oracle, in the first quarter of 2002, has already made use of Web Services technologies to better integrate business logic across the applications that make up Oracle11*i*.

Where Oracle, SAP, and PeopleSoft see Web Services as a foundation for better integrating applications within their own suites, others see Web Services as an industry-standard infrastructure that will facilitate business-logic integration across diverse best-of-breed applications on a global scale.

Another aspect that cannot be overlooked is that since Visual Studio .NET has been released, we should see a significant increase in the development and integration of Web Services. Visual Studio .NET makes it so easy to do, and so cheap: it's only a question of time now.

The following table summarizes the Service Oriented Architecture offerings that the major vendors have, with which all of them aspire to capture a piece of the pie.

Competitor	Environment	Expected Date	Status	Offerings
SAP	J2EE and ABAP in the same kernel	2002	Nearly Done	R3, mySAP.com
Oracle	Java	2002	EOY	11i Suite, Java APIs

Table continued on following page

Competitor	Environment	Expected Date	Status	Offerings
PeopleSoft	Tools for SOAP and UDDI	2002	Nearly Done	PeopleSoft8
Microsoft	.NET and Passport	2001	Done	Bcentral
Siebel	Business Services	2001	Done	Siebel7

Technology Issues

The high-level architecture of a Web Service-enabled ERP solution could primarily take two forms:

❑   Information integration/exchange

❑   Functionality Enhancement or Substitution through the hosted-application model

We will cover both these architectures in detail here.

Web Services-ERP based model: Architecture for Information Integration/Exchange

This architecture can be employed in two business scenarios:

❑   When information native to an internal ERP system has to be made public or shared with other business partners.

❑   When a small company goes in for a Try and Buy approach for an ERP implementation.

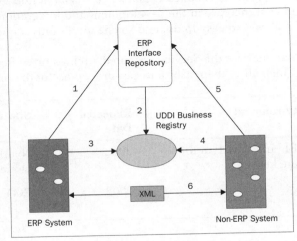

The following are the transactions that happen in this architecture:

1. XML interfaces are published in the Interface Repository.

2. Interfaces are now registered as Service Types with the UDDI business registry.

3. Users register their Business with references to Service Types.

4. Another user discovers a suitable business.

5. The user downloads Service Type Descriptions.

6. Electronic business conducted

To reduce the difficulty of connecting their systems with other vendors' applications, customers have pushed their primary ERP providers to adopt a more open and flexible architecture and to support standards-based computing. Most big ERP providers have responded by migrating their architectures to component frameworks based on such standards as COM, DCOM, and CORBA. In the vast majority of cases, however, it's still quite difficult, expensive, and time-consuming to integrate enterprise software. The technology to make this easier is on its way. Not only Web Services, but also .NET's remoting will help to this end.

Still, when it comes to opening architectures, vendors think twice. On the one hand, they need to respond to customer demands for easier integration. By supporting integration with other vendors' software, they can add diverse functionality to customers' ERP systems without having to develop every new application that comes along. For example, SAP does not have adapters or connectivity to PeopleSoft or Baan. This is where an Integration vendor comes into play and offers such functionality through a Web Service. On the other hand, it's easier for vendors to provide efficient and reliable software when they control all the pieces. ERP vendors also earn higher profits when they sell more modules to individual customers. While the trend is definitely toward increasing openness, it won't happen overnight. Vendors can't abruptly migrate to a new architecture because doing so would disenfranchise customers with legacy systems.

Before making a decision on ERP packages, we must make a list of software with which we need to integrate and the specific functions, business process, and data that need to be married. Although by using XML the need to integrate disparity or remove incompatibility barriers are minimized or negated, we need to adopt a pragmatic approach here and carefully determine how much work is involved to integrate the packages. It would also help if we have a clear understanding of the vendor's timetable for supporting the integration of any functions that are problematic right at the outset.

Web Services-ERP based model: Architecture for the Hosted Application Model

This architecture is suitable for organizations that already have an ERP infrastructure in place and merely want to augment it by franchising outsourced functionalities.

Such an application would follow the same development life cycle as discussed for the earlier architecture.

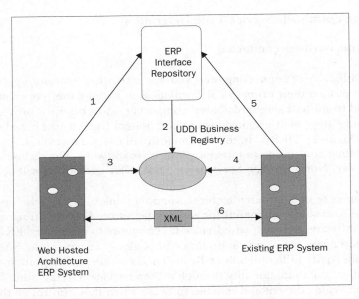

There has been a perception for years that ERP is not meant for the midmarket because of its reputation of having long and expensive implementations. Applications based on this architecture that are hosted and largely not customized, however, have helped ERP shed its reputation.

Comparison

This is a comparison between the current day ERP solutions and the Web Service-based ERP solutions:

Parameter	Traditional Solution	Web Service Solution
Scalability	Low	Very High
Time Frame for implementation	Very High	Moderate
Maintainability	Low	Very High

Parameter	Traditional Solution	Web Service Solution
Reliability	Moderate	High
Portability	Low	Very High
Cost to Enter	High	Moderate
Cost to Maintain	High	Low
Total Cost of Ownership	High	Low
ROI	Moderate	Very High

Beneficiaries of ERP Web Services

Two entities immediately spring to mind as being direct and immediate beneficiaries of ERP solutions using a Web Services methodology:

❑ Medium-sized companies.

❑ Small companies.

These entities are usually grouped into the SME category, but we would consider them separately to see how they benefit from this model. For medium-sized organizations, the Web Services methodology is the cheapest and easiest way to implement an ERP solution. It offers substantial cost savings as we shall see in the subsequent section. One of the major advantages for these organizations is that an ERP system can be literally built off the shelf.

Small companies benefit similarly, using their limited resources to outsource ERP solutions and curb expenditure.

SAP reports that more than 43% of SAP installations are at companies with less than $200 million in annual revenue, and more than 60% take place at companies that have less than $500 million in annual revenue. Small and medium businesses don't have different needs from larger companies, but they generally can't afford customized solutions.

One third of PeopleSoft's new customers are from the SME category. At the present, PeopleSoft has more than 1,000 customers in the midmarket. One-third of Oracle's sales in North America are to companies with less than $500 million in annual revenue. Worldwide, small and midsize companies are 25% to 30% of Oracle's sales.

As with PeopleSoft, Oracle has also come to rely on the hosted-application model to drive down costs and produce rapid implementations for its midsize customers. Much of this is done through the company's FastForward program, which offers customers a subset of Oracle's software suites. In Oracle's fiscal year 2001, which ended in May, 85% of Oracle application implementations via its hosted model were completed in less than 150 days. Such a fast delivery methodology promises rapid breakeven in an ERP implementation.

Economics of ERP Web Services

Web Services are not free, they cost time and money to develop – even those that are being offered for free currently. They are, though, cheaper than their "bricks and mortar" counterparts. Legacy data or information has to be "wrapped" to become a Web Service, which can require a fair bit of custom programming work. This is an item to be considered under the cash-out flow column. Apart from this, however, there are substantial savings in other aspects of ERP Web Services.

In a recent Meta Group study encompassing the total cost of ownership (TCO) of ERP, including hardware, software, professional services, and internal staff costs, among the 63 companies surveyed – including small, medium, and large companies in a range of industries – the average TCO was $15 million (the highest was $300 million and lowest was $400,000). The TCO numbers include getting the software installed and the two years afterward, which is when the real costs of maintaining, upgrading, and optimizing the system for business are felt. While it's hard to draw a solid number from that kind of range of companies and ERP efforts, Meta came up with one statistic that proves that ERP is expensive no matter what kind of company is using it. The TCO for a "heads-down" user over that period was a staggering $53,320.

The TCO for a similar Web Service solution would be substantially lower. This is due to the fact that the following costs normally incurred in a traditional ERP solution are alleviated or reduced in this approach:

- ❑ Deployment costs.
- ❑ Consultancy costs.
- ❑ Future expenses due to migration and scalability issues.
- ❑ Training costs.
- ❑ Integration and testing costs. We benefit from the "componentware" paradigm Web Services offer.
- ❑ Data Conversion costs.
- ❑ Data Analysis costs.

The rapid turn around time of a Web Service solution promises higher yield and ROI, lesser investment, and faster break-even point.

Interrelation

During the last three years, the functional perimeter of ERP systems has expanded into its adjacent markets, such as supply chain management (SCM), customer relationship management (CRM), product data management (PDM), manufacturing executions systems (MES), business intelligence/data warehousing, and e-business. The major ERP vendors have been proactively developing, acquiring, or bundling new functionality so that their packages go beyond the traditional realms of finance, materials planning, and human resources.

We should soon begin to witness symbiotic Web Service offerings from all the major vendors.

The Road Ahead

To judge from a recent Accenture survey of executives in mid-sized and large companies, ERP still looms large on the radar screens of business decision makers. The Accenture study shows that 22% of the executives surveyed believed ERP implementation to be the most beneficial technology investment over the last two years for their organizations.

A growing number of small and midsize companies are deploying enterprise resource planning applications. In the past, many of these companies, typically with an annual revenue of less than $500 million, didn't have the budget or time to consider implementing large, complex, and expensive ERP packages. With the increasingly vast array of software vendors such as Oracle, PeopleSoft, and SAP to choose from, a lot of smaller companies are rethinking their options, which now include less expensive, modular, Web-architected, and hosted versions of ERP software.

Within the next two years, ERP will be redefined as a platform enabled by Web Services globally. Originally focused on automating the internal processes of an enterprise, ERP systems will begin to include customer and supplier-centric processes as well. ERP Web Services will become universal business applications that will encompass front office, business intelligence, e-commerce, and supply chain management.

Conclusion

ERP is a great concept, but like so many of these great ideas, conditions apply. It seems very likely that future ERP applications will not be either products or services, but rather combinations of products, services, and "loosely coupled" applications. These applications are another form of hybrid because they combine locally installed product functions with distributed service functions delivered electronically over the Internet.

Hybrid models offer a best-of-both-worlds solution. They provide fast, locally installed product functions combined with on-demand remote services that take advantage of the Internet. They help maintain private data ownership, while making select data public in a controlled manner. They deliver simple customization of applications through the addition of Web Services channeled via service broker hubs, which focus on the needs of a specific ERP suite.

Authors: Liang-Jie Zhang and Henry Chang

- Process Integration

- E-Logistics Processes Integration Framework

- Example

- Working B2B System

E-Logistics Processes Integration Using Web Services

With globalization and the resulting need for faster and more flexible communications, a company needs a framework to establish itself in no time or make best use of its legacy applications and run efficiently at minimal cost. This case study presents such a framework called ELPIF (E-Logistics Processes Integration Framework) for e-logistics processes integration based on Web Services via incorporating a:

1. Common alliance interface.

2. Adaptation layer.

3. Dynamic data binding mechanism.

This framework can be adopted as a new service delivery model that uses a design pattern, business process inheritance, and solution templates. The interaction between the e-logistics processes and the business process manager that orchestrates e-logistics processes in an e-business solution will be described in this paper. An example of transportation planning in the purchase order management process of a B2B solution is used to illustrate the usage of ELPIF by encapsulating United Parcel Service of America (UPS) Online XML Tools as Web Services.

In the last couple of years, various online shipping tools have been developed for e-commerce application developers. Take the example of the transportation industry: United Parcel Service of America (UPS) provides several online XML tools and HTML tools (UPS OnLine E-Commerce Tools, http://www.ec.ups.com/), and Federal Express (FedEx) provides in-house web tools (FedEx API, http://www.fedex.com/) for developers in order to facilitate the development of online shipping tools. We have not, however, seen a common service interface to allow users to easily hook up with existing tools.

The developers of client applications usually are forced to construct by hand multiple requests for different backend servers requiring a great deal of time and effort, although integration software vendors have been addressing this issue for years. Different shipping carriers might require distinctive implementations and could have proprietary platforms and their own constraints.

In order to expedite the shipping process and minimize costs, the shipping solutions provided by a value-added service provider specializing in the transportation industry must empower the customers and suppliers with the ability to rate, ship, and track shipments. Many solutions in today's competitive market have been able to achieve the above goals but they still have some deficiencies:

- Most of them are platform-dependent and unique to a specific shipping carrier. Since the shipping solutions are not generic, they could not be considered as a candidate for standards that can be followed by the rest of the players in the industry.

- Because most Windows-based applications are standalone applications, users have no choice but to purchase or evaluate them before actually using them (for examples of shipping automation, see, http://www.kewill.com/). Moreover, Web-based solutions are distributed over the Internet, implemented as servlets or CGIs. The interfaces for integration are not suitable for advertising or data exchange.

With the development of Web Services, it becomes technically feasible to define a uniform interface for the solution developers, which leads to potential business opportunities for technology vendors, service providers, and solution software providers (see http://www.ibm.com/services/uddi/). The framework, ELPIF, presented in this paper proposes a common generic interface for all the Shipping Service Providers, allowing all providers to build their Web Services on this interface and then deploy those services in the Universal Description, Discovery, and Integration (UDDI) Registries for other companies to find and use. Note that the common generic interface should cover all the possible services provided by the shipping industry. Only some of them will be implemented or provided by a shipping carrier. Though we are focused on the shipping industry, the principles embodied in ELPIF can be applied to other domains.

Blending the Web Services and the dynamic XML data binding approach will lead to what could be considered a generic shipping service. This is critical since it allows a shipping service client to design and deploy code to use the generic shipping model, and then at run-time use the dynamic data binding mechanism to invoke a specific implementation of a shipping service. Because Web Services can be implemented in any programming language, developers are not obliged to change their development environments in order to generate or use Web Services. If the shipping service carriers have their own special services that differentiate themselves from others, we also recommend them to publish their service interfaces to the UDDI Registry or use Web Services Inspection Language (WSIL) documents so that their e-logistics expertise can be made available to e-commerce sites and e-marketplaces as cost-effective services. At this point, the common interface for the shipping industry could be extended to encapsulate these new services. Consequently, any client application can benefit from the characteristic of architectural independence that is embraced in our framework and other people's work on Web Services-based application integration.

For most integration architecture, XML plays a role of trivializing the exchange of business data among companies by providing a cross-platform approach in the areas of data encoding and data formatting. For example, Simple Object Access Protocol (SOAP), built on XML, defines a simple way to package information for exchange across system boundaries. UDDI Registries, on the other hand, allow programmable elements to be located in a central repository or in web sites, which others can access remotely. By adopting the above technologies, not only do we get interoperability for our customers but also we can use our multi-platform approach to provide better offerings and solutions with the help of which any industry can accomplish their transactions efficiently and profitably.

ELPIF serves as a Web Services model such that any user could easily access the services it provides through a standard SOAP protocol. ELPIF helps shipping businesses act more quickly and more efficiently, and it also provides a methodology for automating process integration resulting in reduced integration time and cost, increased efficiency of service delivery, and competitive advantage in the marketplace.

This paper is organized as follows: Section 1 discusses e-logistics processes integration after reviewing e-logistics processes, and also presents our proposed integration framework, ELPIF, by introducing the common alliance interface, adaptation layer, and dynamic data binding mechanism. Section 2 gives an integration example using UPS On-Line XML Tools in a purchase order management process. Section 3 shows a working B2B system using e-logistics Web Services.

E-Logistics Processes Integration

When it comes to logistics, the challenge has always been how to deliver products to customers as quickly and safely as possible. Logistics is concerned with the flow of materials in the supply chain, from source through the industrial process to the customer, and then on to reuse, recycle, or disposal. By coordinating all resources, logistics have to ensure that service-level agreements with customers are honored. Efficient logistics can result in cost savings, which can be passed on to the customer, often resulting in increased business.

E-logistics is defined as the mechanism of automating the logistics processes and providing an integrated, end-to-end fulfillment and supply chain management service to the users of logistics processes. Those logistics processes that are automated by e-logistics provide supply chain visibility and can be part of existing e-commerce or workflow systems in an enterprise.

The typical e-logistics processes include Request For Quotes (RFQ), Shipping, and Tracking. As shown in the following diagram, e-logistics interacts with the business process manager in an e-commerce server such as a B2B (business to business) or B2C (business to consumer) server.

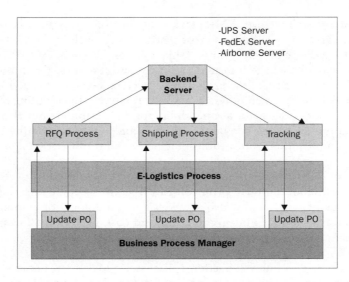

The business process manager invokes the RFQ process for the basic services such as getting the quotes in an e-logistics process. Whenever the response is obtained, the purchase order (PO) will be updated. The shipping process is also invoked by the business process manager and will update the corresponding PO upon completion. Along with the shipment of goods, a tracking number will be given to the customer and that tracking number will be bound to the PO number in the processing e-commerce system. Customers can track their shipment with the help of that number. The interaction diagram of e-logistics and business process manager shown above represents the high-level view of ELPIF. It is worth noting at this stage that although FedEx and Airborne are both webMethods customers, the ELPIF presented in this paper is a framework, not a real service. Thus, value-added service providers who adopt ELPIF could work with FedEx, Airborne, or other shipping service providers.

ELPIF Components and Services

As mentioned earlier, there are three main components to ELPIF, and we shall discuss each in turn. After looking at the general architecture of the framework, we shall examine the Web Services it provides.

Common Alliance Interface

Common Alliance Interface is a higher-level service interface that encapsulates the clients from multiple transportation carriers and provides an abstraction layer for available services. Such an interface would contain the method signatures of the functions that need to be implemented by the Web Services published by different Shipping Service Providers such as UPS, FedEx, and Airborne. The published Web Services communicate directly with their legacy applications using the adaptation layer and dynamic data binding mechanisms introduced in this article. These methods require XML as an input and their result is also XML. As a multi-carrier connector, the Common Alliance Interface makes the overall shipping processes simpler than current practices because:

❏ A set of common interfaces is available to all the shipping carriers, and would ease the work of conducting service requests. All a service requestor has to do is issue a single service request using standardized interfaces, as opposed to composing and sending different complex requests to multiple targeted service providers.

❏ It would also ease the development task of the client application. Developers only need to develop one single piece of code for all the Shipping Service Providers.

❏ From a shipping carrier's perspective, a set of standard interfaces provided by the Common Alliance Interface of ELPIF can be used as a means to increase the customers' awareness of their quality of services and products in terms of reliability and efficiency.

❏ It would reduce the development effort by reusing the Common Alliance Interface and allowing easier adaptation to new service requirements or technologies. This last point is key, because without adoption of the service it will flounder and not be successful.

The Common Alliance Interface is implemented by all the shipping carriers, and the resulting Web Services are published in the UDDI Registry so that trading partners and customers can search and retrieve those services.

Adaptation Layer

The adaptation layer is a key connector between the Web Services and corresponding legacy applications in an industry. The adaptation layer works as a service dispatching broker and service aggregation broker. It is responsible for manipulating the requests from the user and the responses from the server. When a user invokes a Web Service, the request is sent to the adaptation layer which then performs the method signature mapping between application client and Web Services methods, conducts protocol transformation (from SOAP to HTTPS, say), and dispatches the request to an appropriate shipping carrier server (legacy application). Responses from the server are also aggregated by this layer and will be sent back to the requestor. The adaptation layer plays an important role in aggregating responses from several shipping carriers to the service requestor.

Dynamic Data Binding

The adaptation layer binds the "dynamic data" (the live and updated data) from the Shipping Service Provider's server to the response XML. For instance, the quote for a service is not hard-coded in the implementation of a Web Service. The quote information will be connected to the transporters' backend servers when this method in the Web Service is invoked. The adaptation layer is used to create a connection template while the dynamic data binding mechanism integrates real-time data into the defined connection template.

ELPIF Architecture

The ELPIF backend architecture in the following diagram shows the interaction between different layers. The Web Services of different Shipping Service Providers provide implementations of the methods that are defined in the Common Alliance Interface. The user finds the appropriate service with the assistance of the UDDI Registry and sends its XML-based service request to invoke a service. The request is then sent to the appropriate Shipping Service Provider (SSP) server and the response (XML) is sent back to the requestor by the adaptation layer and Web Services Layer.

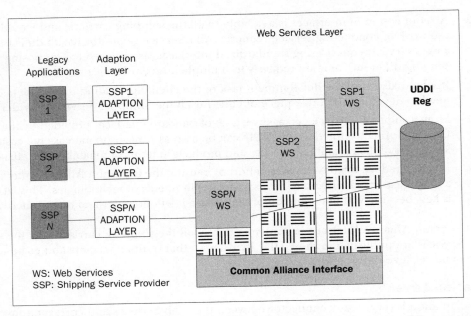

For example, for a RFQ Web Service, the Common Alliance Interface could contain a method such as:

```
public String getServicesQuotes(String xmlInput)
```

This method could be implemented in the Web Services of the various Shipping Service Providers. It would then be called by the Service Requestor to obtain quotes from different providers. This method takes XML as an input and returns XML as an output. An example of such Request and Response XML is given later in the paper.

ELPIF serves as a service model using the design pattern in which all Web Services are built on the Common Alliance Interface and the requestor invokes the desired Web Service after finding an appropriate one. The whole complexity of the interactions among the Web Services, Adaptation Layer, and the legacy applications are transparent to the application developer or the requestor of the service.

ELPIF provides three Web Services to each Shipping Service Provider in order to connect their existing applications to a shipping e-marketplace that is empowered by UDDI registries and Web Services:

- RFQ Web Services.
- Shipping Web Services.
- Tracking Web Services.

They are briefly described as follows.

RFQ Web Services

Any B2B application can send a request to the RFQ Web Services. The RFQ Web Services then dynamically bind the data entered by the requestor (such as shipping destination and weight) to the input XML template, and send the request to the adaptation layer. The adaptation layer dispatches the request to the appropriate server and gets the response from the backend server. It then binds the live data received from the server with the response XML template and sends it back to the B2B application. The authentication of the user will be verified at each step by examining the user ID and password associated with the application. For example, this RFQ process is actually used by the service requestor, such as a shipping agent, to compare the different available services so they can select the most favorable one. As an end user, you can use your user ID and password to sign into a value-added-service providing portal, which uses an intelligent shipping agent that is authorized to invoke all the RFQ Web Services. Before they use the intelligent shipping agent, the user has to be authenticated by a policy-based authentication system such as Tivoli Policy Director.

Shipping Web Services

After the user selects the transportation service provider, the next process is sending a shipping request to the Shipping Web Services. The Shipping Web Services provided by the service provider then dynamically bind the data entered by the service requestor (such as shipping destination and weight) to the input XML template and send the request to the adaptation layer. The adaptation layer then sends the request to the shipping server and gets the response from the server. It then binds the live data received from the shipping server with the response XML template and sends it back to the B2B application.

The customer will be given a tracking number embedded in the response. Once the goods are shipped, the tracking number is mapped to the purchase order ID in a B2B application. Similarly, the service requestor application is authenticated by verifying the provided user ID and password.

Tracking Web Services

The supplier, buyer, or any party in the supply chain may want to check on the status of the shipment corresponding to a specific purchase order. After the commerce server gets the shipping status from the Tracking Web Services, it will update the manifest information in the purchase order database. The Tracking Web Services talk to the backend server to retrieve the detailed shipping status through the adaptation layer and hence can track the status of the shipment.

E-Logistics Example: UPS Integration

In this section, an e-logistics example is given for encapsulating UPS Online XML Tools into Web Services.

The portion to the left of the dotted line in the following diagram represents the creation and details checking of a purchase order:

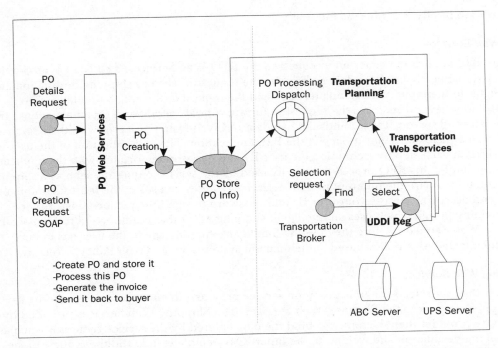

Once we have created the purchase order, it will be processed further by the downstream components. One issue that needs to be looked into is the transportation planning. This is a vital issue as it is concerned with many factors such as lowest shipping cost, easy availability, and so on. The transportation broker is an intelligent agent that dynamically creates a response list from the available service providers such as UPS and FedEx who meet the criteria of the requestor most efficiently. All shipping carriers should have their own Web Services published in the UDDI registry so that they can be easily found from a central place. The selection request made by the customer is sent to the transportation broker that finds the appropriate service from the UDDI Registry and the result is bound to the requestor. The transportation Web Services may include ABC Transportation Web Services, UPS Web Services, and so on.

The following diagram depicts the integration architecture of a shipping carrier. UPS is taken as an example of a shipping carrier. UPS Web Services like RFQ, Shipping, and Tracking are explained in this paper, although there can be many more services such as warehouse management Web Service, transportation management Web Service and so on. These Web Services interact with the UPS XML Online tools:

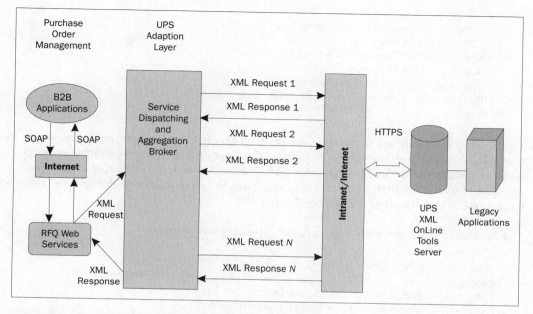

When a Web Service, such as the RFQ Web Service for UPS, is invoked by a SOAP call, it binds data, such as country of dispatch, source, and weight, to the XML Request template. The XML Request is then sent to the Adaptation Layer, which works as a service dispatching broker and service aggregation broker. Once it receives an XML Request, which might be the aggregation of multiple requests such as lookup for Next Day Air Service and Standard Service by UPS, it sends these requests to the UPS Server. The adaptation layer will aggregate the responses received. After mapping the live data received to the response XML template, the adaptation layer will send the response back to the requestor.

The Request XML template can have the following structure:

```
<?xml version="1.0">
<AccessLicenseNum>123</AccessLicenseNum>
<UserId>upsuser</UserId>
<Password>2ppp4</Password>
<Shipment>
  <SourceAdd>
    <City>Charlotte</City>
    <State>NC</State>
    <PostalCode>28213</PostalCode>
    <CountryCode>US</CountryCode>
  </SourceAdd>
  <DestinationAdd>
    <City>White Plains</City>
    <State>NY</State>
    <PostalCode>10603</PostalCode>
```

```
      <CountryCode>US</CountryCode>
    </DestinationAdd>
    <ServiceCode>11</ServiceCode>
    <ServiceCode>14</ServiceCode>
    <PackageWeight>100</PackageWeight>
    <UnitOfMeasurement>lbs</UnitOfMeasurement>
  </Shipment>
```

This request is dispatched to the appropriate UPS server by the adaptation layer, which then sends the received response to the requestor. If the request is an aggregation of multiple services such as Quote for Next Day Air and Ground Service, the response from the server is aggregated by the adaptation layer and is sent back to the requestor of the service. The service code number is mapped to the Service Name.

The Response XML template can have the following structure:

```
<?xml version="1.0">
<Response>
  <PackageWeight>100</PackageWeight>
  <UnitOfMeasurement>lbs</UnitOfMeasurement>
  <RatedShipment>
    <ServiceCode>11</ServiceCode>
    <Charges>
      <CurrencyCode>USD</CurrencyCode>
      <MonetaryValue>300</MonetaryValue>
    </Charges>
    <DaysToDeliever>1</DaysToDeliever>
    <DelieveryTime>10:00AM</DelieveryTime>
  </RatedShipment>
  <RatedShipment>
    <ServiceCode>14</ServiceCode>
    <Charges>
      <CurrencyCode>USD</CurrencyCode>
      <MonetaryValue>250</MonetaryValue>
    </Charges>
    <DaysToDeliever>2</DaysToDeliever>
    <DelieveryTime>11:00AM</DelieveryTime>
  /RatedShipment>
</Response>
```

The following screenshot shows the deployed service information about UPS RFQ Web Service. The ID of this Web Service is urn:ups_gcb-service, which is a Java application with 13 methods. You can invoke some of them or all of them depending on your requirement and business context:

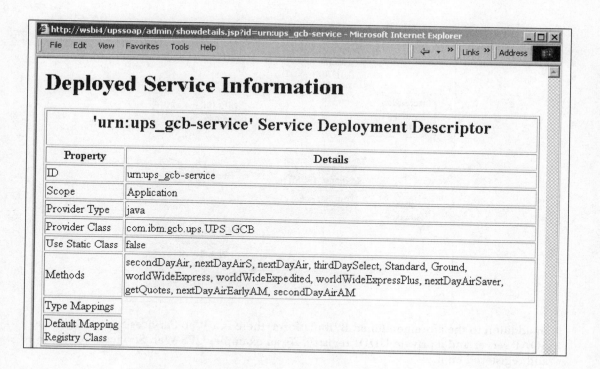

A Working B2B System Using ELPIF

The B2B system is shown on the left side of the following diagram. The detailed description can be found in Bhaskaran *et al* (see *Reference*). The Interaction Manager (IM) that houses the solution components is responsible for driving the client interaction. This is a model-view-controller framework consisting of a set of JavaBeans, JSP (JavaServer Pages) templates, and Servlets. The Trust and Access Manager (TAM) houses the Organization Model that forms the basis for client authorization, which is the process of determining whether an authenticated client has the right to perform an operation on a specific resource in a secure domain. The Business Flow Manager (BFM) externalizes the flow definitions (control flows and data flows) and the business rules that drive the process choreography:

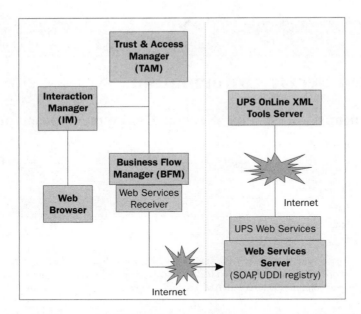

In addition to the aforementioned B2B platform, there is a Web Services Server including a SOAP server and a private UDDI registry. As an example, UPS Web Services are deployed and registered on it.

Requests from the Web browser will be sent to the TAM first to finish the single sign-on process. Single sign-on is a mechanism whereby a single action of user authentication and authorization can permit a user to access all computers and systems where they have access permission, without the need to enter multiple passwords. Single sign-on reduces human error, a major component of systems failure, and is therefore highly desirable but difficult to implement. For more details on single sign-on, see http://www.opengroup.org/security/sso/. The subsequent pages in the application will automatically attach the user credential information to BFM that will invoke a command to search the UDDI server or invoke a Web Service based on the business context.

The following scenario describes a prototype of Web Services integration with the above B2B system. Stage one represents a business process implemented by the B2B system as a Web Service; stage two is an example of using Web Services as building blocks for business process solution based on ELPIF.

Stage One: Submitting a Purchase Order

1. John, the purchasing agent of Fabulous Furniture Outlet (an example buyer for the B2B system), opens the procurement system client.

2. John submits a purchase order for 78 hardwood chairs. Using Web Services, it is submitted to the BFM for processing.

Stage Two: Processing a Purchase Order

1. Mary, the sales manager for BookCase Corporation, (an example supplier for the B2B system) logs on to check new purchase orders.

2. Mary discovers John's purchase order as she proceeds to process the order. As part of order processing Mary must authorize a transporter to ship bookcases from their manufacturing center in USA.

The following screenshot illustrates the screen of the details of a specific PO. This information is derived from the purchase order database:

KEPEX PO Details -> 50-260.1010162303218	
Supplier Article Description	Hardwooden Chair
Kepex Article Num	4
Supplier Id	999
Customer Name	Sears
Qty	78.0
Dispatch Country	USA
Port of Loading	New York
E T D	2002-02-10
Transport Service Provider	

Get List of Transporter (E-Hub Memebers Only)

The Dispatch Country is USA and the port of loading is New York. Based on this information, the transportation broker will search the UDDI registry to get a transporter list of service providers in the United States. Each service provider may provide multiple services. For each service, Mary can invoke the Web Services to get the quotes.

The following screenshot illustrates the response from three service providers: ABC Transportation Inc, Sunshine Transportation Inc, and UPS. These Web Services are built on the ELPIF. The UPS Web Services, for example, are directly connected to a live UPS XML Tools Server through the adaptation layer of ELPIF. In our application, seven methods have been invoked to get their quotes:

Supplier Portal -> Transporter Quotes List for PO

PO ID: 50-260.1010162303218

Transporter	Service Name	Service Invoked	Quote (USD)	Select
ABC Transportation Inc.	ABC_Transport_Service	getTransportationQuote	245.38	○
Sunshine Transportation Inc.	Sunshine_Transport_Service	getTransportationQuote	219.87	○
UPS	Next Day Air, FROM Hawthorne, NY 10532 TO San Francisco, CA 94102 (Your Packaging, 120 pounds)	nextDayAir	308.04	○
UPS	Second Day Air	secondDayAir	206.03	⦿
UPS	Third Day Select	thirdDaySelect	144.27	○
UPS	UPS Ground	Ground	58.17	○
UPS	Next Day Air Saver	nextDayAirSaver	275.3	○
UPS	Next Day Air Early AM	nextDayAirEarlyAM	335.75	○
UPS	Second Day Air AM	secondDayAirAM	231.12	○

Accept

After Mary reviews the quotes, she can select one as a transportation service provider for this specific purchase order. Then the purchase order information will be updated. The updated purchase order information is shown in the following screenshot. At the same time, the notification will be sent to the buyer, supplier, and shipping company. The PO ID has been mapped to the real tracking ID generated by shipping carrier so that it can be used for tracking:

KEPEX Supplier Portal PO: Selected Transporter Review

PO ID: 50-260.1010162303218

Kepex Article Num	Hardwooden Chair
Supplier Article No	Hardwooden Chair
Supplier Article Num	4
Supplier Id	999
Cust num	597
Qty	78.0
Dispatch Country	USA
Port of Loading	New York
E T D	2002-02-10
Transport Service Provider	UPS

The PO is finalized. The notification will be sent to the buyer, shipping company and supplier.

From this working B2B solutions development, we have learned that Web Services are emerging e-business applications that can connect and interact with one another on the Web more easily and efficiently, eliminating much of the time-consuming custom coding currently required in B2B environments. At the same time, they enable development of powerful business services supporting dynamic, collaborative B2B activities and facilitate dynamic business process brokering and intelligent agents with open, real-time business services based on ELPIF.

Conclusions

An e-logistics framework ELPIF is presented in this paper. ELPIF can be adopted by shipping carriers or marketplaces. Based on ELPIF, a shipping service can be designed in a standard way. Shipping service providers can make optimum use of their legacy applications and run efficiently with minimal cost input.

We have introduced and explained the concept of Common Alliance Interface, Adaptation Layer, and Dynamic Data Binding mechanisms. The Common Alliance Interface serves as an isolation layer separating the service requestors and service providers and hence reduces complexity by minimizing the number of interfaces to requesting applications. The Adaptation Layer, which is the mediator between the alliance layer and the service providers, manipulates the request and response accordingly.

ELPIF exploits Web Services as the building blocks that distinguish ELPIF from other existing integration solutions, most of which are either standalone applications or hard-wired with existing platforms. Hence, we argue that ELPIF contributes to the area of business process integration by providing a new service delivery model using a design pattern and solution templates, for the shipping industry in particular and whole industry that demands business integration in general.

Reference

Kumar Bhaskaran, Jen-Yao Chung, Terry Heath, Santhosh Kumaran, Raja Das, and Prabir Nandi, An e-business Integration & Collaboration Platform for B2B e-Commerce, Advanced Issues of E-Commerce and Web-Based Information Systems, IEEE WECWIS, 2001, pp120-122.

Author: Bilal Siddiqui

- Requirements of E-Commerce models
- Starting an Electronic Marketplace
- Architecture using UDDI and WSDL
- Reducing Costs
- Common Business Protocols

UDDI-based Electronic Marketplaces

Electronic Marketplaces (eMarketplaces) are supposed to bring together businesses on the Web. Buyers and sellers should be able to interact with each other inside an architecture that is easy to use and maintain. eMarketplace owners can implement several types of processes depending upon their target audience, operations, and finance models. The greatest benefits lie with cost reduction for all players and the ability to reach otherwise untapped business prospects. This paper discusses how UDDI (Universal Description, Discovery and Integration) and WSDL (Web Services Description Language) work together to form the core architecture of the next-generation e-commerce model.

Take conventional eMarketplaces like http://www.verticalnetmarketplaces.com/ for example. They are trying to provide an edge to their customers by aggregating their otherwise fragmented buying power. This means bringing together service providers (in various manners, the most common example of which is supply chain management) for easier access to products and better value for money.

There are certain entities that are common to most e-commerce models of today, for example Buyers, Sellers, and Marketplaces. Buyers are the customers who want to make use of the products and services that sellers offer. Throughout this paper, we will refer to buyers as eBuyers. Sellers have the role of supplying products and services. We will refer to them as eSuppliers. The Marketplace is the virtual place that resides somewhere on the Internet, where eBuyers and eSuppliers can meet. We will call it an eMarketplace.

While discussing UDDI-based eMarketplaces in this paper, we will also discuss the present-day mechanism for interaction between eBuyers and eSuppliers at existing eMarketplaces. Interaction between eSuppliers and eBuyers is normally referred to as B2C (Business to Consumer). eSuppliers can also interact with other eSuppliers through B2B (Business to Business). An important point to notice is that the idea of eMarketplaces is a subset of e-commerce. E-commerce can also happen if a company decides to sell its products online through its own web site without any B2B. On the other hand, an eMarketplace allows multiple eSuppliers to offer their products and services to eBuyers, and other eSuppliers.

There are various ways of bringing together buyers and sellers, which we will discuss shortly, but some common requirements of possible models have been identified. Let us see these common requirements first.

Some Common Requirement of All E-Commerce Models

There are two prime requirements that we shall consider here, those of content management and interoperability.

Content Management

Whatever model you choose, an eMarketplace will be required to provide eBuyers with access to eSuppliers' data. For example eBuyers will need pricing and product information. In present day e-commerce, this is done through one of the following two methods:

1. eMarketplaces have an interface for eSuppliers, where they can update changes in their internal content. These changes will be presented to prospective eBuyers on request.

2. All service providers who want to become partners of an eMarketplace will integrate their content management systems with that of the marketplace. This would mean they do not have to re-enter information into the eMarketplace's content management system.

The pros and cons of these options are obvious: the first has approximately zero initial cost but has a high operational cost (as it requires duplication of content management effort), while the second is the other way around (high initial cost, low operational costs). Both initial and operational costs are either borne by an eMarketplace owner or the eSuppliers. What if we want to reduce the total cost of our eMarketplace? We somehow need to reduce both the initial and operational costs. We'll show how UDDI and WSDL give us the best of both worlds.

Interoperability in E-Commerce

No business (eSupplier) can serve the entire needs of its customers (eBuyers) alone. It has to coordinate with other eSuppliers. This is the famous Business-to-Business (B2B) concept. An eMarketplace owner will be interested in allowing one eSupplier to invoke the services of other eSuppliers. For example many eSuppliers will use the services of forwarding or shipping companies. They will therefore invoke the freight-related services of shipping companies.

In present day e-commerce, this is very costly to achieve through an eMarketplace. The simple reason for that is that every business has its own workflow and resource planning systems, and the cost of integrating them in most of the cases is not worth the benefit. On the other hand, the concept of Web Services reduces the cost of interoperability to such an extent that hardly any business will remain out of the eMarketplace domain.

We are now going to discuss eMarketplace models and features in detail. We will also discuss the UDDI option for building an eMarketplace, its advantages and architecture. Before going into detail on UDDI and WSDL, let us first briefly discuss some of the popular models that are currently available for e-commerce over the Internet:

1. **Online procurement portals:** These work for the benefit of buyer members. They provide product and price transparency to buyers. In addition to that they provide value added services like quality recommendation, comparison reports, benchmarks, etc. to their customers. An example of this category is http://www.buy.com/.

2. **Vertical Exchanges:** These portals are buyer and supplier neutral, which means that they do not act for the benefit of any one side. Exchanges like http://www.paperspace.com/ and http://www.esteel.com/ are examples of this category. These portals cover specific vertical markets and try to attract more business partners (eSuppliers) as well as customers (eBuyers) by providing natural market conditions where supply and demand conditions prevail.

3. **Sell-side eMarketplaces:** These act like distribution channels over the Internet, for example http://www.aspentech.com/. Suppliers become their members and these eMarketplaces work for their benefit by providing access to otherwise untapped buyer groups. These marketplaces provide comprehensive services to eSuppliers ranging from developing strategies to implementing operational plans.

Supply Chain Management Solutions as a Special Case of e-Commerce

Supply Chain Management is a special topic in B2B e-commerce and we will use this model to elaborate on UDDI-based eMarketplaces.

Supply chain management optimizes the way eSuppliers respond to market needs. Therefore eBuyers only interact with eSuppliers at the eMarketplace. In order to fulfill the needs of eBuyers, though, eSuppliers utilize a supply chain management solution.

We have shown this idea in the following diagram. It illustrates a supply-chain example starting when an eBuyer needs a price offer. The eBuyer searches the eMarketplace for information about eSuppliers who are capable of performing the required job (eSupplier discovery process). The eMarketplace responds by sending eSupplier A's information. The eBuyer now raises a service invocation request to eSupplier A. On receiving the request, eSupplier A searches the eMarketplace for its trading partners (other eSuppliers such as manufacturers, distributors, and retailers) who can assist in fulfilling the job. The eMarketplace responds by sending the details of eSuppliers B and C. eSupplier A invokes the services of eSuppliers B and C (sublevel requests to dynamically located eSuppliers who can act as trading partners):

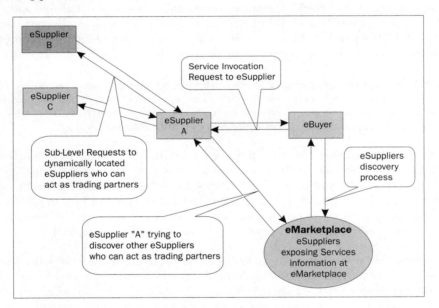

Every eSupplier wants to find the best sources to buy from. Similarly, they also want to match their inventory to market requirements (perhaps through some Just In Time concepts). These types of optimization criteria can be handled by eMarketplaces. For example, the eMarketplace can allow an eSupplier to communicate their delivery dates and estimates before dispatch of goods.

An eSupplier becomes registered with one or more eMarketplaces, from where they can sell their goods or services to other eSuppliers, who in turn sell their good or services to the eBuyers (perhaps the end users). The eMarketplace puts them together in one place, just like the original marketplaces where people traded their goods.

What Is a UDDI-based eMarketplace?

A UDDI based eMarketplace provides the same level of information and the same level of breadth of services to its customers that a conventional eMarketplace would have offered. It defines, however, flexible standards for interoperability in order to manage growing complexity and dynamism in relationships (which means an eSupplier's internal workflow and content management systems will remain independent of the eMarketplace). It also provides a significant cost reduction for the implementation of eMarketplaces. This cost reduction is twofold: due to the existence of a standard UDDI specification, best-of-breed implementations will be available off-the-shelf (cost reduction for eMarketplace owners), and B2B Integration for eSuppliers will also become cheaper due to interoperable standards for Web Services (cost reduction for eSuppliers).

Think of UDDI as a standard process in which you can search for required services, and once found ask them to serve you. As discussed above, an eSupplier may need to invoke other services in order to fulfill requirements from eBuyers. At our eMarketplace, one eSupplier may become a customer (essentially an eBuyer) for other eSuppliers.

If we are able to define industry-wide standards for doing this (searching for and invoking services), the entire process will appear seamless to its users, although it is distributed all over the Internet. UDDI (for searching) and WSDL (for describing how services are to be invoked) are the standards for this purpose.

The only step remaining is to build user-friendly, Web-based interfaces around UDDI and your eMarketplace is ready.

How Customers and Businesses Participate in a UDDI based eMarketplace

According to the UDDI specification, two actions can be performed on a UDDI registry: publishing and inquiry. There are APIs (Application Programming Interfaces) provided to accommodate these actions. They are in the form of messages going to or coming from a UDDI registry, messages that are human-readable text (a concept called SOAP messaging, described in the next section). As human-readable text is supported in all platforms and in all programming languages, there is no problem in supporting the UDDI APIs on any platform.

The Publishing API is for the use of service providers. Using this API, a business (an eSupplier) can expose (publish or advertise) its services to our eMarketplace where their prospective customers (eBuyers) can search for and make use of their service.

The Inquiry API will be used by eBuyers, to search for products or services of interest at a UDDI-based eMarketplace. This API specifies several methods to perform general to detailed (drilled-down) searches.

121

A Real-Life Example for a UDDI-based eMarketplace

Take for example the tourism industry in which there are a number of entities that interact with each other. At an eMarketplace dedicated to tourism, tour operators (eSuppliers) will offer vacation tours, and eBuyers will buy vacation tours. The tour operators will need to interact with hotels and car rental services in order to fulfil tour requirements. All these entities (tour operators, hotels, and car rentals services) are eSuppliers.

How Can We Start a UDDI-based eMarketplace?

A UDDI registry will sit at the heart of our eMarketplace. UDDI is actually a normal database with a special interface for read and write operations. We can think of the Inquiry API as UDDI's way of reading or searching through records. On the other hand, the Publishing API is intended for writing records to the UDDI registry. These records will constitute the database that contains information about eSuppliers and their products or services.

Why does UDDI define a special mechanism for reading and writing? Why not use some popular technology like ODBC? Let's go through the sequence of events in history that led us to the development of UDDI APIs.

The Internet emerged with HTTP among the top enabling technologies. Once the Internet had gained popularity, many techniques emerged for Electronic Data Interchange (EDI) between applications over the Internet, eventually giving way to XML (which is human-readable text) as the de facto standard for all EDI over the Internet. With the simplicity of XML, processing tools emerged making its application possible in every industry. If we consider B2B interactions over the Internet, proprietary and expensive formats have given way to XML-based EDI.

The next logical step was to combine XML with HTTP, which gives rise to direct messaging between software objects. Think of XML as the language or grammar used to write business correspondence and HTTP as the mail or courier service. These two together will allow XML- and HTTP-aware software components to write letters to each other and respond to each other's requirements, thus fulfilling business needs.

SOAP (Simple Object Access Protocol) is the name of the technology that makes use of XML and HTTP. It can transport XML documents between software components. This transport is called SOAP messaging.

SOAP provides a framework for business communication that is independent of the platform on which it is used, programming language used for implementation, web and application servers deployed, and data formats used for back-end data storage. Therefore a UDDI-based eMarketplace might use some ODBC-compliant database at the back end, but it will use SOAP messaging to expose its functionality to eBuyers and eSuppliers.

UDDI utilizes SOAP messaging for communication between the UDDI registry and users. Both Publishing and Inquiry APIs are based on XML grammar and currently SOAP is the only available transport mechanism.

On top of the UDDI registry, our eMarketplace will contain two graphical user interfaces (GUI) in the form of web sites or another way of interfacing with users graphically. The search/inquiry interface will deal with eBuyers coming to our eMarketplace, so that they can search for services of interest; this GUI will invoke the UDDI Inquiry API. The publishing GUI will interface with eSuppliers (publishing their services), so that they can introduce their services at our eMarketplace; this GUI will use the UDDI Publishing API.

Let's talk about these interfaces one at a time.

How Will We Enable eBuyers To Use Our eMarketplace?

The search/inquiry GUI will invoke the Inquiry API of our UDDI. It may be normal ASP/JSP/PHP or any other form of Web page. The GUI should contain search and indexing options similar to any typical or conventional existing eMarketplace. The main difference lies with what happens when an eBuyer has found the service they are interested in. Unlike most conventional eMarketplaces, the search GUI will not redirect eBuyers to the eSupplier's site blindly. It will rather display the eSupplier's interface details to the customer and allow them to invoke services. It will also bring the resulting message back to the eBuyer after invocation. This means that our eMarketplace will be linked to eSuppliers, so that eBuyers will dynamically access their content management system when they invoke a service.

How Will We Enable eSuppliers To Serve eBuyers At Our eMarketplace?

This is the place where UDDI's Publishing API is used. Our eMarketplace should provide a Graphical User Interface to cater to publishing requests. Using this GUI, eSuppliers will publish the details of their businesses and services they offer. They also have the option of editing their profiles later.

The Publishing API contains certain XML structures. These structures are used to register a business, publish services, and bind services to any technical model (we will discuss this API later). Using these XML structures, first of all an eSupplier registers itself. Then it will publish its services (a single business entity may contain one or more services). The next step would be to publish WSDL interfaces at the UDDI. This is done through Binding Templates and Technical Models. A **Binding Template** binds a service to a WSDL interface. UDDI refers to that WSDL Interface as a **Technical Model**.

In simple English, services of any service provider are exposed in terms of one or more interfaces. These interfaces are described by a grammar called Web Services Description Language or WSDL for short. In UDDI terminology, all interfaces are called Technical Models. An example of this type of interface is given and described later in the section *How WSDL Servers work*.

A Binding Template binds the interfaces of a service provider with their back-end implementations. In order to do this, each binding template creates instances of the Technical Models. Each instance is called a **Technical Model Instance**. A Binding Template can have any number of Technical Model Instances. A Binding Template also contains the URL address of a SOAP server. This SOAP server hosts the implementation of all the services described by the Technical Model Instances contained in this Binding Template.

Each of these entities (business, service, binding template, and the technical model) has a unique key for reference. UDDI identifies them through the key.

What Is the Role of UDDI in Our eMarketplace?

The eSupplier that wants to register itself to a particular conventional eMarketplace has to write its interface according to the architecture of the eMarketplace. For each eMarketplace, it will have to rebuild the interfacing requirements separately. With UDDI-based eMarketplaces, participating eSuppliers have to write their WSDL interfaces only once and they can get themselves registered with any other UDDI-based eMarketplace without further effort and cost.

As far as the role of UDDI in an eMarketplace is concerned, the UDDI acts like a central repository where eSuppliers can register themselves, expose their services and market their products. The UDDI-based eMarketplace makes B2B integration less costly. We will see this in more detail in the next section.

What Is the Role of Web Services Definition Language (WSDL) in an eMarketplace?

WSDL is the grammar in which a business can describe its services. For our UDDI-based eMarketplace, it provides an interface between the UDDI registry and the business logic of the eSuppliers. The WSDL file provides not only details about the services of an eSupplier but also contains information about how to invoke these services, what methods you can call, what parameters you have to pass to these methods, and what formats will be returned by different methods.

When a UDDI-based eMarketplace takes an eBuyer to the doorstep of an eSupplier, the attendant at the business gate is SOAP, with whom the eBuyer will talk using WSDL. The eMarketplace actually links the customer with the business services interface (the WSDL interface). We will learn more about WSDL shortly.

Architecture of a UDDI- and WSDL-based eMarketplace

At this point, we have already identified the components of a UDDI-based eMarketplace. Let's list them in one place and discuss the role of each:

1. UDDI Registry Interface for UDDI users.

2. Web-based Publishing Interface.

3. Web-based Inquiry/Search Interface.

The following diagram shows a UDDI-based eMarketplace, its Web-based interfaces, its UDDI APIs, back-end data storage, eSuppliers, and eBuyers:

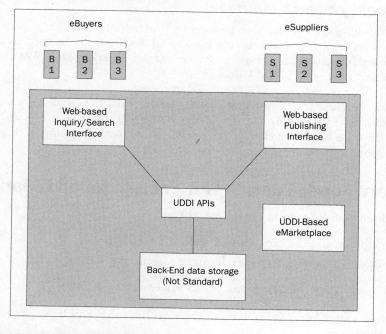

UDDI Registry Interface for Users

The UDDI specification only defines a set of APIs and does not care about back-end data format. This component will provide a standard UDDI interface and is not aware that it is being used as part of an eMarketplace. It is simply an interface to the UDDI registry.

Web-based Publishing Interface Module

This module should provide all the functionality that is required by eSuppliers (companies who want to sell products/services at our eMarketplace). This should include GUI components to allow the following:

1. Publish company information.

2. Publish services.

3. Publish technical models or WSDL interfaces that the user wants to expose.

4. Provide the URL address of their services.

5. Advertise according to classification and categorization of services.

Web-based Inquiry/Search Interface

While the Publishing GUI is meant to be used by professionals who are expected to have technical knowledge of Web Services, the Inquiry GUI will mostly be used by eBuyers, who may be ordinary Internet users (valued customers of our eMarketplace). We cannot expect them to have any type of technical knowledge.

Therefore, the design of the Web-based Inquiry/Search GUI needs special care for ease of use. This search GUI is more like a "Search Engine". Refer to my article "*UDDI as a Search Engine*" at WebServicesArchitect.com, which provides in-depth discussion of this subject (see http://www.webservicesarchitect.com/content/articles/siddiqui01.asp).

UDDI is Very Good, But it is Not Enough for an eMarketplace.

The above discussion leads us to the points where:

❑ An eSupplier has the capability of exposing their services.
❑ An eBuyer in need of these services can search for them.

There are two important things missing in this discussion up till now:

1. How an eSupplier will implement their services that can be exposed at an eMarketplace.

2. How our eBuyers in search of services will actually invoke or make use of these services.

These two things are outside of UDDI's domain, so they have to be handled by other enabling technologies. Before we carry on with our discussion of how to achieve this, let us look at the following diagram, which explains the sequence of operations that completely explains this scenario:

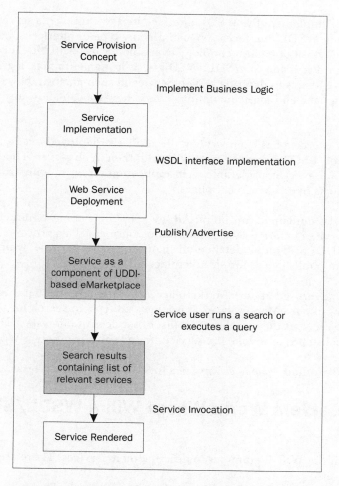

All components and actions shaded are within the UDDI domain. What about the rest? Let's examine them.

Any business (eSupplier) can start with an idea or a business concept. Naturally, the first step is to implement the business logic associated with that concept. Our UDDI-based eMarketplace does not impose any restriction on this implementation. You can use any technology, Operating System, web server, programming language, design methodology, or architecture for implementing the business logic. A UDDI-based eMarketplace will bring together the business logics of different eSuppliers, therefore it hardly matters where the business logic resides. This also means if you have an existing service already implemented on the web server in whatever way, you can proceed with the next step.

The next step is to implement the WSDL interface for the eSupplier's service. UDDI does not mandate using only WSDL interfaces. We can use any type of interfaces, but for the time being WSDL is the most popular technology available for use with UDDI registries. Therefore we will restrict our discussion to WSDL. WSDL is, as its name implies, a grammar to describe Web Services. The idea is to describe a Web Service in such an abstract way that it remains independent from back-end implementation. This is how we can allow any type of business logic implementation.

Once the WSDL interface has been written, the service is deployed over a SOAP server. The eSupplier will need a SOAP server compatible with their Web server. There are SOAP servers available for every considerable web/application server ranging from Microsoft's IIS to high-end products like IBM's WebSphere.

We enter the UDDI domain at this point. All the eSuppliers at our eMarketplace will need to advertise their services before they can start online business. This process is called **Publishing** Web Services. UDDI provides a detailed mechanism for this purpose, which eSuppliers will follow to get them published at our eMarketplace.

Once published/advertised at our eMarketplace, we can safely say that the Web Service is now a component of our eMarketplace. This allows eBuyers to search for the Web Service. When an eBuyer receives the search results (list of services of interest), UDDI's job is finished. The next and final step is to invoke the services found. This is purely a WSDL task.

We are now ready to find *"how to do"* answers for the above defined tasks.

How WSDL Servers Work: Where Will a WSDL/SOAP Server be Located?

An eSupplier can use WSDL grammar to describe their services. There are four important aspects to doing this:

1. The name of the service and names of various procedures in the service. For example an eSupplier may be a goods-forwarding company interested in exposing procedures like `getQuotation` and `shipToDestination`.

2. A description of the service and each procedure in simple English. These descriptions will be presented to eBuyers for their easy understanding and ready reference. WDSL allows a separate description of each procedure. For example, an eSupplier may give the following description of their `getQuotation` procedure/method: "This method will calculate the total cost of your package from source to destination".

3. Information that an eSupplier needs from an eBuyer before they can make use of the service. If we take the freight-forwarding example discussed opposite, the information required will be source and destination places, weight and dimensions of the packet, and whether the packet contains fragile equipment. This information will become the parameters that eBuyers will send when invoking Web Service procedures.

4. We also need to specify the format in which our service will respond. For example, our service may respond by sending a message as shown in the following diagram:

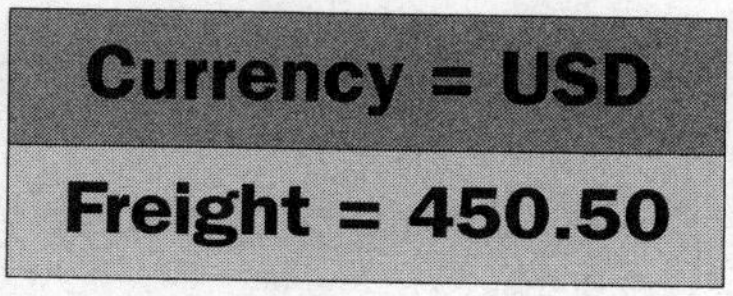

```
Currency = USD

Freight = 450.50
```

An eSupplier may choose to implement their service in any way, so that there can be any number of fields in the response. They can also specify complex structures having fields within fields (boxes within boxes).

WSDL grammar is designed to specify each of the above four aspects. We have written a sample WSDL interface in the form of our boxes within boxes structure. The structure is meant to be self-explanatory (the primary purpose of WSDL) so we do not include any descriptive notes for this WSDL in our paper:

Name of WSDL Interface: Quotation
Description: Use this service to get the prices of computer hardware components.
URL Address of WSDL File: http://www.ourcompany.com/quotation.wsdl

List of Methods:
1. Get List of Items
2. Get Models
3. Get Prices
4. Get Complete Quotation

Method Name: Get list of Items
Description: Use this method to get a list of all items our company sells

Method Name: Get Models
Description: Use this method to get a list of all models for selected item

Input Parameters	Output Parameters	Input Parameters	Output Parameters
No input parameter will be taken	**Name:** Item Names **Type:** List of Strings **Description:** Item names will be a list of products that we sell	**Name:** Item Name **Type:** String **Description:** Item name will be the name of the product of interest. First use the *Get List of Items* method to get a list of all items that we sell	**Name:** Model Number **Type:** List of numbers **Description:** Models of the selected item that we sell
			Name: Features **Type:** List of Strings **Description:** List of features against each model number

Method Name: Get Price
Description: Use this method to get the price of a particular model

Method Name: Get Complete Quotation
Description: Use this method to get a complete quotation of selected models of various items

Input Parameters	Output Parameters	Input Parameters	Output Parameters
Name: Model Number **Type:** Number **Description:** Unique model number of interest	**Name:** Price **Type:** Number **Description:** Price of the selected model	**Name:** Model Numbers **Type:** List of Numbers **Description:** The list of model numbers for which you want to get a complete quotation	**Name:** Price **Type:** List of Numbers **Description:** Prices of the selected models
	Name: Validity Period **Type:** Date **Description:** The date up to which current quoted price is valid		**Name:** Validity Period **Type:** Date **Description:** The date up to which current quoted price is valid

So we have described our service, but it is still an abstract description without any back-end implementation bound with it. This binding of abstract description with implementation is the job of a SOAP server.

All WSDL files have to be deployed on SOAP servers (SOAP is the only binding option available for now, however WSDL allows a flexible framework where other future bindings can also work). This deployment means the URL address of the SOAP server. SOAP servers work on simple Web and Application servers like Apache or IBM's WebSphere. Therefore SOAP URLs can be simple Internet addresses like
http://www.myservicedeployment/myfirstbinding/mySOAPserver/.

Interoperability in SOAP

It is natural that a SOAP server will talk to a SOAP client on the other end. This SOAP client will be a part of our eMarketplace. The following diagram represents this simply:

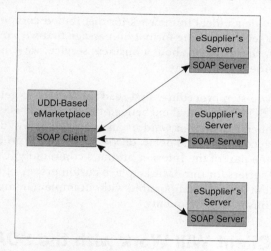

In the diagram you can note the following points:

❑ The SOAP servers of all eSuppliers are OUTSIDE the domain of our eMarketplace.

❑ There is a SOAP client within the domain of our eMarketplace. This SOAP client is capable of communicating with all SOAP servers of eSuppliers.

Curious readers may have two questions at this point:

1. What are the business processes in our UDDI-based eMarketplace that require a SOAP client?

2. SOAP servers are outside the domain of our eMarketplace. This means our business partners are at liberty to choose any SOAP server. Then how can we make sure that SOAP servers will correctly interact with our SOAP client?

We will answer these questions in turn.

Responsibilities of SOAP in Our UDDI-based eMarketplace

The primary purpose of our SOAP client is to allow eBuyers to invoke services provided/offered by eSuppliers. As explained earlier, WSDL-based services are deployed on SOAP servers.

WSDL is only capable of describing services in terms of four points that we showed earlier in our WSDL illustration. Once described, WSDL leaves it to the SOAP binding to allow access to service implementation. It is our SOAP client that will coordinate with web site users to do this in a user-friendly manner. An eBuyer is not expected to know anything about the technology behind SOAP, WSDL, or UDDI. It is therefore important that our eMarketplace presents a user-friendly GUI that hides the technical details at the back end.

WSDL and SOAP provide an ideal framework for distributed computing. WSDL can tell us names of methods in a service and the format of message that we can exchange with that service. Once we know these details about a business service, we can use SOAP to access the objects of service providers.

Therefore, we have a two-step procedure: first read the WSDL to get a description of the services, and then use SOAP for actual exchange of messages. This is the basic concept of **loosely coupled** components. Different vendors and companies will design and implement software components according to the needs of specific business procedures. These components will become part of the Internet business community. Users of these components will either be Internet surfers (or our eMarketplace customers) or other software components. B2B and B2C integration is next to impossible without implementing the concept of loosely coupled software and business components.

How Our SOAP Client Will Work with the SOAP Servers of eSuppliers (SOAP Interoperability)

SOAP interoperability is still not 100% trouble-free. The latest version of SOAP is 1.2, published at W3C as a working draft on December 17, 2001. Most SOAP implementations available for the time being claim to be SOAP 1.1-complaint. We expect SOAP to become a W3C recommendation some time in late 2002. Until then, there are a few issues that may hinder interoperability in some places. All these issues are highly technical and therefore beyond the scope of this paper. Following are web sites that contain more information about SOAP interoperability:

- ❏ http://www.xmethods.net/soapbuilders/proposal.html (SOAP interoperability Test specification).
- ❏ http://www.whitemesa.com/interop.htm (SOAP builders interoperability lab).
- ❏ http://www.xmethods.com/ilab (SOAP builders interoperability lab).
- ❏ http://www-106.ibm.com/developerworks/webservices/library/ws-asio/ (An article on SOAP interoperability).

How Will Businesses Get Involved in Our eMarketplace?

UDDI provides a mechanism that allows eSuppliers to publish or advertise their services. The process is not very different from entering information about their company into our database. This information also includes registering their WSDL interfaces at our eMarketplace. Once information about our partners is inside our database, the users of our eMarketplace can search it; they can also invoke services of interest after searching for them. Some readers may think this is the same old process found in all conventional eMarketplaces, but there are two marked differences:

Every conventional eMarketplace has implemented its own model for categorization or classification of products and services. They do not follow a uniform standard for this purpose. On the other hand UDDI has proposed using the well-known product classification architecture of UNSPSC (http://eccma.org/unspsc/). It also allows using other classification methods, where each classification method will be identifiable from the other. This would mean that our business partners would register at our eMarketplace through an already well-known classification technique.

Without the concept of WSDL interfaces or Web Services, eSuppliers can only publish at an eMarketplace and cannot integrate their content management systems with ours without bearing the high costs of B2B integration.

We will now discuss these two aspects in detail, specifically the classification (taxonomical) architecture of UDDI and the methodology to bring down the cost of B2B integration.

Taxonomical Architecture

Without proper classification and categorization, large content cannot be managed effectively and browsing through it will be very difficult. When we discuss an enterprise scale where data consist of millions of records, it will be almost impossible to find any specific piece of data without categorization.

With the advent of the Internet, a huge amount of data is summed up. Search engines make it possible to find information from the Internet, by categorizing information under certain headings and storing the information for a quick keyword-based search. Any web user can browse through categories to reach the required information. Using a search engine such as Google, a customer can drill down through categories and subcategories to select the desired product.

Now consider eMarketplaces like buy.com. Each existing eMarketplace develops its own structure for categorization. There is no standard architecture available which can accommodate the categorization needs of an e-business community. This creates problems for both eBuyers and eSuppliers. This problem is further aggravated when we are discussing B2B integration. In this case, we would like software tools to browse and search through product categories. B2B integration will only be possible if the involved parties are following a standard classification technique.

The idea of Web Services needs to address all aspects of B2B integration. UDDI is the part of Web Services where all the data is stored. There is, then, a need for such a flexible architecture for categorization that it can accommodate the needs of all e-communities. UDDI's classification technique allows communities to use well-known categorizations. It is actually a flexible architecture where new categorization systems or structures can dynamically be updated and be part of a system which UDDI calls its taxonomical architecture.

In UDDI taxonomy, any organization can register their categorization architecture, which will be made available to all users of that registry. Instead of developing their own taxonomical architecture, which itself needs special expertise, UDDI adopts all the well-known taxonomical architectures that have matured with time. An eSupplier is free to use any taxonomical architecture they feel fit for their business.

How Do UDDI and WSDL Bring Down the Cost of B2B Integration?

The major point where WSDL-based B2B integration reduces cost is the use of standards. An eSupplier will implement their interface once and can then be registered with all UDDI registries, ours and others. Equally, our eMarketplace can read WSDL interfaces from other UDDI registries and make their services available at our eMarketplace. In fact, there is a standard mechanism available for data exchange between registries.

We will now discuss the methods that our business partners will use to expose or publish their services at our eMarketplace.

Mechanism for Publishing at Our UDDI-based eMarketplace

UDDI offers the following methods for publishing services. These will be utilized by eSuppliers to publish their services. Our eMarketplace should have a comprehensive GUI for this purpose. Note that we have slightly simplified the technical details associated with these methods, maintaining our focus on the business requirements of a eMarketplace:

1. Get Authentication Token.

2. Save Business.

3. Delete Business.

4. Save Service.

5. Delete Service.

6. Save Binding.

7. Delete Binding.

8. Save Technical Model.

9. Delete Technical Model.

Get Authentication Token: This is the first method to be called by a publisher (an eSupplier). Using this API call, a publisher provides the Operator site with a username and password against which they get an authentication token. The information in this authentication token is then provided with every API call to the Operator site.

Save Business: This API call is used to create a new business entry or edit any existing business entry. This is the first entity to be created and all the other entities will be created within a business entity. The Save Business message contains two parameters: first is the authentication token obtained by the Get Authentication Token message, and second is a Business Entity structure. The Business Entity structure contains general information about the business, such as business name, address, contact details, description of business, etc. It also contains information about taxonomies used by this business. This method sends back a unique business key through which a business can be referred to in the future.

Delete Business: This API call removes a business entry from a UDDI registry. This message takes two parameters from the publisher: one the Authentication Token element, and the second the unique business key (returned by Save Business API call).

Save Service: This API call is used to add a new business service or updates any existing one. A business service can only be added to an existing business entity. It takes two parameters: the Authentication Token, and the Business Service structure. A business can contain any number of services it feels like. Each service will contain a name of the service, its description, and a list of Binding Templates (each template will contain the URL of a SOAP server, where the service is deployed). This call returns a unique service key.

Delete Service: The Delete Service API call is used for removing business service/services from a UDDI registry. It takes the two parameters: first is the authentication token, and second is the unique service key, which the publisher got while saving the service for the first time.

Save Binding: The Save Binding API call is used for saving a new Binding Template or update an existing one. Each service contains at least one binding template, which binds the service to a Technical Model Instance. This API call takes two parameters: the Authentication Token, and a Binding Template structure. The Binding Template structure contains a description and an access point (the address of SOAP server deployment of the Binding Template). This Binding Template structure should contain all the Technical Models Instances that the service wants to bind with one particular SOAP server.

135

Delete Binding: This API call is used to remove a binding template. It takes two parameters: the Authentication Token, and the binding key returned by the Save Binding API call.

Save Technical Model: This API call registers or updates a Technical Model. A Technical Model can be the WSDL interface from a company, a fingerprint (discussed in the next section, *Common Business Protocols and Practices*), or the categorization/taxonomy architecture. It takes two parameters: first the authentication token, and second a Technical Model structure (containing a name, description, and address of a document that may be a WSDL file). This method will return a unique key, which will be used to identify the technical model later on.

Delete Technical Model: This API call deletes the technical model. It will take two parameters: first is the authentication token, and second is the Technical Model key returned by the Save Technical Model API call.

Common Business Protocols and Practices

So far we have discussed B2B integration through UDDI- and WSDL-based eMarketplaces. But there is another dimension of this idea yet to be explored. Think of the business operations of one particular business, a shipping business for example. The business process of one shipping company is not expected to be very different from any other shipping company. For example the Get Total Freight method in the WSDL of one shipping company will take roughly the same parameters, no matter who implements them. Similarly, a Get Per Night Charge method in the Web Service of a hotel will generally be similar to the same method in any other hotel's service.

This gives rise to the concept of Common Business Practices or Protocols. It is possible to build standard WSDL interfaces for any particular business sector. These protocols will reflect and cater for all the needs of that particular business community and all businesses will use that protocol. This is what UDDI calls a **Fingerprint**.

But who will design these fingerprints? Naturally it should be some expert in their community, someone who knows all the requirement of their business discipline. Perhaps the most popular fingerprint will come from standards organizations through the well-known community process where all interested parties work on the draft of the proposed protocol before it can become a standard. The organization that designs fingerprints will also be responsible for maintaining them so that they remain relevant in a dynamic business world.

We have proposed a sample fingerprint for the Computer Hardware industry in our WSDL illustration. It is only an example to support UDDI's idea of fingerprints and is not intended to fulfill actual professional requirements. Readers will notice that fingerprints are just the WSDL interfaces that are accepted as standard interfaces of a particular business community.

We have drawn our WSDL illustration so that it can be used as a template or a form. Business experts can fill it in with their business ideas. Software analysts and designers can use the completed (filled in) forms for WSDL and service implementation.

Readers may question the practicality of the idea of Common Business Protocols, especially when supply chains may have very small companies acting as eSuppliers. In the past, large players in every industry have managed to dominate the standardization processes. This one point may hamper the lowering of B2B integration costs.

Advantages of Common Business Protocols

The advantages of this idea are threefold:

- ❏   Businesses will have a reliable and relevant interface made by experts suitable for both their business needs and the requirements of going on-line. If there were no Common Business Protocols, every business would have to experiment to arrive at best practices. This is one point where cost reduction is likely.

- ❏   We will have known requirements to cater for at our eMarketplace. Without fingerprints, eBuyers would have to read and understand different interfaces from similar businesses. Fingerprints allow uniform behavior for all businesses that implement them.

- ❏   We can also expect that best-of-breed implementations will be produced for popular fingerprints. Buying an off-the-shelf solution is normally a cheaper and better option than developing from scratch.

This does not stop businesses (eSuppliers) from implementing more than one fingerprint. They can implement any number of fingerprints, as they like.

How To Publish Fingerprints at a UDDI Registry

UDDI uses Technical Models to publish fingerprints. The standards organization that designs a WSDL interface to be used as a Common Business Practice will publish it once. Any eSuppliers interested in implementing that fingerprint will register an instance of it.

This means eSuppliers will use the WSDL interface of the fingerprint, implement it on the Web server (or buy an off-the-shelf implementation), and include a reference to that fingerprint on our UDDI-based eMarkeplace as part of their services.

Every fingerprint receives a unique Technical Model key at the time of being registered at our UDDI registry (recall the Save Technical Model API call we discussed in the last section). This technical model key will be utilized to refer to this fingerprint while creating its instances. An eSupplier may also register the instances of their fingerprints at more than one eMarketplace. In fact most eSuppliers would like as much exposure as they can get: implement once and be exposed everywhere is a very attractive idea.

At this point we would like to discuss the impact of defining fingerprints on two of the present-day e-commerce models: vertical exchanges and supply chain management.

Vertical Exchanges

Portals like http://www.esteel.com/ or http://www.paperspace.com/ are primarily B2B eMarketplaces serving very specific business communities (esteel serves only the steel industry and paperspace covers only the paper industry). As they cover the supply chain of a specific industry from top to bottom, they are referred to as Vertical exchanges.

This type of B2B portal can work around a family of related fingerprints. They are specialized in their field and therefore need only a few fingerprints registered at their UDDI registry. They also have an option of getting their eMarketplace exposed at other eMarketplaces. For this purpose, UDDI allows a mechanism for one registry to exchange its data with others. Therefore specialized eMarketplaces can have their members automatically listed at their friendly (partner) eMarketplaces.

Is there any possibility we could have achieved this level of B2B integration with conventional eMarketplaces? It seems unlikely.

Supply Chain Management

Fingerprints are also of paramount importance for supply chain management in all types of e-commerce. You may wish to refer to our first diagram where we have shown an eBuyer making use of the services of an eMarketplace.

The eSupplier will become an eBuyer for other businesses. We will now see how a fingerprints-based supply chain works. WSDL allows loose coupling between components and considerably reduces the cost of integrating your workflow with the output of your suppliers. In the absence of common business protocols, businesses will need to study the WSDL interfaces of each of their B2B suppliers. Every company will implement its own business interface. This means if you are a service provider at our eMarketplace and you want to make use of services provided by other businesses, you will need to incorporate the WSDL interfaces of each of your suppliers separately. Additionally, there is always a chance of finding more competitive suppliers in the future, which means implementing new interfaces is an on-going job.

This one problem will remain an obstacle in B2B integration until online business communities agree on common business practices. Once we have common protocols to work with, all our B2B suppliers will automatically become integrated with our supply chain. We will need to implement tools to coordinate with fingerprints instead of interfaces from individual suppliers. The rest of the process will not change. Fingerprints will follow the same WSDL grammar and therefore the process of invoking specific methods in an interface will be the same.

No business can imagine working without using e-mail. Why? The cost advantage ratio is such that you cannot avoid using it. What about e-commerce? Most companies can survive without doing online business. UDDI and WSDL, though, will reduce the cost of B2B integration to such an extent that it will be a rare company that chooses not to go online.

The Next Generation Dot Com

Web Services are targeted at lowering the cost of B2B integration through the standardization process. Cost reduction naturally results in a favorable cost-benefit and feasibility analysis. This does not mean, though, that Web Services can do magic to make every investment idea feasible and justified.

B2B integration with conventional e-commerce was accompanied by a lot of media hype. The result was unjustified investments that led to the failure of many dot com ventures. The lesson to be learned by prospective eSuppliers from previous mistakes is to consider the amount of value addition and extra advantage gained by going online at a UDDI-based eMarketplace. The same applies to eMarketplace owners as well. Lowered costs of B2B integration at UDDI-based eMarketplaces needs to be compared to specific gains in particular industrial sectors.

A Pragmatic Approach To UDDI-based eMarketplaces

We have already discussed the roles of eMarketplace owners and eSuppliers. UDDI and WSDL together can ensure B2B integration by providing the concept of components loosely coupled with each other through interfaces. But this is not enough for practical B2B to happen on a UDDI-based eMarketplace. The following are two important requirements without which no B2B or eMarketplace can happen:

❑   Security.

❑   Transactions across enterprises (from one eSupplier to another eSupplier).

The W3C has released two specifications (XML Encryption and XML Digital Signatures) that control various aspects of end-to-end security in Web Services (authentication, exchange of keys, encryption, etc.). Refer to http://www.w3.org/ for more details.

Cross-enterprise transactions are an interesting topic, where standardization can offer a few features that were not possible without having interoperable interfaces. This is the concept of long-life electronic transactions, in which eSuppliers can invoke the services of each other as part of a B2B transaction.

A complete transaction consists of a sequence of service invocation requests. The result of any single service invocation request can affect the entire transaction. A transaction can exist for days or weeks before concluding. Refer to the OASIS web site (http://www.oasis-open.org/) for details about Business Transaction Protocol (BTP).

139

On a pragmatic analysis, UDDI, WSDL, SOAP, XML Encryption, and XML Digital Signature will be needed to implement a complete eMarketplace. Soon interoperable implementations of all these will be available off-the-shelf. Thus, an eMarketplace implementation will largely be a system integration task.

Conclusion

We have discussed several technologies in this paper. Together they can form a UDDI-based eMarketplace. We will summarize the technologies involved:

- ❑ UDDI is a set of APIs for publishing and search operations.
- ❑ We can build eMarketplaces around UDDI registries.
- ❑ WSDL is a grammar to describe interfaces for Web Services.
- ❑ Service providers will use WSDL interfaces to expose/publish their services at our eMarketplace.
- ❑ Customers (users of our eMarketplace) can invoke services through their WSDL interfaces.
- ❑ Fingerprints are standard WSDL interfaces for specific business communities. Fingerprints can standardize the way in which businesses interact with each other. This will considerably reduce the cost of B2B integration.

Author: Kunal Mittal

- Technical Challenges
- Current Shortcomings
- Web Services Benefits
- Uses for UDDI, SOAP, WSDL
- Case Study

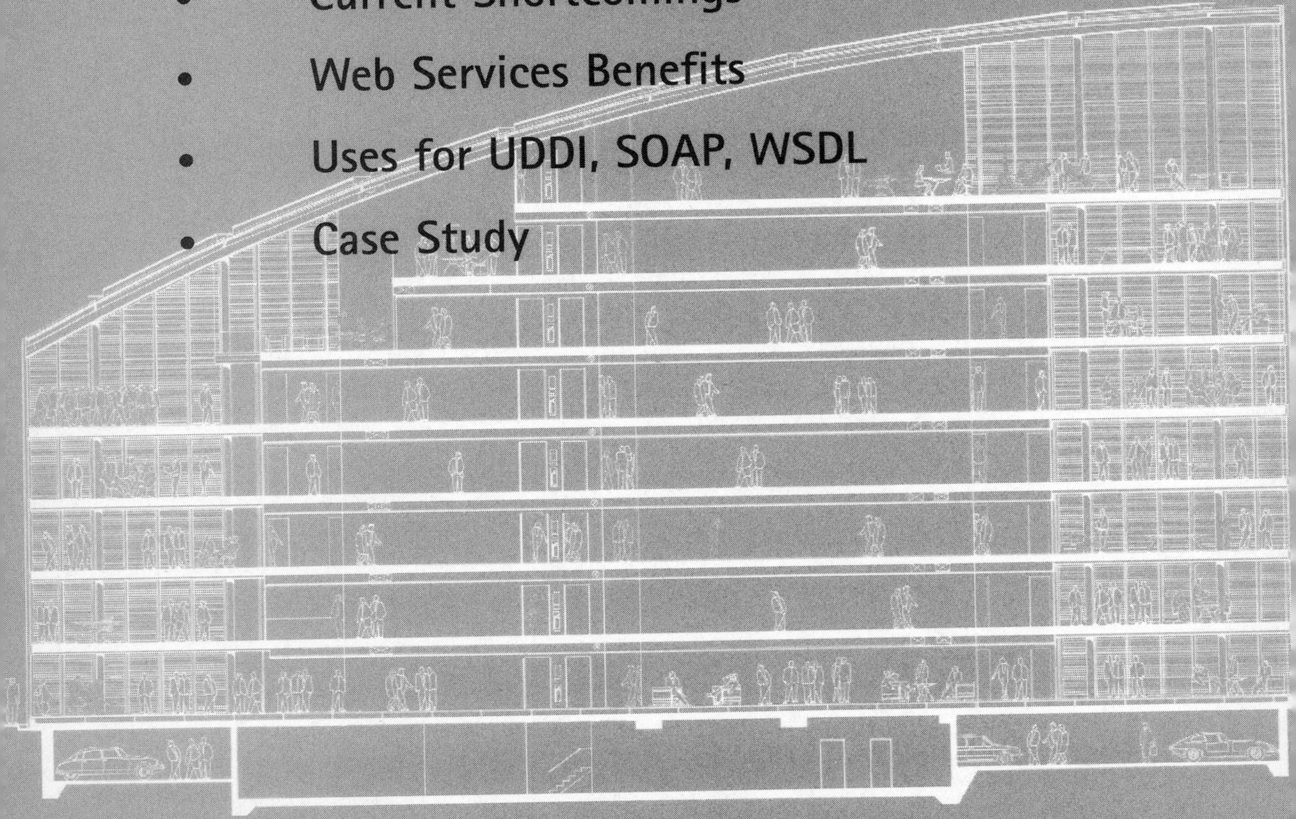

Web Services and the Real Estate Industry

Web Services is a technology with tremendous potential. In selected industries, such as Financial, Insurance, and Travel, companies are already beginning to tap into the power of Web Services which enables them to integrate easily with new business partners, provide powerful new services to consumers, and position themselves for long term growth. Web Services can also provide the following benefits:

- ❑ Faster time to market, increased employee productivity.
- ❑ New and value added services, at lower costs.
- ❑ Quicker and dynamic partnerships, with efficient B2B Collaboration.

This paper focuses on how Web Services can revolutionize the real estate industry. We concentrate on the residential real estate industry, identifying the complex nature of a real estate transaction. It emphasizes the fact that the number of distinct people involved in a single transaction, and the coordination and management of these people to serve the best interests of the buyer and seller, is an intricate process. We present ideas on how Web Services can be used to streamline these interactions. The concepts described in this paper can be similarly applied to the commercial real estate industry.

Technological Challenges Faced By the Real Estate Industry

The rapid change in technology affects the interactions between the different parties involved in a single real estate transaction, such as the buyer, seller, their agents, their mortgage and title companies, and various other parties such as home inspectors, property appraisers, notaries, home insurance agents, and so on. Web Services technology allows these individuals or companies to interact and achieves a better, faster, cheaper, and more reliable way of conducting business. Seeing the number of people involved within a single real estate deal, it is easy to see the benefits of a cross-platform and asynchronous solution to address these complications.

Individuals seeking to buy or sell a house are getting more "Internet savvy". They are using the Internet to explore their options, such as choosing a real estate agent. Hence, it is becoming increasingly important for realtors to provide online services to win more clients. For example, they might want to provide statistical information about the various properties listed for sale, comparable sales, etc. from accredited sources, all at the click of a mouse. Realtors need more power than the Multiple Listing Service (MLS) system to present their clients with the best possible options. The MLS system allows the listing of a property for sale, to be viewed by multiple realtors. Many realtors poll this system and display a subset of listings on their own sites. Access to this MLS system, however, is not simple and is difficult to automate. The Internet evolution has brought sharp competition between realtors, forcing them to tailor their services according to the needs of the client.

After the difficult task of choosing a realtor to help the buying or selling process, an individual has to go through hundreds of sheets of papers – understanding legal jargon, various clauses regarding the deal, understanding all the provisions, etc. In addition, the individual also has to deal with various third parties to be able to buy or sell the house.

Various businesses such as agents, contractors, mortgage companies, and insurance companies involved in the real estate process now provide their services on the Internet. Real estate communities are emerging to provide a subset of the services required for a single transaction. These services, however, do not follow any standards and do not integrate with other services to provide a one-stop, best-of-breed shop to a person trying to initiate a real-estate transaction. Individual businesses involved in some aspect of a real estate deal use different technologies. Their internal processes are often not fully automated and integrated with their service offerings. Even as a standalone service, they might not be making the best use of technology. Thus, integrating one service or business another is not on the horizon for such companies, mainly due to the prohibitive costs of implementing technology.

The following diagram shows the typical interactions for the purchase or sale of a single home. Everybody needs to talk to everyone else. The amateur buyer or seller is stuck in the midst of various real estate professionals:

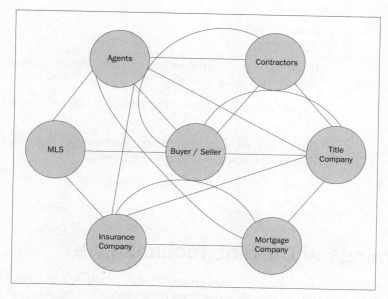

Individuals seeking to engage in some sort of a real estate deal go online and get quotations from various real estate agents, and can read a lot of interesting articles and tips on how to choose an agent, how to buy or sell a house, and so on. One such site is Home Gain (http://www.homegain.com/). From there they can go to another web site, such as Priceline (http://www.priceline.com/), where they provide financial information and have various mortgage companies bid for their loan. Then they could go to a third web site such as ImproveNet (http://www.improvenet.com/), to find contractors for home repairs. After all this, there are still large amounts of paperwork involved as well as the management of finances, taxes, and insurance. When the interest rates drop, they are back in the market looking for the best ways to re-finance their loans.

As an end user, they need a real estate portal or community that provides them with all of the above and much more without their having to go through all the trouble. A community portal that can provide these features seamlessly to a client will be best positioned for long-term success. A community portal could offer various services, implemented as Web Services. A sample list of services is shown below:

Real Estate Service	Description
Listing of Real Estate Agents	Dynamically generated list of agents based on the user criteria.
Mortgage Companies	Dynamic application process for the pre-approval of a loan, and then the final loan approval.

Table continued on following page

Real Estate Service	Description
Contractors	Dynamic list of contractors to provide appraisals, inspections, repairs, and other services.
Insurance Companies	Dynamic list of companies providing home insurance services.
Utilities	List of utility companies (Water, Electricity, Garbage, Gas and Phone) providing services to the house.
Value-added Services	Statistical data on the locality, house, schools, etc.

Shortcomings of Current Technologies

Current technologies, at best, allow the real estate industry to follow some sort of a Community Model. Businesses like Home Gain are expanding their service offerings to provide a single one-stop shop for a buyer or seller. They are expanding services to allow the management of the complete or a major portion of the real estate transaction from their web site.

This, however, is not enough. Any business that wants to offer services has to register with the community site and follow certain rules and regulations. This process is tedious as the new business might be using a different set of technologies to the site offering this community service. The average time to integrate a new business could be several weeks to several months for both the community site as well as the business.

Furthermore, the new business might be required to follow certain templates, pricing procedures, and other restrictions that might not allow them to be as competitive as they would like. Many times, the business might be required to pay a commission or fee to be listed on the community site. It would retain little or no control on how people find and choose their services amongst the other competitors. This is the primary reason the above list of services needs to be provided as Web Services.

Benefits from Web Services

Why would the real estate industry want to use Web Services? Web Services is the first technology that truly addresses the issues outlined above. The power of Web Services such as dynamic discovery of services (UDDI), common messaging platform without language dependencies (XML-based SOAP), and dynamic description of services (XML-based WSDL) allows for easy interactions with other required services to complete the transaction successfully. Services can find each other, negotiate service-level agreements (SLA), and exchange the required data, all without the need for traditional Enterprise Application Integration (EAI).

If businesses expose their services using Web Services standards (SOAP, WSDL, and UDDI), a quick e-Marketplace of services can be formed, where individuals can potentially describe their requirements and allow the entire e-Marketplace of businesses to bid on their contract. This process can happen dynamically without ties to any community site, and without being restricted by the businesses that the community site has registered. This is, however, a long-term vision. We do not see an e-Marketplace forming in the real-estate industry for at least the next two to three years. Although it takes merely hours to implement Web Services, the real return on investment (ROI), particularly for such an e-Marketplace, will not be seen until there is a critical mass of real estate service providers that wrap their services using Web Services technologies.

In the short term, more traditional style community sites will prevail. Thus, we still need to be able to justify the ROI in order to get widespread adoption of Web Services as the new standard for real estate applications. How can community sites differentiate themselves by the use of Web Services? What are the short-term benefits of Web Services?

Business Drivers

Currently, any new real estate firm (individual realtor, mortgage company, title company, home insurance broker, etc.) that wants to integrate with any of the existing real estate communities needs to spend weeks to months with traditional EAI. EAI is difficult as the underlying applications can be built on different technologies such as Visual Basic, C++, Java, etc. Thus, companies can extend the life cycle of existing applications by wrapping their existing business services as Web Services.

Web Services are built on top of XML, which provides a language-independent integration platform. It allows an enterprise to expose some core services so that third parties can combine these and resell value-added services. It shifts the focus from integration to concentrating resources on its core abilities and providing enriched homogeneous environments. Web Services enable a more consistent and uniform experience for the buyer or seller, and allow them to aggregate and personalize data and services from a variety of service providers.

The use of Web Services allows real estate firms to focus on new services, and provide a faster time to close a deal in order to gain competitive advantage and more exposure to clients.

Technical Drivers

There are significant technical drivers that push Web Services to become the technology platform of choice for real estate applications:

1. **Standards-based development** – easy to build, manage, extend, and integrate.

2. **Flexibility of solution** – clients can combine the services to meet their needs.

3. **Infrastructure** – Standards-based application server vendors, such as BEA and IBM, provide technology containers to deploy and manage the applications.

4. **Common language communication** – Web Services technologies allow different services to communicate in a common language.

5. **Interoperability** – Web Services technologies allow different services to communicate using a common language.

Web Services Technologies

Here, we will briefly describe the primary three new technologies that enable Web Services. Using UDDI, SOAP, and WSDL, an application developer can easily create and interact with Web Services. These technologies are built on top of XML that provides a language-independent grammar for negotiation. HTTP, HTTPS, or other protocols (such as SMTP) can be used as the transport layer to pass information between Web Services over the wire.

Protocol	Description
UDDI	Allows the discovery of a Web Service
SOAP	Message exchange protocol for the interactions between the Web Services
WSDL	Defines what the Web Service can do

The following diagram shows how these technologies can be used in a typical flow of messages between a buyer and the real estate agents and mortgage companies:

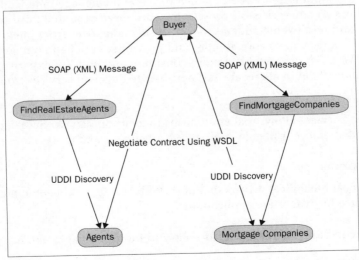

A SOAP message can be sent to a "find real estate agents" service with some search criteria. This service is one provided by a community site as described later. The services can then use UDDI to return a list of agents. The contract between the buyer and agents can be negotiated using WSDL.

Dynamic Discovery Using UDDI

UDDI (Universal Description, Discovery, and Integration – http://www.uddi.org/) is the current technology enabling dynamic discovery of Web Services. As Web Services are adopted, real estate services can list themselves in UDDI repositories provided by companies such as IBM, Microsoft, and others.

A typical UDDI listing for a real estate agent would include the following:

1. Name of Agent.

2. Discovery URL.

3. Contact Information.

4. Search Criteria.

To see samples of these registries, visit the UDDI repositories on the Internet (for more details, see the IBM site at http://www-3.ibm.com/services/uddi/, or the Microsoft site at http://uddi.microsoft.com/). These UDDI repositories serve as yellow pages, and communities can dynamically search these repositories and find services based on the needs of the users.

With UDDI, prospective Web Services providers can identify the businesses they are considering and catalog what services they can provide. UDDI outlines the mechanisms of finding and connecting to different real estate services, but it does not define the interactions that can take place between these Web Services. Thus, Web Services use UDDI in conjunction with other technologies such as SOAP and WSDL, to define the protocol and syntax of the transaction.

Message Exchange Using SOAP

SOAP (Simple Object Access Protocol, http://www.w3.org/TR/SOAP/) is an XML-based language for exchanging messages. It is a mechanism for Web Services to talk to each other over HTTP or other transport protocols, and it is language independent. A real estate service could use its Visual Basic application to talk to a J2EE application using SOAP (via XML serialization).

The previous diagram shows that the buyer can send a SOAP message to the FindRealEstate Agents service to invoke the search for real estate agents. This message needs to contain the SOAP XML headers (see a developer-oriented paper for how this would look), and the search criteria of what they are looking for. This could include some selection criteria to rank the resulting list of agents. Thus, using the SOAP protocol it is possible to integrate the communications between the different real estate services via a community portal.

Defining Contracts Using WSDL

WSDL (Web Services Description Language, http://www.w3.org/TR/wsdl/) is an XML-based language used to describe the services provided and methods to access these services.

149

We can, for example, negotiate the contracts between the mortgage companies and the buyer. The buyer would pass all their financial information and other information needed to have a loan approved as a SOAP message. How, though, do we find out what information is needed? The list of information needed by a mortgage company to process a loan application is defined in a WSDL file. The mortgage company defines the format for the input data, as well as the format and contents of the data it will return as a result of the loan processing. The Web Services orchestration platform will know how to interpret the WSDL file between the buyer and mortgage company.

This basic introduction to Web Services technologies demonstrates how real estate services can be wrapped using Web Services. We will show this using a case study, which should shed light on how Web Services can be used in a simplified real estate transaction.

Case Study

As an example, we will show how a basic Real Estate Community can be created using Web Services technologies.

Problem Description

In our example, we try to describe a community site that will manage and orchestrate real-estate transactions using Web Services technologies. We will describe how the following real-estate process can be converted into a collection of Web Services, and orchestrated through a community site. Our example shows a relatively simple five-step process for buying a house.

Process	Notes
1) Preparatory work: **In parallel and asynchronous**	
a) Get a credit report (Source: http://www.creditreport.com/)	Can use UDDI here.
b) Estimate your buying power (Source: http://www.interest.com/calculators/)	Can use UDDI here.
2) Retrieve a list of real-estate agents based on location (city/state or zip), accreditations, etc. (Source: http://www.realtor.com/)	Can use UDDI here.
3) Offer Process (Both steps must take place)	
a) Make offer on house (Source: Manual)	This process is manual, as it requires interaction and negotiation between the buyer and seller, and is traditionally mediated by their agents.

Process	Notes
b) Offer accepted (Source: Manual)	Buyer and seller agents use faxed offer contracts and manually update community site for notifications.
4) Escrow: Under contract with accepted offer. **In parallel and asynchronous**	
a) Get an appraisal (Source: http://www.appraisalreferrals.com/)	Or buyer's agent can have a recommended list of appraisers.
b) Get an inspection (Source: http://www.ashi.com/)	American Society of Home Inspectors (or buyer's agent list).
c) Apply for a mortgage (Source: http://www.lendingtree.com/)	Just like current loan demo app – several banks make offers, the customer selects one.
d) Transfer money to mortgage bank (Source: Manual)	The buyer must contact their bank and have the money wired to the mortgage bank. There is definitely scope to expand this into a Web Services offering.
5) Close of escrow!	Manual confirmation by lender.

Some of the processes can be carried out in parallel, and asynchronously. This means that the services can be initiated simultaneously, and one does not need to wait for a reply from one service before going on to work on the other service:

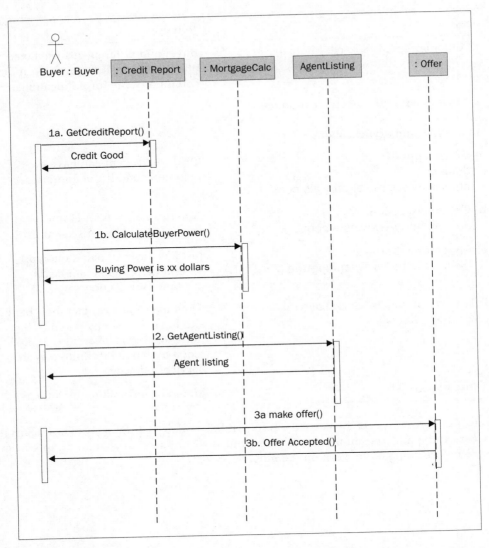

Step 1 is the pre-processing step. The buyer decides to get a credit report as well as estimate their buying power. Neither of these activities has any relation to the other, so they can be done in parallel. The buyer goes to the community site to start these processes. The community site allows the buyer to get a credit report from one of many credit-reporting companies. These companies list their services in a UDDI registry. The buyer is also able to choose from a list of mortgage calculators that provide different levels of functionality.

The next step is for the buyer to find an appropriate real estate agent to help them in the buying process. Realtors list themselves in an UDDI repository and the community site searches these listings based on some search criteria given by the buyer. This can include years in profession, number of houses sold in the last year, commission rates, etc. Once the buyer chooses an agent, the agent helps them find a house. This process is not covered in our example. The buyer looks at different houses and chooses one. The agent and buyer get together and make an offer to the seller. This is step 3 of our process. Once the offer is accepted, we enter a contract mode. This is the beginning of a transaction, and the steps are highlighted in the following diagram:

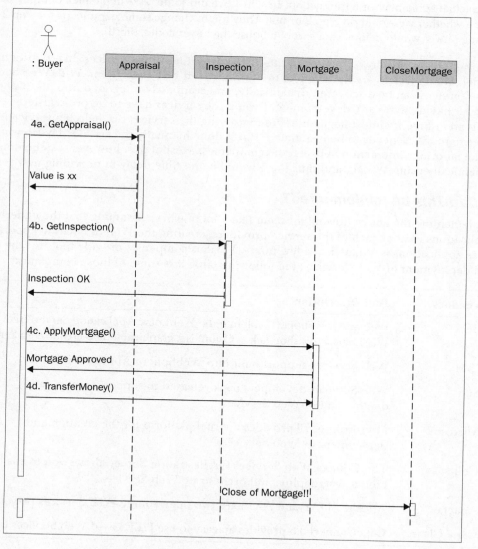

Step 4 of the home-buying process is where we need transaction support. Based on the successful return of the three services (Appraisal, Inspection, and Mortgage), we will either close the deal and the buyer will have a new house, or the process will be canceled. At each step however, the buyer is calling a Web Service. For example, in step 4a, the buyer calls an Appraisal Web Service and then chooses from a list of people who provide appraisal services. They then interact with that appraisal service. In parallel, they can do the same to order a Home Inspection. These processes are asynchronous, so we do not need one of them to finish before we start the next. We do, however, need to define a contract or transaction that says we can only move to step 5 if step 4a through step 4d succeed. This was not necessarily the case for step 1. Step 1 did not need a contractual agreement or a transaction. In step 1, we did some tasks in parallel, but they did not define whether we would do Step 2 or not. They might change some parameters for step 2 (the buying power would define what sort of a house the buyer could afford).

At any point in this flow, we need to interact with various other services. In a traditional model, these services are hard coded, or pre-registered with the system. With Web Services, these services can be discovered dynamically, and seamlessly integrated into the system without having to do any development. Even if the services have to be pre-registered, the integration time is almost negligible. Pre-registering the services can help if a service level agreement (SLA) needs to be negotiated. If it is done manually, it can take days to weeks due to the laborious interaction between the companies. Most of this, however, can be done dynamically using WSDL, and thus there would be no time delay in providing new services.

How Can This be Implemented?

Implementing the above flow might seem like a lot of work. Assuming that the underlying applications exist at each of the service providers, creating the Web Services wrappers to these applications is a matter of a few hours. Various companies provide tools for the creation and deployment of Web Services; the following table lists some of those companies:

Vendors	Tool Description
BEA	Web Services support built into the WebLogic Application Server. BEA WebLogic Workshop (a.k.a. Cajun) is a graphical tool to create Web Services.
IBM	Web Services support built into WebSphere Application Server.
Sun	Web Services developers pack released to support creation and deployment of Web Services.
Microsoft	Microsoft .NET provides a visual platform for the creation and deployment of Web Services.
Collaxa	The Collaxa Web Services Orchestration Server allows you to easily create, test, deploy, and orchestrate Web Services.
Apache	Apache SOAP and AXIS are two open-source Web Services projects.
Cape Clear	CapeConnect 3.5 provides an easy-to-use J2EE-based Web Services toolkit.

Collaxa has a full working example of this case study (for more details, see http://www.collaxa.com/dispatch.jsp?ref=wsa_app_source). Interfaces to various Web portals and services are implemented with XML Web Services leveraging the Collaxa Web Service Orchestration Server™. Full sourcecode for this example is available from the Collaxa site. **Note:** This paper does not intend to recommend one product over the other, and merely uses the Collaxa product as a way of showing a real example.

Conclusion

Web Services will be the next revolution in the real estate B2B and B2C application space. In order to remain competitive, real estate businesses and portals must develop Web Services interfaces to their applications. Using these emerging standards, the total time and complexity to complete a real estate transaction can be decreased considerably with minimal integration costs. Real estate firms need to understand their existing applications and identify the functionality that needs to be exposed as part of their Web Services offerings. The use of standards such as XML, HTTP, and SOAP allow for easy integration with other services.

Implementing Web Services does not require huge amounts of financial or time commitment. Many vendors, as described in this paper, provide software tools to support the creation and deployment of Web Services. Ramp-up time for developers to learn these technologies is minimal as these tools do most of the grunt work for you. It should only take a matter of hours or days for companies to wrap their existing service offerings as Web Services.

The resulting integrated systems will allow the end-customer, a person trying to buy or sell a house, to be shielded from all the complexity of interacting with the various entities involved in this complex transaction.

Author: David O'Riordan

- B2B and EAI Processes
- ebXML BPSS
- XLANG
- WSFL
- BPML
- Convergence

Business Process Standards For Web Services

The convergence of two major trends is creating a rapidly growing demand for a new breed of software that facilitates automation of business processes both between enterprises and within the enterprise.

The first of these trends is Web Services technology: a collection of XML-based standards that provide a means for passing information between applications using XML documents. The ability of Web Services to reach beyond the firewall, the loose coupling between applications encouraged by Web Service interfaces, and the wide support for core Web Service standards by major enterprise software vendors are the key reasons why Web Services technology promises to make integration of applications both within the enterprise and between different enterprises significantly easier and cheaper than before. Loose coupling means that not only can applications be implemented on different platforms and operating systems, but also that the implementations can readily be changed without affecting the interfaces.

The second of these trends is a business driver. In order to increase an organization's agility in responding to customer, market, and strategic requirements, the information flow between the IT systems that carry out these business operations must be streamlined. This includes not only the organization's own IT systems but also those of its partners. It is the task of electronic business integration to automate this information flow as much as possible in order to streamline operations. Historically, organizations have generally focused on integrating their own IT systems.

If, however, the information flow between the organization's own IT systems and those of its partners (particularly in the supply chain) is not also streamlined, then the overall agility of the business is still restricted. Therefore, many enterprises also strive to integrate their partner's IT systems with their own in order to more fully automate critical business processes such as sales, procurement, and research and development. The benefits of the increased agility resulting from business process automation are extensive. For example, operational costs are decreased, inventories are reduced, customer satisfaction is increased, and products are brought to market faster.

A whole new set of tools has arisen to facilitate the integration and automation of business processes. These include graphical process modeling tools, middleware technologies such as CORBA and JMS, integration brokers, Business Process Management Systems (BPMS), and B2B servers. Unfortunately, until recently the investment required by organizations to integrate the IT systems both inside their organization and across the firewall has been very high. This is mainly because the different proprietary interfaces and data formats used by each application have meant that integration projects have had to invest considerable resources in expensive integration tools as well as in the time and expertise to perform the integration.

Web Services technology promises to change this by replacing proprietary interfaces and data formats with low-cost, ubiquitously supported standards for interfaces and data that work as well across the firewall as within it. The first generation of Web Services technology, though, has largely focused on the messaging foundation supported by SOAP and WSDL. While this foundation is sufficient for some internal application integration needs, it is not sufficient to support the complete automation of critical business processes. This requires the ability to specify workflow, security requirements, transaction management, and other critical information related to the business process context. Such information is generally specified in a business process model.

The Need for Business Process Standards

We require standards for business process models that are built on Web Service architectures. These would enable processes to be modeled, deployed, executed, and managed by software from various vendors. Without such standards, a number of undesirable consequences arise. These include:

❑ Vendors are likely to offer support for such features as proprietary extensions to Web Service standards, leading to vendor lock-in.

❑ Collaborating enterprises may choose incompatible means of defining the shared process models, leading to inefficiencies and error-prone operations.

❑ Reuse of proven processes and patterns across products from different vendors is difficult if these can't be specified in a standard way.

❑ The emergence of best-of-breed tools for modeling and for execution of processes will be hampered.

B2B and EAI Processes

Business processes can be divided into two distinct but converging domains:

- **Public processes** are those that an enterprise shares with its customers, suppliers, or other partners. This is the **business-to-business integration (B2Bi)** domain.

- **Private processes** are those that are internal to the enterprise. This is the **enterprise application integration (EAI)** domain.

Solutions for these two domains share many common characteristics. For example XML document exchange between applications is used in both the EAI and B2B domains for loosely coupled integration of applications. Additionally, in any enterprise, public and private business processes combine to perform the overall operations of the business. These facts drive the demand for a single business process standard that encompasses both the B2B and EAI domains.

There are, however, some important differences between the domains. For example, stricter legal and security requirements will apply to public processes. On the other hand private process models stipulate execution details that are not present in public process models, such as how a purchase order is actually processed by various enterprise applications.

Business Process Features

A business process standard that provides comprehensive support for both public and private processes should consider the following features:

- **Collaboration-Based Process Models**
  Experience in both EAI and B2B process modeling has led to the increasing adoption of collaboration-based process models, usually based on UML. In collaboration-based process models, processes are described as a set of collaborations between various participants, including organizations, applications, employees, and other business processes. Usually participants can be abstracted in model descriptions using roles. The ability to recursively decompose process models is generally required.

- **Workflow**
  The workflow defines how the participants in a process work together to execute a process from start to finish, and is also called choreography or orchestration. Most workflow standards support subprocesses, which allow activities within a workflow to be implemented as another workflow. Workflow descriptions can be generated from collaboration models, or specified independently. Recursively decomposed process models can be mapped to workflow descriptions using subprocesses.

There are two complementary parts to workflow: the **control flow** and the **data flow**. The control flow defines the sequencing of different activities in the process. The data flow defines how information flows between activities.

❑ **Transaction Management**
Transactions are crucial building blocks of any business process and a comprehensive business process standard must provide a means for specifying how transactions are managed. Long-running transactions that may take hours or weeks to complete must be supported. If an enclosing transaction fails after an enclosed transaction is completed, some compensating actions may be needed. For example if a hotel reservation is canceled after a payment has been authorized, a compensating action may be required to cancel the payment. Time constraints for receiving responses or acknowledgements may also be required.

❑ **Exception Handling**
If an exception is raised during the course of a business process, then it is important that the model allow appropriate recovery actions to be taken.

❑ **Service Interfaces**
Web Services provide a basis for passing messages between participants in collaboration-based processes. Some recently proposed business process standards such as WSFL and XLANG use WSDL interfaces to describe the loosely coupled services exposed by participants.

❑ **Message Security and Reliability**
For mission-critical processes, reliable and secure message delivery is required. Additionally, B2B messages may need to be digitally signed and authenticated. These quality-of-service semantics may vary for different transactions.

❑ **Audit Trail**
It is generally very important for legal purposes in B2B processes that an audit trail of certain business transactions is kept. This means that a trading partner is unable to claim that a transaction was not accepted when in fact it was; that is, it ensures non-repudiation of the transaction by the partner. Digitally signed receipt acknowledgements of messages may be demanded.

❑ **Agreements**
The notion of agreements is specifically for B2B processes. An agreement represents a contract between two or more partners to carry out specific functions (identified by roles) in a public business process.

❑ **Execution**
Public processes describe only how information should flow between organizations. In order to be able to fully automate the execution of the business process within an organization, the complete information flow within that organization as well as across its firewalls must be specified. This requires the process models to fully describe the private as well as the public activities of the organization.

A powerful approach supported by some standards is Web Service aggregation, whereby one Web Service is used in the implementation of another. For example an organizational workflow that handles purchase orders might receive the orders from customers via one Web Service and then call an internal ERP application via another Web Service to help process the order. Such an approach should become significantly less expensive than traditional EAI methods.

The Web Services Stack

In order to describe how Web Service standards relate to the above features, it is useful to begin by looking at a representative Web Services architecture.

Web Services architecture is built from layers of technology and standards on which services can be implemented and deployed. Each layer on this Web Services stack depends on the layers below it. There are many variations of this architecture, but each variation generally includes the features described in the previous section in addition to the basic messaging and service description foundation layers.

The following diagram illustrates a generic Web Services architecture, and how it maps to specific architectures from prominent organizations or companies. The next section examines some of the business process specifications in more detail:

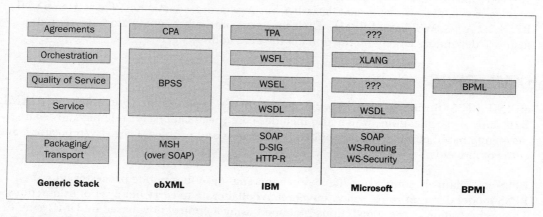

In this generic architecture we have the following layers:

❑ **Packaging/Transport**
This enables information to be packaged into messages and transported reliably and securely between participants. It is sometimes just called the **messaging layer**.

❑ **Service**
This layer describes the operational interfaces of a Web Service.

   ❑   **Quality Of Service**
This layer describes non-operational aspects of services, including reliability and security characteristics.

   ❑   **Orchestration**
This layer describes how services interact with each other in business processes using workflow descriptions. This layer is also sometimes referred to as the **choreography layer**.

   ❑   **Agreements**
This layer describes how specific trading partners will collaborate to perform some shared business process.

This generic architecture is of course a highly simplified representation. It omits some important elements that are not the focus of this article, for example service discovery.

It should be noted that BPMI deliberately only defines the process layer, as it is intended that BPML process models can bind to complementary standards from other stacks (see *BMPL* for more details) .

The Candidates

Now let's examine those specifications that address the orchestration layer of the Web Services stack, the core layer that describes business process semantics. These are ebXML BPSS, XLANG, WSFL, and BPML. Each supports some subset of the aforementioned features, depending largely on the domain they are addressing.

ebXML BPSS

ebXML BPSS (Business Process Specification Schema) is part of the comprehensive ebXML B2B suite of specifications, which also includes core specifications for reliable and secure messaging based on SOAP, collaboration agreements and profiles, a registry/repository, and core components.

BPSS is a relatively simple but effective schema that describes public processes only. In a BPSS model different roles (seller, buyer, etc.) collaborate to carry out a set of transactions. The orchestration of the transactions is defined using a control flow based on UML activity graph semantics. There is no explicit support for describing how data flows between transactions.

The transaction part of the model is based on a proven, robust model for long-lived e-commerce business transactions used by previous B2B standards such as RosettaNet. There is explicit support for specifying quality-of-service semantics for transactions such as authentication, acknowledgements, non-repudiation, and timeouts:

Feature	Support
Collaboration-Based Modeling	BPSS describes public processes as collaborations between roles, with each role abstractly representing a trading partner. There are two types of collaborations: binary collaborations between two roles, and multi-party collaborations between three or more roles. Multi-party collaborations are decomposed to binary collaborations. Recursive decomposition is further supported through nesting binary collaborations inside other binary collaborations, making for a flexible solution.
Workflow	BPSS workflow is described by assigning a public control flow based on UML activity graph semantics to each binary collaboration. The control flow describes the sequencing of business transactions between the two roles. The control flow can specify sequential, parallel, and conditional execution of business transactions. There is also a limited facility for describing control flow across multi-party collaborations.
Transaction Management	BPSS supports a long-running business transaction model based on robust, proven e-commerce transaction patterns used by previous standards such as RosettaNet. A business transaction consists of a request and optionally a response. Each request or response may require that a receipt acknowledgement be returned to the sender. Additionally for contract-forming transactions such as purchase order requests, an acceptance acknowledgement may need to be returned to the requester. Time constraints can be applied to the return of responses and acknowledgements. If a business transaction fails on either side, the other side is notified so that both sides can carry out any actions necessary to process the failure in their internal systems. Transactions are not nested and there is no support for specifying compensating transactions.
Exception Handling	BPSS defines a number of possible exceptions and prescribes how these are communicated and how they affect the state of the transaction. They generally cause the transaction to fail. Transitions exiting from a transaction can be enabled based on whether the transaction failed or succeeded. For example if a quote request transaction fails, a procurement process might transition to completion, whereas if it succeeds the process might transition to a purchase order transaction.

Table continued on following page

Feature	Support
Service Interfaces	BPSS process models implicitly contain service interface descriptions for each role. The service interfaces support specific asynchronous request and response operations, each with a defined message content. That content can consist of any number of specified XML document types and MIME attachments. The service interface also implicitly supports generic acknowledgement and exception messages. Organizations can advertise their support for particular roles (service interfaces) in ebXML collaboration profiles and agreements, which include the location of the services.
	WSDL descriptions of the service interfaces for each role could be readily generated although there is no standard mapping at this time.
Message Security And Reliability	BPSS assumes that processes will use reliable and secure messaging services such as the ebXML messaging service. For each request or response, it can be stipulated that the identity of the originator must be checked for authorization purposes. For document security, it can be stipulated whether each document or attachment in a request or response must be encrypted, whether it must contain a message digest to prevent tampering, and whether a digital certificate is required. For each transaction it is possible to specify whether guaranteed delivery of messages is required. Default settings for these properties can be specified as attributes of transactions in a BPSS model, and these defaults can then be overridden in a CPA (collaboration protocol agreement) between two partners.
Audit Trail	For each request or response, it can be stipulated that the sender must save a copy of the message contents. Additionally it can be stipulated that a digitally signed receipt acknowledgement must be returned to the sender, who then saves it. This provides a high degree of non-repudiation of transactions. Default settings for these properties can be specified as attributes of transactions in a BPSS model, and these defaults can then be overridden in a CPA between two partners.
Agreements	A BPSS process model can be referenced in an ebXML CPA. This provides details on which trading partner supports which role in a specified process model in the context of some business agreement.
Execution	As a public process schema, BPSS provides no support for internal execution semantics.

See also http://www.ebxml.org/specs/ebBPSS.pdf.

XLANG

XLANG is Microsoft's proposal in this space, and like BPSS is currently focused entirely on public processes.

XLANG uses WSDL to describe the service interfaces of each participant. The behavior is specified with a control flow that choreographs the WSDL operations. There is no means for specifying data flow between operations. Long-running transactions encompassing multiple operations are supported and can be nested. Compensating operations for transactions can be specified. Exceptions can be caught and recovery operations specified. Acknowledgements and timeouts can be flexibly incorporated. Some support for agreements is provided in XLANG by contracts, which defines how to stitch together Web Services of collaborating partners.

XLANG does not define quality-of-service characteristics of Web Services such as non-repudiation and authentication, or guaranteed messaging requirements.

Feature	Support
Collaboration-Based Modeling	XLANG describes processes as interactions between Web Service providers so collaboration-based process modeling tools are possible. The block-structured control flow descriptions of XLANG are more suitable for generation from flow-chart tools than UML tools, but the latter is possible. Recursive decomposition of XLANG processes is facilitated by actions that are implemented by subprocesses.
Workflow	In XLANG the workflow associated with each Web Service is defined by an XML `<behavior>` element. This defines a control flow based on a block-structured approach. The control flow supports sequential, parallel, and conditional actions. Actions can include WSDL operations, timed waits, and the raising of exceptions. There is no support for specifying data flow between actions.
Transaction Management	XLANG provides a flexible and comprehensive long-running transaction model. Transactions are scoped by context blocks, within which any number of actions can be defined. Transactions can be nested to any level. Compensating blocks can be associated with each transaction context. If a fault occurs in a transaction then the compensating actions of all nested transactions that have completed will usually need to be executed. XLANG allows flexible specification of the order in which such actions will be executed, but the default is reverse order.

Table continued on following page

Feature	Support
Exception Handling	XLANG provides flexible exception-handling facilities. Exception handlers can be specified for any block of actions, and explicit recovery actions specified including the compensating blocks of specified transactions. Exceptions can also be raised at any point in the control flow.
Service Interfaces	XLANG uses WSDL to describe the service interfaces for each participating Web Service.
Message Security And Reliability	There is no support for security and reliability semantics in XLANG.
Audit Trail	There is no support for non-repudiation semantics in XLANG.
Agreements	XLANG supports the notion of business process contracts, which could provide the foundation for business agreements. These specify how two or more XLANG-enabled Web Services are stitched together to describe a shared process between particular participants.
Execution	XLANG is focused on public processes and omits some details required to automate execution of a process, for example data flow constructs.

The following diagram illustrates a sample three-party contract in XLANG:

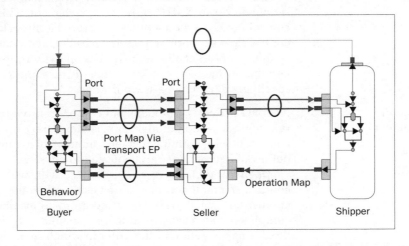

See also http://www.gotdotnet.com/team/xml_wssspecs/xlang-c/default.htm.

WSFL

WSFL (Web Services Flow Language) is IBM's proposal in this area. It covers both public and private processes. WSFL is primarily focused on describing Web Service compositions, and like XLANG uses WSDL to describe the service interfaces.

A **flow model** describes the workflow for a process. Both control flow and data flow can be defined using a state-transition model. Transactions and exception handling are not explicitly supported, but some of the semantics can be implemented using conditional transitions. Activities in a workflow can be exported as Web Service operations, and activities can also be implemented by delegation to a Web Service. In this way WSFL supports Web Service aggregation.

A **global model** defines how the various Web Services are linked together in the process. It is similar therefore to the business process contracts of XLANG.

Quality-of-service characteristics are delegated to a separate specification called WSEL (Web Services Endpoint Language).

Feature	Support
Collaboration-Based Modeling	WSFL describes processes as interactions between Web Service providers, which can be abstracted using roles so collaboration-based process modeling tools could certainly be used to generate WSFL descriptions. Recursive decomposition of WSFL processes is facilitated because WSFL flow models can be exposed as Web Services, which in turn can be used in the implementation of activities in other flow models.
Workflow	In WSFL, a flow model defines the workflow associated with each service provider (collaboration role). This defines both a control flow and a data model. The control flow is based on transitions between activities. Transitions can specify XPATH conditions on particular messages that enable or disable them, thus directing the process flow to different activities depending on the content of the messages. Data flows can extract data from different activities using XPATH expressions, transform them using XSLT, and aggregate them for input into other activities.
Transaction Management	WSFL doesn't support transactions. Transactional characteristics of Web Services are being addressed in another IBM project (WSTx), which might end up contributing to the complementary WSEL specification. See http://www.research.ibm.com/AEM/wstx.html for more details on WSTx.

Table continued on following page

Feature	Support
Exception Handling	WSFL can support handling different exceptions that are indicated in the content of messages by specifying transition conditions that examine the message for these exceptions. In this way the process flow can be directed to different activities for different exceptions.
Service Interfaces	WSFL explicitly uses WSDL to describe the service interfaces for each participating Web Service.
Message Security And Reliability	There is no support for security and reliability semantics in WSFL. This is delegated to the separate WSEL specification.
Audit Trail	There is no support for non-repudiation semantics in WSFL. This is delegated to the separate WSEL specification.
Agreements	In the IBM Web Services stack, agreements are a separate component (TPA) but WSFL global models give a foundation that could be used for business agreements.
Execution	WSFL provides execution capabilities for activities through Web Service invocations or through Java, CICS, or EXE/CMD-based implementation.

See also http://www-4.ibm.com/software/solutions/webservices/pdf/WSFL.pdf.

BPML

BPML (Business Process Management Language) is a specification from the BPMI.org (Business Process Management Initiative) organization. BPML aims to provide a comprehensive means of specifying the processes of an enterprise. It is positioned as complementary to public process standards such as ebXML BPSS – the BPMI FAQ (from the BPMI.org web site, http://www.bpmi.org/faq.esp) states:

"**What is the relationship between BPMI.org and ebXML?**
BPMI.org and ebXML are addressing complementary aspects of e-Business process management. While ebXML provides a standard way to describe the Public Interface of e-Business processes, BPMI.org provides a standard way to describe their Private Implementation."

BPML describes comprehensive control flow and data flow constructs. It supports both short- and long-running transactions with compensating activities. It also supports exception handling and timeouts. It does not provide a means to specify characteristics that are important to B2B processes, such as authentication and non-repudiation.

Feature	Support
Collaboration-Based Modeling	BPML describes processes as XML message exchanges between participants. Participants can be abstracted using roles and can represent organizations, applications, employees, or other processes. Participants can be assigned statically or determined dynamically at runtime. In essence the private process represented by a BPML process interacts with participants through a set of collaborations. Such descriptions are amenable to generation from collaboration modeling tools. Recursive decomposition is supported through nested processes.
Workflow	BPML provides comprehensive control and data flow support. A process consists of a simple or a complex activity. Simple activities include sending or receiving an XML message, invoking a Web Service operation, or raising an exception. Complex activities include block-structured control flow constructs for sequential, parallel, and conditional execution of other simple or complex activities. Activities can be scheduled to start at a future date, and time constraints can be assigned to the duration of the activity. Data flow between activities is accomplished by assigning data from messages to state variables and vice-versa. Rule sets express complex conditions based on XPATH expressions that can be used to filter input messages to activities.
Transaction Management	BPML provides comprehensive support for both ACID (coordinated) and long-running (extended) transactions. A transaction can be associated with any complex activity. This implies that transactions can be nested. Compensating activities can be associated with both coordinated and extended transactions. If a transaction is aborted, any compensating activities within the same context will be executed in reverse order.
Exception Handling	The exception-handling capabilities supported by BPML are robust and quite similar to XLANG. Exceptions are propagated upwards to enclosing activities until caught. If not handled within a transaction, the transaction is aborted.
Service Interfaces	The service interfaces exposed by participants in collaborations can be described in BPML using abstract processes. An abstract process need not fully specify how the participant implements the process, but does specify aspects of their behavior relevant to the overall process model. Thus BPML abstract processes are analogous to descriptions of participant behavior in purely public process models such as ebXML or XLANG. Conceivably, mappings could be performed between these standards and BPML abstract processes. The service interface part of abstract processes is very similar to WSDL so that part of a mapping should be quite straightforward.

Table continued on following page

169

Feature	Support
Message Security And Reliability	There is no support for security and reliability semantics in BPML.
Audit Trail	There is no support for non-repudiation semantics in BPML.
Agreements	There is no support for agreements in BPML.
Execution	Participants in BPML processes can represent IT systems, applications, or users within an organization, or external service providers. Thus, by exchanging messages with these participants the detailed implementation steps of a process can be specified. BPML does not specify all details for binding such participants, for example messaging transports or application programming interface bindings. Such details are left to vendors. If legacy applications are already exposed as WSDL Web Services, then they can be incorporated as participants in BPML processes by vendor tools that map the WSDL interfaces to BPML abstract processes and route the messages at run-time using SOAP. Such processes would then look very similar to the Web Service composition approach facilitated by WSFL. It is conceivable that such an approach could be standardized in a future version of BPML.

See also http://www.bpmi.org/.

Convergence

As outlined above, the business drivers point to a convergence of private and public business process model standards based on Web Services. How might this convergence occur in practice?

It seems likely that both ebXML BPSS and BPML will remain focused on their complementary domains for the time being, which are the B2B and EAI domains respectively.

On the other hand, Microsoft and IBM are clearly moving towards a set of specifications that would address both B2B and EAI requirements. It has been widely speculated that they will collaborate to produce a single proposal or set of proposals in this space that could then be submitted to the W3C for inclusion in its Web Services architecture stack in the process layer.

There are, however, significant obstacles to be overcome for this to happen. Technical obstacles include the different approaches to control flow modeling (in XLANG control flow is described using a block-structured approach best represented graphically using flow charts, while WSFL uses a state-transition approach best represented graphically using UML activity or state graphs). This is not just an argument about the technical merits of the respective approaches – both vendors have significant investments in these technologies in their respective product lines (WebSphere from IBM and BizTalk from Microsoft).

Given these obstacles and the time it takes for any new proposal to become widely supported in products and in the marketplace, the widespread adoption of a single Web Services-based standard for B2B and EAI processes is some time away.

Although the standards convergence process is ongoing, this does not necessarily mean that enterprises should wait before adopting one or more of these standards. The potential return on investment from automating business processes means that it might be quite costly for enterprises to wait until the standardization process has settled before adopting business process modeling and automation tools. The best way to protect investment in such tools is to ensure that the vendors are committed to a standards-based approach. For the moment an enterprise should focus on the standards that best support the domain that it is most urgently seeking to automate. If seeking to integrate public and private processes, an approach based on using complementary existing standards should be considered.

OMG EDOC

At this point it is worth mentioning another relevant emerging standard that applies to the modeling of business processes for Web Services. This is the EDOC (Extended Distributed Object Computing) standard from the OMG (Object Management Group, http://www.omg.org/).

EDOC essentially defines a modeling framework that supports the OMG MDA (model-driven architecture). It aims to support collaborations between loosely coupled systems in both the B2B and EAI domain, and to enable the reuse of business components from different distributed object technologies in these collaborations, such as CORBA, EJB, and Web Services.

EDOC is based on UML and defines several complementary subprofiles, including a Component Collaboration Architecture. This profile defines the core concepts that can be used to describe collaboration-based process models. Such models could be mapped to the different business process standards described above that are then used to drive the execution of the collaborations. Thus EDOC is clearly complementary to these standards.

Conclusion

It is clear that businesses are increasingly moving towards comprehensive automation and integration of their private and public processes, and that Web Services is becoming increasingly popular for use as the integration infrastructure. This scenario drives the demand for Web Services-based business process standards. Over the next couple of years we can expect to see continuing activity to address this demand.

Authors: Gunjan Samtani and Dimple Sadhwani

- STP Critical Parameters

- Web Services for STP

- Web Services Example

- Advantages

- Where to Start

Web Services and Straight Through Processing (STP)

This paper discusses the fundamentals of STP, the need for, driving forces behind, and benefits of STP, the current state of technology supporting STP, and the relationship of enterprise and business-to-business application integration and business process management with STP. It also looks at the critical parameters for the success of STP, presents an introduction to Web Services including its participants and operations, and examines the application of SOA-based framework to STP. There is a detailed discussion on the usage of Web Services for STP, and an example of the usage of Web Services for a real-world STP-related matching utility for mortgage and government-backed fixed income instruments.

We would like to bring to the reader's attention the fact that STP is as much about business issues as it is about technology. In this paper, we have tried to keep a balance between these two different, yet interlinked, subjects as they relate to STP. It is worth mentioning that the readership of this article includes senior management (technical and business), business analysts, systems architects, project managers and software developers. Thus, our aim has been to keep a higher-level view of both business and technology issues, making the article useful and worthwhile for each one of you.

What Is Straight Through Processing (STP)?

Straight Through Processing (STP), a solution that automates the end-to-end processing of transactions for all financial instruments from initiation to resolution, is set to revolutionize the financial industry. STP will streamline back office activities, leading to reduced failures, lower risks, and significantly lower costs per transaction. It encompasses a set of applications, business processes, and standards that will redefine the settlement and processing paradigm within the capital markets industry.

STP has the same significance to the financial industry as Supply Chain Management (SCM) has to the manufacturing industry and Customer Relationship Management (CRM) has to the service industry.

The Need for STP

Although the financial industry has reduced its T+5 trading cycle (settlement 5 days after the actual trade has been done) to T+3, it has been a real laggard in any kind of business process management and technological advancement as far as trade settlement and processing are concerned. Decades old, manual, and redundant operational processes are still in place without any sort of automation.

As an example, the following diagram shows the current manual process utilized for derivatives trading. As depicted, there are multiple points within the business process where human intervention is required. Further, the flow and format of data from one system to the other (such as from the Trade Pricing System to the Settlement System) occurs in non-standard proprietary format, even within the company. The issue of non-standard formats is multiplied when communicating with external trading partners, as each company may use a different format:

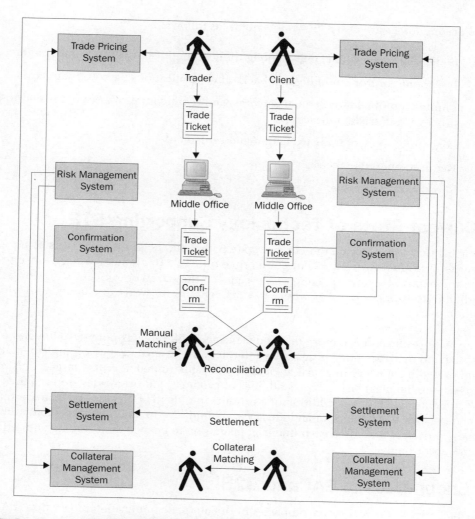

The Drivers and Benefits of STP

There are multiple drivers that are literally forcing the entire industry to bite the bullet of STP once and for all. Some of these key driving forces include pricing and competitive compulsions, higher trade volume growth of approximately 31.6% compounded annually year-over-year, competition from international markets, increased end-user (investor) expectations of service quality, and last but not least the need for greater process efficiency. At the end of the day, it will not be a financial company's prerogative to implement STP, it will be a regulatory requirement – which effectively means that if you want to remain in business you better start working towards the implementation of STP.

These driving forces are also STP's key benefits, as follows:

- ❏   Better electronic connectivity among different entities involved in the trading cycle.

- ❏   Integration of front, middle, and back office applications based on standards.

- ❏   Elimination of a lot of manual activities and redundant processes in the end-to-end processing of trade transactions.

- ❏   Higher accuracy of trade execution and settlement.

- ❏   Reduced operational costs.

- ❏   Shortened trade cycle.

The Current State of Technology Supporting STP

One word that can describe the current state within financial organizations as far as STP is concerned: **confusion.** In a recent conference on STP (16th January 2002), more than half of the financial companies present confessed that they are yet to begin work for STP – mainly due to lack of clarity as where to start, what to do, what to change, and which technology to use.

STP, which was introduced more than a decade ago, still remains point-to-point and is characterized by hard-coded proprietary interfaces. In its current state of implementation within pretty much every financial institution STP, still limited in scope, targets only a portion of underlying financial instruments and lines of products and businesses, and requires a full development cycle for each addition of a product into the STP world. The primary reason for this state of affairs is the lack of an industry-wide initiative to automate and standardize the business processes and force each financial institution to change their trading and settlement systems accordingly.

STP Encompasses EAI and B2Bi

Straight Through Processing encompasses both enterprise application integration (EAI) and business-to-business application integration (B2Bi). EAI for STP, also known as **internal STP**, relates to the trade and settlement processes that are internal to an industry participant (see the following diagram). For example, in the case of a fixed income dealer it would include placing the trade through the trading system, authorizing its execution, and receiving details of executions as they are communicated through the exchange or clearing corporation and allocation process.

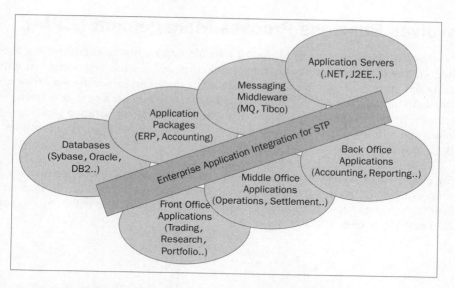

On the other hand, B2Bi for STP, also known as **external STP**, is about connecting seamlessly to all external partners in the trading and settlement process, including the industry-matching utilities such as GSCC's RTTM (Government Securities Clearing Corporation's Real-time Trade Matching) and Omgeo. The external partners include custodians, exchanges, clearing corporations, central security depositories, and other information providers:

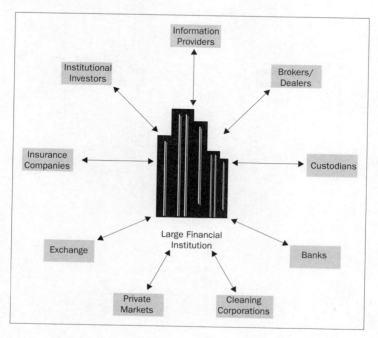

STP Involves Business Process Management (BPM)

Business process management (BPM) for STP would enable financial enterprises to automate and integrate the disparate internal and external corporate business processes. It will do so by supporting dynamic process topologies, which allow the boundary between processes and participants to be determined, either statically or dynamically on a real-time basis. Furthermore, its implementation will provide every financial corporation with the opportunity to redefine and automate core business processes, which would result in streamlined business operations and reduced costs.

BPM for internal STP would enable companies to achieve internal systems that are truly integrated using automated workflows. The business processes that control information flow by coordinating interactions with business applications and systems within an organization, are called **private** or **closed** STP processes:

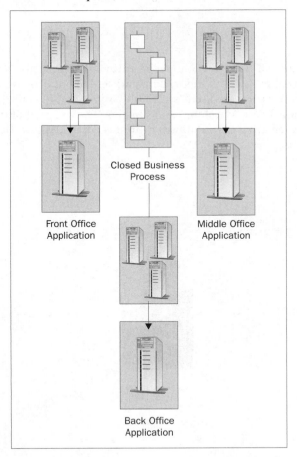

Closed Business
Process

Front Office
Application

Middle Office
Application

Back Office
Application

BPM for external STP would focus on how financial institutions, as a vertical industry, can refine their business processes so that the applications supporting them can be seamlessly integrated across the enterprise. With effective BPM for external STP, financial institutions can become part of a unified business process flow. This would allow the dynamic sharing of trade state information among trading partners, through which all communication can be tracked and recorded. Since STP transactions can span several days, unified workflows become critical in ensuring the completion of automated business transactions. The external business processes that control interactions among independent financial institutions are called **public** or **open** STP processes:

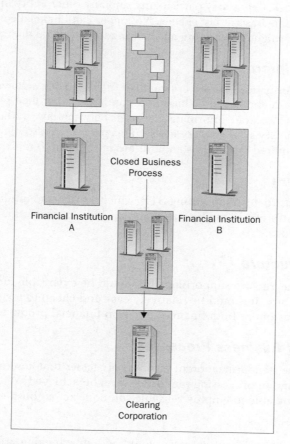

Closed Business
Process

Financial Institution
A

Financial Institution
B

Clearing
Corporation

Critical Parameters of STP

The critical parameters of STP that determine its success or failure across the entire industry are:

- ❑ Speed.
- ❑ Accuracy.

❑ Stable infrastructure.

❑ Extensible infrastructure.

❑ Standardization.

❑ Security.

Speed of Trade Information

In order to achieve STP, the trade information has to be passed between the buying entity, selling entity, exchanges, depository participants, and any other entity involved in the trade processing on a real-time basis at fast speeds. No longer can financial companies have batch programs running overnight transferring and sharing trade-related data among different entities.

Accuracy of Trade Information

Accuracy of trade information is more critical than the speed. To achieve accuracy, the format in which trade data is shared has to be based on standards rather than proprietary formats. Using standards allows accurate information transfer between new trading partners much quicker than if proprietary systems were in use. This parameter also highlights the importance of testing that will be required once new standards are introduced to represent business processes.

Stable Infrastructure

The technology infrastructure supporting STP, which would span multiple networks, applications, and platforms, has to be stable and provide for the fast and accurate processing of complex transactions.

Extensible Infrastructure

The technology infrastructure supporting STP should be extensible for tomorrow's needs. Using this infrastructure, it should be relatively easy and cheap to take the opportunities of tomorrow to mass-customize both financial and non-financial products and services.

Standardization of Business Processes

It is only through the standardization of business processes that key requirements of STP – automation and common processing platforms – can be achieved. Without standardization, companies will not be able to employ reusable solutions across business applications for either EAI or B2Bi.

The standardization of business processes would help in achieving greater business process efficiency, transparency, and control. Let's discuss in detail each of these factors; later in the paper we will discuss how Web Services make BPM easier with all these factors included.

❑ **Efficiency:** STP in itself eliminates the need for manually re-entering any trade-related data, provides intelligence for validating information, and purges risks from all the processes and subprocesses involved in a transaction life cycle.

❑ **Transparency:** Business process transparency is an extremely important requirement of STP. At any stage of the trade cycle and at any time, any entity (if entitled) should be able to determine the state of the transaction. For example, if a trade has not executed after being submitted to the exchange, the buying trader should be able to determine the reason in real time. This may be achieved in many ways, including passing a message (based on industry standards) from the exchange to the buying trader informing them of the failed execution of the trade along with the reason. This message can be propagated from the back office systems right to the front office system into the traders' workstation.

❑ **Control:** It is imperative for STP that the control of business processes is automated as much as possible. There may still be instances where human involvement is necessary, especially in the case of exceptions. It should, however, be fairly easy to add any workflow logic by simply adding on to the layer of the business process control.

Security

Secured interoperability holds the key for STP to become a successful initiative. The security requirements for internal STP are almost a subset of those for external STP. External STP involves significant security risks as it involves the use of the Internet or VPNs, which mandates two levels of security. Firstly, external STP necessitates opening up corporate firewalls to enable cross-boundary communication between enterprises. Thus, financial companies have to secure their internal network against malicious attacks through these open ports. Secondly, the data transmitted over the Internet or any other mode has to be secured. The data may contain classified information, such as corporate information, trade information, settlement information, and thus cannot be left unguarded.

Application of Service-Oriented Architecture (SOA) - based Framework to STP

The financial institutions have to use a solution that provides an STP operations model with high-performance technology to enable the seamless transmission and execution of trades along with high-performance, reliable, extensible, scalable, and open standards-based communication and messaging. The key requirements of an STP solution include:

❑ High availability and scalability to be able to support increased trade volume.

❑ High security as the data exchanged among multiple entities is trade-related confidential data.

❑ Robust business services that can be plugged into any internal or external securities processing application.

❑ Guaranteed messaging to ensure that each and every message surely reaches the destination.

The solution

A standardized SOA-based framework can enable financial companies to achieve their business goals by providing a service-based platform to integrate new and existing applications and systems with STP functionality, implementing industry standards, and building an infrastructure that would support the dynamic financial messaging required for continuous processing for all types of financial instruments. Service-oriented architecture can provide the foundation and Web Services can provide the building blocks for application architecture in order to achieve seamless trade processing.

A SOA-based framework is capable of providing support for multiple XML standards at the same time, such as ISO 15022 and FpML, and adding support for further standards without significant redevelopment effort. With the use of Web Services as an enabling technology, STP-related problems and issues will shift from connectivity among different applications in-house and with trading partner applications to the content and structure of the information that is exchanged. The analogy here will be that Web Services will define the standard postal mechanism along with the envelope and addressing format for exchanging letters. What is inside the envelope (the content of the letter) will be defined by the XML-based business process standard, such as ISO 15022 XML.

Why Use Web Services for STP?

It is important to mention here that Web Services will not be the ONLY technology, but ONE of SEVERAL technologies, which will play a role in STP. Also, as a word of caution, the use of Web Services for STP, especially for transaction-oriented external business processes, is still far away. It is, however, only through imagining an evolving technology that we set the benchmarks and direction for its growth, future research, and, last but not least, its adoption.

There are several benefits of using Web Services as one of the core technologies for STP. As we will see below, the central benefits are:

- ❑   Based on open standards.
- ❑   Easier business process management.
- ❑   Easier integration.
- ❑   More flexible.
- ❑   Better and cheaper customer service.

Based On Open Standards

Since external STP requires integration of business processes across corporate boundaries using exchange of documents or messages, the communication among different systems should be based on open standards.

Web Services fully utilize open standards, including Hypertext Transfer Protocol (HTTP), Extensible Markup Language (XML), Simple Object Access Protocol (SOAP), Web Services Description Language (WSDL), and Universal Discovery, Description and Integration (UDDI). Application-centric Web Services enable companies to integrate business processes without the constraints of proprietary infrastructures, platforms, and operating systems.

At this stage of the paper, we will introduce the standards for the financial industry that will enable STP for all financial instruments. The principal standards we will look at are:

❑ FpML.

❑ FIX.

❑ SWIFT.

❑ ISO 15002 XML.

These standards will work together with Web Services, rather than in competition, as they address the orchestration layer of the Web Services stack. In other words, they provide the core layer that describes business process semantics for STP. These trading standards are still evolving as a result of the re-engineering of the core business processes underlying STP, but once matured they will standardize the trade-related data that is shared between multiple applications for internal STP and with the trading partners for external STP.

Financial Products Markup Language (FpML)

FpML, based on XML, aims to standardize e-commerce activities in the field of financial derivatives, swaps, and structured products. All categories of over-the-counter (OTC) derivatives will eventually be incorporated into the standard. It aims to streamline the processes, such as electronic deal confirmation with external counter parties, quantitative modeling, and risk management, supporting trading activities in the financial derivatives by describing these products and associated business interactions, based on industry standards. See http://www.fpml.org/ for more details.

Financial Information Exchange Protocol (FIX)

The Financial Information Exchange protocol (FIX) is a language that defines specific kinds of electronic messages (pre-trade and trade messages) for communicating securities transactions between financial institutions, primarily investment managers, brokers/dealers, ECNs, and stock exchanges. The most important feature of FIX that differentiates it from other protocols in the financial industry is that FIX is a connected, session-based protocol. See http://www.fixprotocol.org/ for more details.

SWIFT

SWIFT is the industry-owned cooperative supplying secure messaging services and interface software to 7,000 financial institutions in 192 countries. It currently totally dominates the messaging services used by banks, brokers/dealers, and investment managers. The average daily value of payment messages on SWIFT is estimated to be above USD 5 trillion and SWIFT carried over 1.2 billion messages in 2000. See http://www.swift.com/ for more details.

ISO 15022 XML

ISO 15022 XML is a result of the convergence of the most important messaging protocols in the financial vertical industry – FIX, FpML, and SWIFT. It is kind of a superset covering the domains of these existing messaging protocols. ISO 15022 XML is being developed via the use of business modeling with an XML-based representation of the business processes, leveraging the expertise of FPL in the pre-trade and trade (orders and executions) domain and SWIFT in the post-trade domain.

ISO 15022 XML will play a major role in STP, as it brings together the different parts of the trade life cycle and ensures that business items are represented in a standard way. This would be the key to the solution to move towards shortened settlement cycles.

The following diagram shows how ISO 15022 XML can eliminate the current manual processes required for settlement, matching, and reconciliation:

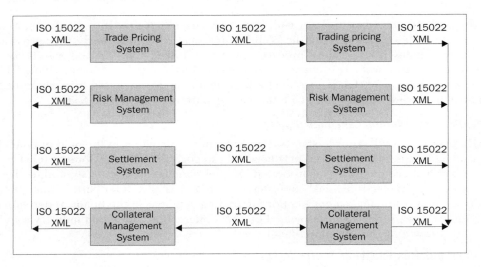

A few very important points:

1. The migration to ISO 15022, which started on the SWIFT network in 1997, will be gradual and cannot happen on an overnight basis. Furthermore, financial institutions cannot directly implement ISO 15022 XML and skip ISO 15022, as the current series of ISO 15022 messages available on SWIFT are not expected to be available on SWIFTNet before the end of the migration to ISO 15022.

2. The creation of ISO 15022 XML would eventually mean the elimination of SWIFTML. The financial institutions should start migrating towards ISO 15022 XML, if they have not already started to do so.

3. The emergence of ISO 15022 XML does not mean that the investment in adopting ISO 15022 standards will be a waste. Financial companies will be able to fully leverage their investment if they have already built an internal dictionary of business elements. It is only the syntax of the message that will change from here on and the business applications should be independent of it. The messaging part provided and supported by messaging applications should be flexible enough to add any XML-specific processing.

See http://lighthouse-partners.com/xml/proj_iso15022xml.htm and http://www.15022.org/ for more details.

Easier Business Process Management

Web Services help to clearly separate business process logic and the participating business services for both internal and external STP, thereby making the development, execution, and management of these services much easier. The main advantage of Web Services is that companies can use Web Services interfaces for process management, logic transformation, and integration for legacy and packaged applications, instead of writing non standards-based custom code for each application.

A Web Service can be implemented as its own business process, or it may be composed of many business processes (both public and private) with each business process being implemented as a Web Service in itself. Each activity comprising the workflow of a business process is logically linked to a Web Service.

Apart from easier application integration, user-centric Web Services make the human intervention (which may be an activity in an STP business process workflow) easier by providing personalization, interface customization, and support for multiple languages, greatly enhancing the user experience. It is important to mention that human intervention, especially in the case of exceptions such as a broker entering wrong trade data, can never be eliminated irrespective of the level of automation.

The key technologies and specifications that will enable the orchestration of internal and external STP-related business processes as Web Services include Web Services Flow Language (WSFL), Business Process Modeling Language (BPML), XLANG and FpML, FIX protocol, and ISO 15022 XML.

Easier Integration

A typical business process related to STP may be supported by multiple diverse applications such as C++, Java, or Excel VBA-based front-end systems; Java, C, or C++-based middle office systems; and AS400 or mainframe-based legacy systems. It is virtually impossible to manage a workflow and execute the different tasks associated with it, which may require using APIs of other systems or exchanging messages with them, unless the underlying technology provides easy integration facilities. XML-based Web Services are an ideal technology for integration in such a diverse environment as they allow applications to communicate across the Internet or intranet in a platform- and language-independent fashion.

Whether the underlying STP applications are integrated synchronously or asynchronously, Web Services enable both types of integration and provide substantial advantages over the traditional technology for achieving them. Through Web Services Definition Language (WSDL), a Web Service can be defined to have an invocation style as document (asynchronous) or RPC (synchronous).

Asynchronous message-oriented applications have a different design and architecture from stateful and synchronous function/method-oriented applications. It is the application architecture, business requirements, and partner agreement (between in-house groups for internal STP and partner companies for external STP) that would dictate whether the integration should be synchronous or asynchronous.

Since application integration forms the backbone of STP, it is worthwhile discussing the benefits of Web Services for both synchronous and asynchronous integration.

Benefits of Using Web Services for Synchronous Integration

Web Services technology solves some of the shortcomings of RPC-and API-oriented synchronous integration (non-XML standard-based), as follows:

❑ RPCs and APIs offer a static solution for function-level integration, even if they use XML for client/server communication. Web Services offer a dynamic approach for integration, where the services can be discovered, bound to, and used dynamically. This is primarily enabled due to the fact that Web Services are found using a defined standard – UDDI.

❑ RPCs and APIs can use any proprietary protocol, but Web Services are built and used over existing, universal protocols such as HTTP and SMTP. This new distributed computing solution exploits the openness of specific Internet technologies to address many of the interoperability issues of CORBA and DCOM.

❑ RPCs and APIs do not offer servers a standard way of exposing their public methods to clients. Each server program may have its own implementation. Web Services, on the other hand, are always exposed by the servers in a standard form using WSDL. Thus, the clients and servers do not have to implement their own proprietary format for using and publishing public methods.

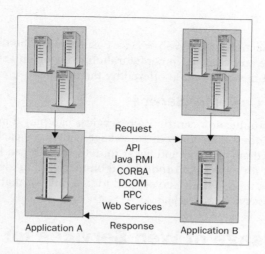

Benefits of Using Web Services for Asynchronous Integration

Web Services can be used for achieving loosely coupled asynchronous integration among applications. In this scenario, the body of SOAP messages exchanged between the Web Services client and Web Services provider contain arbitrary XML documents, which can also be described in WSDL and validated using XML Schema.

Web Services will be used hand-in-hand with existing messaging technologies and protocols including Java Messaging Service (JMS), J2EE Connector Architecture (JCA), IBM's MQ Series, and Microsoft's .NET platform and MSMQ. For example, if a company has an existing J2EE infrastructure, its STP solution should have the capacity of exchanging SOAP documents and JMS-based messages over HTTP, HTTPS, and (in future) HTTPR using JCA for integration among disparate systems, while providing a secure communication.

The benefits of using Web Services for asynchronous communication among STP-based applications include:

❑ The flexibility to define loosely coupled interfaces based on standards.

❑ The underlying language used to represent the data within the messages is XML. It will be necessary to map data representations between internal and external applications supporting STP. Thus, irrespective of the style of XML used to connect the applications, the very fact that it is XML will guarantee the flexibility and ability to create this mapping.

❑ The fact that it is only through the use of technologies such as Web Services that the real goal of service-oriented architecture (configure rather than code) can be achieved. Services-based architecture will yield tremendous cost savings in terms of flexibility, reuse, and speed of making any changes, the key requirements of STP.

Flexibility

Service-oriented architecture-based Web Services can provide the required flexibility for STP in terms of architecture and changes in configuration, control, and standards in the business processes. This type of flexibility is **not** offered by the middleware existing today.

Better and Cheaper Customer Service

Both user-centric and application-centric Web Services can play a major role in customizing a range of financial and non-financial product packages suited for each customer's specifications, making them cheaper and faster to deliver. This can be achieved by assembling Web Services targeted for each such product and bundling them together. Of course the assumption here is that there will be servers and tools available that will make this orchestration of Web Services possible.

An Example Usage of Web Services for STP

*In this example, we will be discussing and using the **Real-time Trade Matching (RTTM)** services introduced by **Government Securities Clearing Corporation (GSCC)** and **Mortgage backed Securities Clearing Corporation (MBSCC)** in the last quarter of 2001 and first quarter of 2002. We will also discuss the shortcomings of their current implementation and how Web Services alleviate them.*

In this example, we will discuss how Web Services can potentially be used in a real-time matching utility for mortgage and government-backed securities. The matching utility provides automated Just-In-Time trade information and a messaging network from pre-trade to post-settlement for all trade participants including the buying entity, the selling entity, the exchange, and the central counterparties.

Matching Utility Description

The matching utility application enables the participants to submit and compare executed trade terms in real-time. This matching utility allows users to submit trades upon execution and achieve binding confirmation upon successful matching. It provides more certainty, reduces execution/market risk and eliminates the redundancy between the verbal checkout process and the clearing corporation's matching process.

The different entities involved in the matching application include the following:

- ❑ A clearing agency, which provides post-trade comparison, netting, risk management, and pool notification services for the financial instrument presented in the example (government and mortgage-backed securities).
- ❑ A buying entity, which can be any one of the following: commercial banks, government-sponsored enterprises, institutional investors, insurance companies, international organizations, investment managers, inter-dealer brokers, mortgage originators, private investment companies, or registered brokers or dealers.

❑ A selling entity, also known as a counterparty of trade, and can be any of the entities listed opposite.

An Example Business Process

There are multiple business processes involved in the matching utility, each requiring exchange of messages among the participants mentioned in the previous section. The complexity and number of messages exchanged will largely depend on the buying and selling entities involved in the trade, for example dealer-dealer vs. brokered trades, and the sanity of trade data exchanged (the data comes in the right and normalized format, whether it requires modification or cancellation of trade, etc.).

For sake of simplicity, however, we will discuss a very basic business process involved in the matching utility. In this business process, a dealer-dealer trade is submitted bilaterally for matching. The following diagram shows the messages that are exchanged among the different entities:

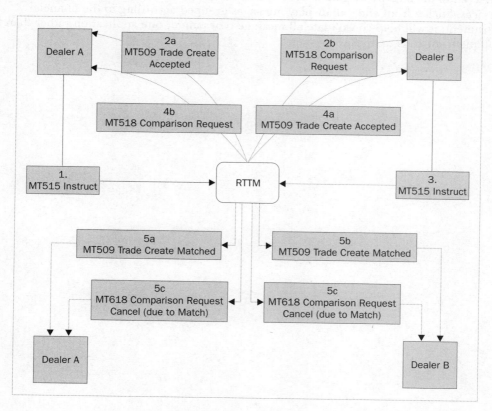

The Use of Web Services

Let's discuss the usage of Web Services for a RTTM application right from the front office trading application, to the middle office operation's application, to the back office matching application to the MBSCC's RTTM application, and finally to the trading partners back-office matching application. It will involve the use of Web Services for both EAI and B2Bi for an STP-related business process.

In this example, a fixed income broker for Dealer A enters a trade through the Web-based trading application. The trade data is passed from the trading application's backend to the matching application. Dealer A's matching application invokes a trade matching Web Service published by MBSCC. Their RTTM application in turn invokes the trade counterparty's Web Service (Dealer B) and passes on the response back to Dealer A's matching application. The entire communication occurs over the Internet, using XML-based standards for RTTM business processes. The messages received by Dealer A's matching application are in turn delivered to the STP Messaging Center Web-based front end asynchounously using Web Services. Such a front end will display messages grouped according to the financial instrument; it will help consolidate all message types under one application rather than having multiple front ends to display messages.

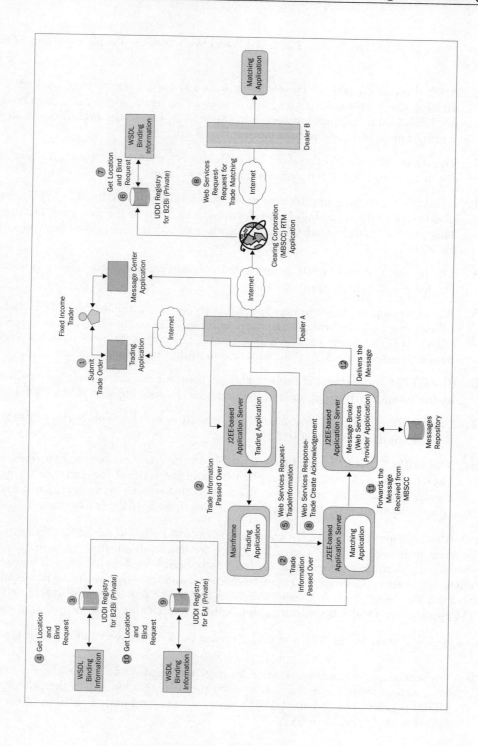

The sequence of steps is as follows for the STP and Web Services for B2Bi portion of the process:

1. A fixed income trader at Dealer A submits a trade for a mortgage-backed security through the Web-based trading application. The trade information is passed from the J2EE-based Application server in the middle tier to the mainframe-based trading application at the backend.

2. The trade information is passed from Dealer A's mainframe-based trading application to the J2EE-based matching application.

3. Dealer A's matching application gets information about MBSCC's Web Service (Real-time trade matching) by performing a look-up in the private UDDI registry. This private UDDI registry is used for all external services (Web Services used for B2Bi).

4. The location of and WSDL binding information for the Web Service is sent to Dealer A's matching application.

5. The matching application invokes the Web Service published by MBSCC to submit the trade information asynchronously. The communication is based on SOAP over the Internet. The MBSCC's RTTM application receives the Web Service request as a SOAP document containing trade information.

6. The RTTM application gets information on the trade matching Web Service published by the counterparty mentioned in the trade data by looking it up in the UDDI.

7. The location of and WSDL binding information for the Web Service is sent to the RTTM application of MBSCC.

8. The MBSCC's RTTM application passes on the trade created acknowledgment back to Dealer A's matching application and the request for trade matching to Dealer B's matching application through Web Services using asynchronous communication. The communication is based on SOAP over the Internet.

It is worth mentioning here that this communication will be based on XML standards defined for business processes for RTTM applications by the financial industry consortium. Furthermore, the binding information for frequently used Web Services should be cached by the client application, to avoid the resource-intensive and time-consuming dynamic binding. In this example, Web Services loosely integrates Dealer A's matching application, MBSCC's RTTM application, Dealer B's matching application, and Dealer A's front-end application.

The sequence of steps for the STP and Web Services for EAI portion of the process is as follows:

9. On receiving the response, Dealer A's matching application gets Web Service information about the message broker by performing a look-up in the private UDDI registry. This private UDDI registry is used for internal services (Web Services used for EAI in STP).

10. The location of and WSDL binding information for Web Services published by the message broker is sent to Dealer A's matching application.

11. The matching application invokes the appropriate Web Service and sends the message received from the MBSCC asynchronously to the message broker.

12. The message broker parses, stores, transforms, builds, and routes and delivers the message through Web Services to the Web-based front end Messaging Center application.

As can be seen from the example with the usage of Web Services, applications that are being integrated no longer have to know the specifics of static information such as how, when, and where. This completely changes the traditional paradigm of point-to-point integration for EAI and B2Bi and will be a huge factor in the adoption of this technology for STP.

UDDI Registry for EAI and B2Bi

A point worth mentioning in this example is that we used two different UDDI registries for Dealer A – one for maintaining information of internal Web Services used for EAI and the second for external Web Services. It is important for companies not to mix information about Web Services used for two separate domains (EAI and B2Bi) to allow easier and secured maintenance and usage of UDDI.

Advantages of Web Services Over the Current Implementation

Although the RTTM service is a big step towards STP as far as government and mortgage-backed securities are concerned, in its current form it has major limitations. The proposed Web Services-based architecture provides several advantages, as follows.

Use of the Internet Rather Than a Proprietary Network

In its current implementation, MBCSS requires using a proprietary network for RTTM services. This effectively forces every participant, small, medium, or large, to use and pay for this network.

Web Services eliminates the need for any proprietary network, as the messages can be encrypted and safely sent over the Internet. It must, however, be noted that Web Services can also be used over a proprietary network.

Security solutions and standards for Web Services are still not mature and are being worked on. There is no question that the next generation of Web Services will allow for the usage of Digital Signatures and other security solutions.

Use of XML Rather Than SWIFT

In its current implementation, MBCSS uses SWIFT ISO 15022 format. The usage and significance of SWIFT to the financial industry is the same as EDI has to the manufacturing industry. The use of XML rather than SWIFT has the same advantages as the much publicized and discussed advantages of using XML rather than EDI. Some of these advantages include:

- **Free from the use of specific vendor software** – with XML, financial companies can integrate business processes with their trading partners without having to use specific vendor software required for SWIFT.

- **Flexible standards** – XML is based on simple, flexible, and open standards, while SWIFT standards are very strict and inflexible. As a result, financial companies will be able to automate the exchange of business information, dramatically improve efficiencies and reduce operating costs with the use of XML.

- **Cheaper** – the initial setup and operational costs of SWIFT are very high. XML enables loose integration at a fraction of the effort and cost of traditional SWIFT.

- **Extensible** – with XML, financial companies do not need to replace or rebuild their applications; instead, they can simply XML-enable the data and systems they already have.

- **Human readable** – XML is both machine and human readable while SWIFT is only machine-readable.

- **Effective use of Internet** – XML effectively uses the Internet to transfer the messages securely, whereas most of the SWIFT message flow occurs through expensive VANs and VPNs.

It is worth mentioning that there are disadvantages of the use of XML rather than SWIFT, as well. Two of the major disadvantages include:

- XML messages can be very large (in some cases five to ten times their corresponding SWIFT messages) making XML much slower than SWIFT. Such a large flow of data over the Internet uses up a lot of network bandwidth and slows down the whole process.

- Several financial organizations and companies are promoting their own flavors of XML standards. This adds to a lot of confusion in the marketplace about the interoperability issues.

Co-existence of SWIFT and XML

At this stage it is worth mentioning that we do not envision the complete replacement of SWIFT with XML. In fact, it will be naïve to even think so, and it is a misleading notion to claim that XML will completely replace SWIFT. It would be prudent for companies to build the XML-world based on the last decades of SWIFT rather than tear it all down.

During these years, 7000 or more financial institutions in more than 190 countries have implemented SWIFT. Collectively, these institutions, active in payments, securities, treasury, and trade services, exchange millions of messages valued in trillions of dollars every business day. SWIFT has also been highly integrated into the core business processes of financial companies. This level of integration required considerable effort.

It is absolutely not possible to undo all SWIFT from business processes and then redo everything based on XML. XML and SWIFT will coexist for a long time. Their interoperability is one of the key success factors for large, medium, and small size companies doing business on the Internet. We have already discussed the ISO 15022, ISO 15022 XML, FIX protocol, and their convergence in the *Based On Open Standards* section.

Elimination of IP-based environments

Web Services will play a critical role in overcoming the communications barriers that exist within the IP-based environments that the securities industry is now embracing. IP-based environments make the integration of applications very static and inflexible, as it uses an X.25 protocol-based packet switched network. The support for this protocol, however, is being withdrawn from November 2002.

Where To Start?

Financial companies should start using Web Services for internal STP at the function, application programming interface (API), or remote procedure call (RPC) level for integrating applications synchronously. This will orient the IT staff with the technology issues involved in using Web Services, which will be very helpful in overcoming the challenges posed later when the company uses Web Services for external STP. It is much easier to control, manage, find, execute, and maintain Web Services within an intranet as compared to using them over the Internet across the corporate firewall. Furthermore, it would help financial companies in identifying business opportunities for using standardized and relatively cheap Web Services solutions as against expensive EAI broker solutions.

Web Services by themselves, however, are not the nirvana for STP. An STP solution within a large financial institution would still comprise multiple solutions that together would offer both non-real time and real-time integration, support for managing semantic transformations, business process integration, and application integration based on open standards and proprietary formats.

Conclusion

STP manages and reduces the settlement time and risks linked to the lead times of cross-border trades and payments for all security instruments including equity, fixed income, derivatives, and foreign exchange. It aims to make trade processing as automated as possible, allowing STP-related business processes to be carried out without any unneeded human intervention, thereby reducing to a minimum the overall processing lead time and the related risks.

Web Services offer a platform-neutral approach for integrating STP applications, so that they can be used to integrate diverse systems in a way supported by standards rather than proprietary systems. The ability of a financial institution to have access to real-time trade-related information spanning multiple companies, in-house departments, applications, platforms, and systems is one of the most important driving factors behind the adoption of Web Services. Financial institutions should first start using Web Services for their internal STP and for business processes that are non-transactional in nature, before they risk using Web Services in external STP.

Authors: Mike Clark and Romin Irani

- Intermediary Services
- Intermediary Architecture
- Intermediary Issues
- Value Added Service Suppliers
- Brokerages

Web Service Intermediaries

We are now at the stage where we are seeing a growing number of Web Services implementations across several industries. These initial implementations have served not only to reinforce the fact that Web Services provide tremendous value, but at the same time to identify pieces in the Web Services puzzle that need to be present in order to effectively implement these solutions.

In this paper, we shall take a look at an entity called the Web Service Intermediary. These intermediaries are increasingly getting recognized as the means to provide value added services like Authentication, Quality of Service, etc. We shall also take a look at the general architecture of an Intermediary and practical issues that Web Services publishers and subscribers will have to grapple with when dealing with an Intermediary. We will then take a look at existing support for Intermediaries in Web Services standards, before moving on to look more closely at a specific type on Intermediary, the Value Added Service Supplier. After this, we will examine the roles that can be taken on by a Web Services brokerage.

What Is a Web Service Intermediary?

An Intermediary is a component that lies between the Service Client (subscriber) and the Service Provider (publisher). It basically intercepts the request from the Service Requestor, provides an intermediary service (functionality) and forwards the request to the Service Provider. Similarly, it intercepts the response from the Service Provider and forwards it to the Service Requestor.

A Web Service intermediary therefore lies between the Web Service Client and the Web Service Provider as shown overleaf:

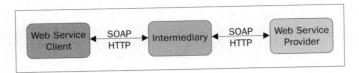

Note that there need not be just one intermediary between the client and the Service Provider. As shown in the diagram below, it is possible to combine Intermediaries in several ways. As we see, a chain of Intermediaries (A and B) intercepts the HTTP Request from the Web Service client. Another Intermediary, C, intercepts the HTTP Response from the Web Service Provider.

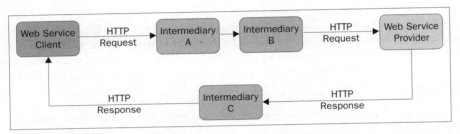

What this means is that it is possible to place Intermediaries in a variety of configurations. A fact to note is that the Web Service Provider (as a part of a Web Service implementation) might utilize other Intermediaries at the back end.

It should now be clear that an Intermediary can be authorized to intercept the calls from the service client to the provider. A Web Service intermediary can in fact be a Web Service itself that provides a certain piece of functionality. Let us now move on to what services these Intermediaries can provide to us.

Intermediary Services

Web Services Intermediaries can provide us with extremely important services as shown below:

- ❑ Authentication Services.
- ❑ Auditing Services.
- ❑ Management Services.
- ❑ Performance Improvement Services.
- ❑ Aggregation Services.

Authentication Services

An Intermediary can provide an authentication service that helps to validate the Web Service client. A well-known example of an Authentication Intermediary is Microsoft, which is providing an Authentication Service called Passport (http://www.passport.com/).

In a sample authentication scenario, a Web Service client will first authenticate itself with the Authentication Intermediary and receive a token to identifies itself. It can then use this token and pass it along in its invocation to the Web Service Provider. The Web Service Provider will use that token and validate it with the Authentication Intermediary again as shown below:

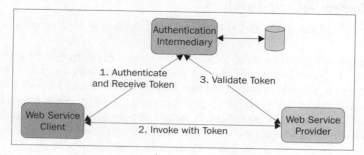

Auditing Services

As Web Services are used between enterprises to perform business operations, it is extremely important that a proper log of messages is kept. An Auditing Service will generally include auditing the activity of the service, its reliability, downtime, etc. An Auditing Service would therefore keep a log that contains information to track all of the above characteristics of the service. It would also serve to track who is using the service and be useful in tracking down any security breaches.

In an Auditing Service scenario, the service interposes itself between the Service Client and Service Provider as shown below:

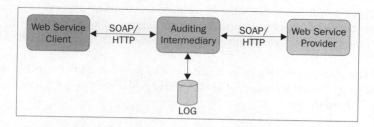

Management Services

A Management Service Intermediary is used to collect a number of useful reports about the Web Service. Some of these reports would include the number of Web Service hits and Web Service client usage (services used, total time usage, monthly/yearly reports, etc.). This would definitely help in identifying if the Web Service were meeting the Quality of Service (QoS) specified in the contract between the two organizations. This intermediary could also track the health of a Web Service and trigger an alert if the Web Service goes down. It functions in a similar manner to the Auditing Service explained above.

Performance Improvement Services

An interesting use of Intermediaries is in the area of Performance Improvement.

A **Cache** Intermediary could be used to store data frequently requested by Web Service clients, for example News Items that change every hour. So, when a client requests this data the intermediary can provide this information from its local cache instead of making an expensive network call to the Web Service. This results in reducing some of the load on the Web Service too. By placing several such "Cache" servers across the network, the response time to the clients will also be improved. Note that we will need a mechanism for the "Cache" servers to regularly update their caches with the latest information.

A **Store and Forward** Intermediary is used in situations where we don't want to overload the Web Service with too many requests. This is similar to the concept of a Batch, where a number of instructions are collected together and sent across at one time. So, what a Store and Forward Intermediary can do is to collect these requests from different Web Services clients and then shoot them off to the Web Service Provider. This would make the Web Service more asynchronous, which is fine if the client doesn't want or need an immediate response.

Aggregation Services

An **Aggregation** Intermediary is a powerful intermediary that can be used to provide a number of value added services that it combines and provides as a uniform service to the client. An Aggregation Intermediary could be used to combine several Web Services into one composite Web Service. An example of Aggregated Services could include transaction management, combining different sources of information into a single unified interface, etc.

In addition to the above services, Intermediaries can provide a host of other services like Reliable Messaging, Transformation of Data (XML/XSLT), Registry Services, Utility Services like Contacts, Calendar, etc.

Now that we have looked at different kinds of Intermediary Services, let us look at the general architecture of a Web Service Intermediary.

High-Level Web Service Intermediary Architecture

Shown below is a very basic set of components that would comprise a Web Service Intermediary. This is by no means a complete set of components but is just to provide you with a glimpse of what it could contain:

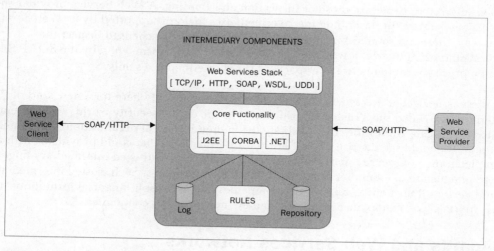

A Web Service intermediary would have the basic **Web Services Stack**, which will allow it to seamlessly plug in to the Web Services invocation route. The **Core Functionality** component is the main functionality of the Web Service. This could be a J2EE application, a CORBA-based application, or .NET component. Similar to Web Services, it should not matter what the platform is or what programming language was used to create this functionality.

The **Rules** component can serve to define the behavior of the Intermediary; how it interacts with different clients, its interaction with other intermediaries, etc. The **Log** database holds all the information on the messages passing to and from the intermediary. Finally the **Repository** can be used not only for its core functionality but also as a source of information about other intermediaries that it needs to interact with.

Web Service Intermediary Issues

As usual, the world of Intermediaries comes with its own set of issues that we need to be aware of. We have seen that Intermediaries intercept the calls from the Service Client to the Service Provider. We have also seen that Intermediaries could be chained together.

What this means is that **Security** is of prime importance whenever intermediaries are involved. For example, if I am a Web Service client, I would like to know which Intermediaries my request is going to go through. Can I trust those intermediaries? Do I need to enforce security through encryption, signatures, to guarantee not only the source of my data but also the validity of my data?

Of equal importance are **Transactions** and **Service Context**. Since there could be a chain of Intermediaries that are present in a single service invocation, care should be taken that the service context is propagated correctly. Also the transaction context needs to be propagated to ensure correct execution of the request.

Other interesting issues are those of **Inspection** and **Routing**. A Web Service provider should have a mechanism for describing the Intermediaries that are supported by its Web Service. This way, there is a standard mechanism for the Web Service client to **inspect** the Intermediaries. Similarly, it would be great to have a mechanism whereby the SOAP Request can be precisely **routed** between a specified set of intermediaries only.

As these issues get addressed, there is definitely an opportunity here for a new kind of Intermediary called the **Trusted Intermediary**. In the digital security world, we have entities called Certificate Authorities that facilitate the authenticating of organizations. In a similar manner, we could see the rise of the "Trusted Intermediary" that could provide us with a complete range of secure intermediary services. Using such a trusted intermediary might be more practical than a number of uncoordinated intermediaries. Such trusted intermediaries could very well turn out to be software companies like Microsoft, financial institutions like Visa, portals like Yahoo, or perhaps a complete new breed of companies.

Standards and Web Services Networks

It is important that each of the above issues be addressed appropriately in any standards that come forth for Web Service Intermediaries. At the moment, there are no standards for Web Services Intermediaries.

As SOAP is being extended to incorporate features like transactions, security, context, etc., it would be advisable to shape these in a manner that the intermediaries can implement too.

The XML Protocol Group at W3C (http://www.w3.org/2000/xp/Group/) is addressing a number of issues relating to Intermediaries. Microsoft has also submitted a WS Protocol that is used to route a SOAP message through a predefined set of intermediaries. The next generation of Apache SOAP called AXIS (http://xml.apache.org/axis/) is going to provide support for intermediaries.

While the standards are being developed, we are seeing the development of Web Services Networks that function as intermediaries for you and provide a set of services like hosting, security, context, maintaining relationships. Web Services network providers include Grand Central (http://www.grandcentral.com/) and Flamenco Networks (http://www.flamenconetworks.com/).

The Birth of the UDDI Value Added Service Supplier

The UDDI registry is still a good candidate for the way forward for businesses today, despite there being moves afoot to quietly drop it out of the picture. One often asked question, however, is how do other independent directory sites such as SalCentral (http://www.salcentral.com/) and XMethods (http://www.xmethods.com/) fit within the overall architecture? We now look more closely at a specific type of Web Service Intermediary: The UDDI Value Added Service Supplier.

Value Added Service Supplier (VASS)

UDDI should be seen as an enormous warehouse full of products. If you go to a warehouse as a customer you are not actually interested in **everything** on the shelves, it would be far better to only visit areas which have products that you're interested in, for example books or CDs.

A VASS can give you as a customer searching abilities that are currently beyond the capabilities of UDDI. A VASS will allow you to access research that has been carried out on behalf of the industry. This enables you to select that "perfect supplier" or Web Service by using selective information such as historic research, validity of information, level of documentation, ease of use, etc. This effectively filters out the invalid entries and gives the user information that's been cleaned, validated, and researched.

All too often we rely on simple categorization and the allocation of keywords to select Web Services. The VASS, however, should be an independent organization that offers the customer impartial advice allowing them to make informed judgments as to the correct supplier or Web Service to choose.

The VASS Business Plan

Currently, UDDI has been misinterpreted as a one-stop shop (similar to a web search engine) for finding, selecting, and keeping track of Web Services and suppliers. This in our opinion is not the case. In fact UDDI is more similar to a data storage device (database) that allows a Value Added Service Supplier (VASS) to sit as a layer above this repository and act as an intermediary between the customer and UDDI by offering additional services that supplement and add value to UDDI. Customers may of course still interact with the UDDI registry directly but simply lose some of the additional services the VASS can supply.

Below is a diagram to show some examples of Value Added Services:

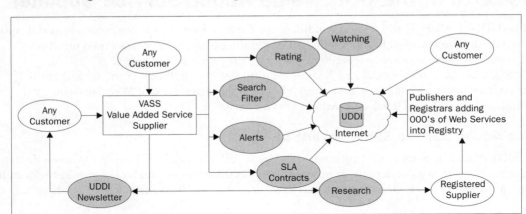

Alerts

Often as a customer you haven't just got one requirement for a business supplier, it's an ongoing requirement. An example of this would be always getting the cheapest quote for stationery. Alerts allow a VASS to e-mail you when a supplier or Web Service is registered within the UDDI that meets your requirements. By asking for an alert on "Stationery and New York", you would receive notifications every time a new stationery supplier from that city joins the UDDI registry. This potentially allows you to get better quotes and lower prices.

Even though we mention here that Alerts are sent to the Customer via e-mail, it is worth noting that this is only one method of providing this information to the customer. Other such notification methods could be:

- ❑ Instant messaging (AOL, Yahoo, MSM, etc.).
- ❑ SMS text messages.
- ❑ Running a predetermined Web Service (this predetermined Web Service could carry out some functionality, such as changing from using a primary Web Service to using a secondary Web Service).

Please note the use of running a predetermined Web Service; this effectively allows a VASS to become part of a 'mission critical' solution for a customer. The ability to instantly notify you by actually changing the way your Web Service functions can be essential in situations of fallback and disaster recovery.

Watching

What if the Web Service fails, what if the supplier moves, changes their tax reference, or a worse case simply changes or moves the Web Service?

Along comes the VASS and allows you to nominate specific UDDI registry entries. Whether it's the organization or Web Service link you're interested in, the VASS will watch the UDDI entry on your behalf and notify you automatically when it changes.

Organizations are using UDDI as a repository for information to allow customers to find suppliers. Because UDDI is capable of containing technical information concerning a Web Service, however, this can be used by the VASS to poll that Web Service on a regular basis to make sure that it's available and working correctly. This regulated information can even be used to form part of the Service Level Agreement.

Rating

Ratings allow all the information that a VASS gathers (such as availability and research on a Web Service and organization) to be signified as a single value that denotes its overall performance and usefulness. This rating can then be used effectively by the customer within the search filter, to only select Web Services that have a good rating.

As far as who rates a Web Service or UDDI registry entry, a number of rating agencies will probably come about, although a number of factors will dictate their success:

❑ Public opinion.

❑ Category suitability (some agencies may provide ratings for UK companies only).

❑ Formal and public acceptance by other corporations (such as Microsoft, IBM, etc.).

Search Filter

The UDDI registry is only as good as the data it contains. Research towards the end of 2001 showed a snapshot of the Production UDDI registry with over 48% of the links invalid. This kind of figure makes searching for information within the registry difficult, to say the least.

The VASS can act as an independent filtering system, which only displays the UDDI registry entries that are valid. It can do this by scanning through each UDDI registry entry daily and making a note of the key values (unique values per UDDI registry entry) that are valid and can be displayed within its own search area.

In addition the VASS will allow additional advanced information searching which is dependent on information gathered from other resources such as Web Service Research (see below), Watching (see above), and Rating (see above). This will give the customer the ability to make a much more informed decision as to which supplier or Web Service to choose and also allow them to more closely scrutinize fewer remaining suppliers.

The VASS contacts new UDDI registry entries and asks the organization to complete a series of questionnaires. This means that first of all the VASS has validated that the organization mentioned in the UDDI registry actually exists (similar to how VeriSign works today with digital certificates). It also means that the VASS can categorize UDDI registry entries as well as supplying potential customers with the ability to search on completed questionnaires.

If a developer then wants to find a business, they can browse through independently verified information with the understanding that a degree of checking and validation has already been performed. For example, if a tax number is entered then the rating supplier can confirm with the country of origin that this tax number is registered to the organization named in the specified registry entry. Phone numbers, fax numbers, and e-mail information can be also verified accordingly.

Research

A VASS will independently research individual Web Services for suppliers. This will mean creating "In The Spotlight" type articles, which systematically give customers the low-down on specific Web Services. These articles will form a benchmark of how a Web Service performs, expected response times, availability, security, and disaster recovery. Along with historic information on how these values fluctuate, which may signify trends, we could ask for example whether the availability of a Web Service is constant throughout the day?

Research will also be performed on suppliers to validate information already supplied within UDDI, such as telephone numbers, fax numbers, and company details. In addition extra information will be obtained which is not necessarily available within UDDI, such as company size, time the company has been trading, last year's accounts, and names of directors.

The information contained within this research could also form the backbone to the Service Level Agreement (see *SLA Contracts* below).

Access to this type of information also can form the basis for a degree of trust between the customer and the Web Service provider. This will significantly shorten the timeline for creating agreements, contractual or otherwise.

SLA Contracts

The topic of Service Level Agreements (SLA) is something which a specialist VASS could consider: as the VASS is separated from the UDDI registry it can simply state that it administers and checks the SLA on behalf of each party. This maintenance of SLA Contracts will require a VASS to police a range of acceptable values that were agreed upon within the SLA. Once one of these values was exceeded such as a response time becoming slower that the agreed limit, all parties would be notified than the agreement has been broken.

The difference between the VASS and an alert type system is that the VASS actually gets a signed copy of the original SLA; and is responsible for setting up and controlling its rules, they are then responsible for making sure that both parties are notified once these rules are breached. Notification will take the form of positive person-to-person interaction, not simply sending off an e-mail message and hoping it arrives.

UDDI Newsletter

Newsletters from a VASS can offer an insight into the UDDI registry and also give a customer first-hand and immediate knowledge of some of the following information on a weekly basis:

- New Web Services being registered within UDDI.
- UDDI 'weather report' showing graphically the data consistency of the registry.
- Specialist research performed on Web Services.
- Ratings being changed for Web Services.
- News on significant changes to the UDDI registry.

All the information included in the newsletter would also be tailored (like web sites do now) to a subscriber's own particular tastes. For example some subscribers will only want to see ratings and Web Services for a specific category, such as Hospitals or Car Showrooms.

Who Pays the VASS?

The VASS has two potential revenue streams.

The first is from the customer who wants to pay for value added information, but often the quantities of users will have to be high to sustain any type of profitable company. It is also notoriously difficult to create an Internet business from the ground up from customer subscriptions unless you already have a critical mass of visitors and are seen as the primary source of information. In addition this type of subscription type service often stifles growth and in turn then affects the following revenue stream.

The second revenue stream is directly from the Web Service Providers. These providers will pay for research on their Web Services and also for specialist services such as using the Alert system as part of an SLA agreement between the provider and the customer.

It does seem that as the UDDI registry grows and potentially becomes unsustainable as a single search engine, the VASS that specialize in specific areas of the industry may well be able to secure themselves a loyal and more willing-to-pay customer base. For example, a customer based in the USA who is looking for a Web Service for sending SMS messages would be far more willing to enter a contractual agreement with an American company than a UK company. The reason is simply that if your agreement does not span country borders, then it is far easier to take legal action against a Web Service provider. If you enter into a commitment with a company in another country, however, then the legal costs alone will probably far outweigh any costs in lost income due to a disruption in a Web Service.

It is likely that many VASS companies will in fact concentrate on country- or industry-specific information and therefore filter the Web Services and UDDI registry entries you see.

Business Architecture for a Web Services Brokerage

SOAP and Web Services may hold center stage of the developing Web industry, as attention focuses on toolkits and multi-platforms; however, this area of the industry is merely the tip of an iceberg, which reaches much further than merely selling utility software. Yet, rather than considering the overall architecture of a Web Services business model, the present trend seems to be for companies to produce development tools for the sake of it, in a market that is still maturing.

For the Web Services industry to succeed, it needs a solid architecture of support and sales services. Both developers and customers need to know what niche they fall into, and how they can interact with other parts of the industry. To fully comprehend the Web Services industry, we need to understand the demarcations between sales, development, and hosting of Web Services.

A main concern in this early stage of the development process of Web Services is that there is no benchmark industry to learn from. The Web Services industry is, possibly, most closely related to that of ASPs (Application Service Providers). As developers get the tools to publish functional Web Services as easily as one can create a HTML web page however, it is likely that the Web Services market will soon overflow. Once Web Services become widely adopted, the large number of RAD (Rapid Application Development) developers, using tools such as VB, Delphi, C++, and the .NET platform will swamp the market with Web Services.

This section of the paper serves as a first stepping-stone for the Web Services brokerage architecture. In it, we bring together the result of eighteen months of research in Web Services, and practical knowledge of building a brokerage (http://www.salcentral.com/).

The term brokerage is used within many contexts; however, in the context of Web Services a brokerage is best defined as an organization, or individual, whose primary activities include the commercial ability to publish, promote, and sell SOAP-based Web Services.

Below are eleven distinct parts of the development process of a Web Service, grouped under four categories: Creation, Publication, Promotion, and Selling.

Category	Definition
Creation	The main players in this category are developers and designers, who have the role to create functional Web Services.
Publication	This category is, primarily, constituted by organizations hosting Web Services.
Promotion	In this category, we find operators that search for and locate Web Services, using general search techniques and Value Added Services.
Selling	Organizations dealing with accounts, sales, and customer contact comprise this category.

Let us now look at an overview of how these categories fit into the architecture of a Web Services Brokerage:

Category	Actor	Description
Creation	Designer	Organization or individual who raises the idea for a Web Service, and is involved in the analysis and design of its functionality.
	Developer	Organization or developer who builds the Web Service.
	Documentation	In-house staff produces technical documentation about a Web Service. The documentation is then used for further in-house development, and for advising other developers, outside the organization, on how to use a particular Web Service.
	Interoperability	A third-party company tests a Web Service's interoperability and ease of use.
	Distributor	Organization who distributes the Web Service, and controls the code warehousing, hosting, and data warehousing of that Web Service.
Publication	Code Warehouse	Third-party storage area for precompiled code and scripts produced by the developer. The version control also takes place here.
	Hosting	Organization that is hosting the compiled Web Service.
	Data Warehouse	Organization that holds the data used by the Web Service.
Promotion	Directory	Provides a means to locate a Web Service by browsing or using a specialist Web Service directory.
	VAS	Value Added Services which enable customers to pick Web Services using a variety of information (see earlier for more details).
	Accreditation	Web Services hosting and development organizations will be given accreditation, based on factors such as organization size and availability of Web Services.

Category	Actor	Description
Selling	Web Service Auditor	Organization that constantly reviews and checks the Web Services their customers are using. With a Web Services Auditor, the customer can make sure that the Web Service conforms to the Service Level Agreement.
	Accounts	Organization that sells access to a customer to be able to run a Web Service, allowing the customer to purchase additional access, and view the customer's current purchases.

In reality, many of these roles are performed by one organization; however, for the purposes of understanding, we will consider them as distinct parts of the development and business process of Web Services.

Creation

The creation of a Web Service will stay in the design, development, and documentation stages (explained in the previous table) until its functionality and design are checked, reviewed, and proved to be satisfactory. The same will happen in most other technical development processes. Already at this early stage in the development process of a Web Service we seem to move away from inherited methodologies and start to tread on new territory.

A Web Service provider can create a client frontend to a Web Service, so that other companies will be able to use it. Interoperability within a Web Service is defined in two distinct layers. The organization that consumes a Web Service is responsible for the layer that controls the user interface. This organization does not have to be the Web Service provider. The second layer is the Web Service, which when separated from the client frontend allows the Web Service provider testing its Web Service to concentrate on business functionality rather than aesthetics or developing a user interface.

This testing process can be performed outside the developing organization. An immediate advantage of this is that third-party organizations, outside the development team of a particular Web Service, can independently test that Web Service. As an organization's Web Service can be made available to other organizations over the Internet, there will be organizations specializing in testing unit functionality and interoperability. External testing, as well as internal, secures high quality of Web Services.

The external organizations testing interoperability will be able to pass a Web Service through a predefined series of tests such as data typing, response analysis, and high traffic, at the end of which they will be able to produce a certificate of assurance that can be fed into a Service Level Agreement (SLA). Without this type of predetermined testing, the customer has to rely only on the developer's skill and judgment. The customer will, in future, have a choice. There will be a definite connection between the most successful and most widely used Web Services and their choice of methods for functionality testing.

The distributor has the most important role in the Creation stage; all information, consisting of code and data, developed in the first parts of the development process, needs to be collated into a single package. This package can then be fed into a Service Level Agreement, which contractually declares that this Web Service performs a certain task. It should be said that not all Web Services need an SLA – it's all about consumer demand.

Customers need to distinguish between many similar Web Services. Quality Assurance and a Service Level Agreement help customers choose the right Web Services. With such quality management, customers can trust the functionality of available Web Services, before trying them out. Furthermore, the distributor is most suited to make choices about the hosting and warehousing of specific Web Services.

Publication

In conversations held with organizations and venture capitalists, looking at the Web Services industry, the one word most consistently raised is 'trust'. For the Web Services development and publication system to work, one must be able to trust other organizations – which may very well be situated in a completely different country – in order to let them administer and back up one's own organization's web site. It's all very well creating an SLA, but what is it really worth if we know that the cost of international litigation far outweighs the cost of hurriedly obtaining another Web Service provider and adjusting our code.

Although some larger corporations may not have a problem with this, the majority of organizations find international litigation an extremely risky venture, even if an organization is in the right. We can expect some extremely detailed Service Level Agreements to be enforced for critical Web Services, but this might not be enough.

One way of solving the problem is to take the original code, compiled Web Service, and data storage, away from the publisher, and place it with trusted intermediaries whose only business function is to administer Web Services. An intermediate organization holds the latest copies of different aspects of a Web Service, independent from the original developer. It offers its customer a secure and safe repository to store a snapshot of the Web Service code, documentation, and all associated files. What makes this model work is that the intermediaries:

- Are trusted by the developer, using a Contract and Service Level Agreement.
- Are trusted by the customer, using a Service Level Agreement.
- Store all the files separately from the developer.

This type of arrangement is similar to the legal and technical binding most web site owners have today when other companies host their web sites. There is, usually, a Service Level Agreement in place, indicating the type of service expected within the terms of your use of that web hosting service.

We would expect that web hosting organizations that host such services, for instance, http://www.brinkster.com/, would only take on Web Services that have been run through favored **interoperability** organizations. This would, in fact, serve to decrease the risk of downtime and potential problems, such as those we have foreseen above, and create a close and essential liaison between interoperability and web site hosting.

Another potential solution to the problem of enforcing a Service Level Agreement is to use the services of a Web Services Auditor. A Web Services Auditor checks that an organization's Web Services match their SLAs, and advise them of any changes in the standard of the service as agreed within the original SLA.

Promotion

Searching for Web Services will become paramount over the next few years. It will be important to have an appropriate method of tracking down the Web Services that we need, out of the potentially hundreds of thousands of available Web Services.

Searching for Web Services includes two sections, which, although they can act independently, are stronger when working collaboratively:

The Web Service directory (UDDI, http://www.xmethods.com/, http://www.salcentral.com/) allows customers to track down a Web Service by using selection criteria. The directory works like a search engine. It enables you to either enter search criteria, or to browse categorized lists, to find a specific Web Service.

In addition to the Web Service directory, there seems to be a place for dynamic Web Service searching tools, to interrogate and locate new Web Services. These would use a similar technique to the current web site spiders, by moving along series of linked XML discovery files, each one describing the location of various Web Services, and any further XML discovery files. These tools would find new and changed Web Services, so that they can be displayed within a specialist search engine or Web Service open directory.

VAS (Value Added Services), for example, at http://www.salcentral.com/ and http://www.xmethods.com/, allow us to select Web Services not only by categorized lists or searching tools, but also by giving additional analysis or general information that would normally not be available. If we, for instance, find two Web Services that perform similar tasks, we can, with VAS, get information about the response rate of each Web Service, and availability over the last six months. This information allows a customer to make an informed judgment as to which Web Service to choose.

Accreditation will, undoubtedly, serve to create a layered approach to Web Services. Customers will make selections based on criteria such as who hosts a Web Service, and whether the hosting company has any accreditation.

Selling

A major problem that the industry will face is the potential abundance of free Web Services. Free Web Services, although providing excellent value for customers, undermine the commercial prospects for the Web Services industry. It is clear that to enable a Web Service provider to sell their services, they need to differentiate their Web Services from free ones.

To do this, an organization needs to use ascertained information such as accreditation and Value Added Services to show that its Web Service is trustworthy. It must, of course, also keep its charges down. Consumers would know that this Web Service has been checked by independent organizations (as described above).

A third-party organization operates as a Web Services Auditor. It makes sure that a Web Service functions in accordance with its Service Level Agreement. The Web Services Auditor constantly checks and re-checks the Web Services it is looking after. If a Web Service fails to reach the standard established in the SLA, the Web Services Auditor notifies its customer, allowing them to take immediate action. The Web Services Auditor look out for new versions of the Web Service being made available, and makes sure that response rates are consistently in line with what is defined in the SLA.

Accounts are simply the money collectors of the Web Services world. They collect monthly or per call, allowing the Web Service developer to use a technical layer to call into accounts, and validate whether the user of a Web Service is allowed to use that Web Service. This technical layer, which validates a user's use of a Web Service on behalf of the Web Service developer, has many advantages:

❑ The developer simply creates a Web Service, and attaches accounts functionality later.

❑ The developer does not need to create a debiting web site to collect money.

❑ A customer can buy usage of Web Services from many different Web Service providers through the same accounts engine, allowing them to have a central point for credit card debiting.

❑ Customers can, at once, view transactions for all the Web Services they use, although they belong to different organizations.

❑ Customers can easily see when use of a Web Service expires.

Even though this area is technically challenging, it seems that the major problems would be those associated with the legal aspects of such transactions; for instance, whether the organization that debits an account is liable for the Web Service's availability.

The clearest type of scenario would be one in which the organization dealing with the accounts is simply an intermediary, and the Service Level Agreement is agreed between the customer and the organizations previously identified as the code warehouse, hosting, and data warehouse.

Conclusion

In this paper, we have looked at what a Web Service Intermediary is and the kind of services that they provides. Web Services intermediaries are here to stay, and with appropriate development of standards for them we should see tremendous activity on the part of component developers and organizations to write intermediaries that seamlessly plugin to Web Services networks, thereby providing value-added-services.

The second section of this paper has come off the back of the data integrity research undertaken on the UDDI registry. This joint research (SalCentral and WebServicesArchitect) is now publicly available at http://www.salcentral.com/uddi/default.asp. From this research it is apparent that the UDDI is really simply a dumb registry; in many ways it forms the basis of the data storage of the millions of pieces of information. To make this information useful, however, someone (the VASS) needs to give the customer and Web Service provider an element of control.

VASS are already starting to appear such as SalCentral and XMethods. Over the long term, however, some may be better suited to tailor their efforts more towards a specific industry solution, such as a VASS for the Hotel trade, which concentrates on Hotel based Web Services or a VASS for a specific country. This change in effort will only appear however when a critical mass of Web Services have appeared.

What happens now is significant, with the expected increase in the size of the registry. Customers and Web Service providers may in fact become disillusioned with the degree of data integrity and therefore the concern is that UDDI may in fact get a bad name for itself, something that can be difficult to shake off.

In addition, some may have noticed the similarity between search engines and UDDI; in fact we may be seeing the birth of the next stage of search engines. This will potentially make existing search engines redundant and allow customers to search and select companies to trade with using specialist filtered lists rather than in that huge cloud called the Internet. As well as this, it seems that existing search engines may in fact be able to hook directly into the VASS search engine.

Finally, we examined what a Web Services Brokerage would include, and who would be responsible for the elements within its architecture. We saw that there are four main areas of activity surrounding a Web Service before it is first used by a customer (Creation, Publication, Promotion, and Selling), and that at each stage a brokerage can be involved.

Author: Romin Irani

- Global Electronic Business Standard

- How ebXML Works

- Industry Support

- The Role of Web Services

- Web Services and ebXML

An Introduction To ebXML

Introduction

Global electronic business is here to stay. In order for businesses, small and large, to exist in the new economy it has become imperative that their systems communicate with each other. Over the last few months, there has been tremendous activity by leading industry standards groups to create processes that will enable inter-company business based on a common protocol.

In this paper, we shall take a look at ebXML, which is a global electronic business standard that is sponsored by UN/CEFACT (United Nations Center For Trade Facilitation And Electronic Business) and OASIS (Organization for the Advancement of Structural Information Standards). We shall cover the following areas:

- ❑ The need for a global standard for conducting electronic business.

- ❑ What ebXML is and how it plans to facilitate global electronic business.

- ❑ Current industry support for ebXML, that is the Standard Bodies, Industry Groups, Vendors, and users.

- ❑ What Web Services are and how they would help in accelerating ebXML implementations.

Need for a Global Electronic Business Standard

In this section we shall take a look at how organizations today conduct electronic business with each other, and discuss why they would benefit if there were a standard for their interactions. We shall also look at what any such global electronic business standard would need to consist of. This will set the background for the next section, when we describe ebXML and how it could achieve the requirements that we set forth in a standard.

State of Things Today

Organizations around the world are going collaborative. It is no longer feasible for any one organization to provide all services to a consumer; every day we hear of organizations announcing partnerships to collaborate with each other in order to integrate each other's business processes to cut costs, time, etc. One of the fundamental requirements is that of interoperability between the electronic systems of partner organizations. But in today's world, interoperability between partner systems (electronic business integration) is done not only in an ad-hoc manner but also using a variety of approaches. Take a look at the diagram shown below:

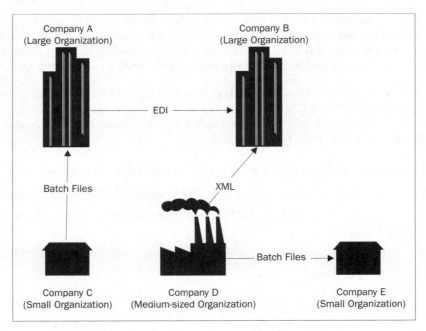

From the diagram, we can see that organizations are using different ways to conduct electronic business. Some of the larger organizations conduct electronic business based on EDI (Electronic Data Interchange) while some of the medium/small organizations still continue to do electronic business primarily via the transfer of raw data.

Advantages of Having a Global Standard

As we see, organizations have not yet decided on a uniform way to do electronic business. Doesn't EDI, though, provide for capture of common data-interchange formats and common business processes in which they are used? Yes, but EDI has proved to be expensive due to the high costs of setting up the network infrastructure to execute EDI transactions. Another big reason for EDI not being popular among small-to-medium sized organizations is that there is usually a dominant business entity that has tried to enforce proprietary integration approaches on all the other partners. What this means is that EDI is meant for large corporations only, unless someone can improve the position for small-to-medium sized organizations.

If we have a common global electronic standard based on open Internet standards, some of the advantages that an organization would gain are as follows:

- ❑ The cost of implementation would be substantially reduced since an organization would now have to implement just one standard that their internal systems can understand and communicate with.

- ❑ An organization would have a variety of implementations/vendors to choose their products from.

- ❑ An organization would be able to gain more business since its business is now exposed to several such organizations that use the same standard.

- ❑ Such business will also be easier to integrate with due to each partner using the same standards.

What Should a Global Electronic Business Standard Consist of?

We now understand the importance of having a global electronic standard for business. But what exactly should such a standard comprise? In other words, what should be some of the common capabilities/issues addressed by a global electronic standard? It is important to understand these points in order to fully appreciate how ebXML provides the same points that we address here.

A global electronic business standard should definitely address the following:

- ❑ Define common business transactions, such as sending a purchase order.

- ❑ Define common data-interchange formats; that is, messages in the context of the above transactions.

- ❑ Define a mechanism for listing your organization's capabilities and the business transactions that your organization can perform in a common repository accessible to all other organizations. In short, an ability to describe your company profile.

- ❑ Define a mechanism to allow organizations to discover companies and look up their profile.

- ❑ Define a mechanism to establish trust and credit worthiness standards among participants.

- ❑ Define a mechanism that allows two organizations to negotiate on the business terms before they commence transactions.

- ❑ Define a common transport mechanism for exchanging messages between organizations.

- ❑ Define the security and reliability framework.

The ebXML Standard

ebXML (electronic business XML) is a global electronic business standard that is sponsored by UN/CEFACT (United Nations Center For Trade Facilitation And Electronic Business, http://www.unece.org/cefact/) and OASIS (Organization for the Advancement of Structural Information Standards, http://www.oasis-open.org/). ebXML defines a framework for global electronic business that will allow businesses to find each other and conduct their business based on well-defined XML messages within the context of standard business processes which are governed by standard or mutually-negotiated partner agreements. The ebXML standard provides support for each of the points that we identified in the previous section, *What Should a Global Electronic Business Standard Consist of?*

How ebXML Works

In this section we shall take a look at how a business would get itself ready to perform business transactions with other organizations, based on the ebXML standard. Shown below are three key phases in the order in which they are supposed to be executed towards meeting that goal:

- ❑ Implementation phase.

- ❑ Discovery of partner information and negotiation phase.

- ❑ Transaction phase.

Implementation Phase

In this diagram, the first thing to note is the *ebXML Repository*. This repository contains industry-defined Business Processes and Scenarios that are commonly applicable to most business transactions. Companies can choose to extend these processes and add scenarios of their own. The repository also contains profiles for businesses that have already registered themselves for performing ebXML transactions with other trading partners.

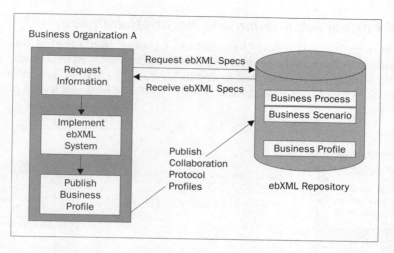

So, what is an Implementation Phase? For Organization A, which is interested in doing electronic business as per the ebXML standard, it consists of three steps as shown in the diagram above:

1. Request Information.

2. Implement ebXML System.

3. Publish Business Profile.

The first step is to request the ebXML Specifications (Business Processes, Business Scenarios) and understand them. Once the organization has digested the specifications, it decides which business processes it would like to implement, following which it needs to implement a system in-house based on those standards. It could either build a new system or build on top of an existing legacy system. The whole idea is to expose a system that understands and talks ebXML. There are several choices available today in the form of third-party applications that can bring various components together and assemble an ebXML system.

Once the system is built, the organization is ready to conduct business with other organizations. To facilitate that, it needs to publish its profile known as a Collaboration Protocol Profile (CPP) to the ebXML Repository for other organizations to discover. A CPP thus enables any organization to describe its profile; which business processes it supports, its roles in those processes, the messages exchanged, the transport mechanism for the messages, etc. Once the CPP is published to the ebXML Repository, it will allow other organizations to access it and learn about the capabilities of Organization A. At any time, Organization A is free to access its own profile, and review and make changes as necessary.

Discovery of Partner Information and Negotiation Phase

We saw in the previous phase how Organization A readied itself for electronic business on the ebXML standard by first implementing an ebXML-compliant system in-house and then publishing its profile, which described its capabilities to the ebXML Repository. In this next phase, we shall look at how Organization A does electronic business with a partner, Organization B.

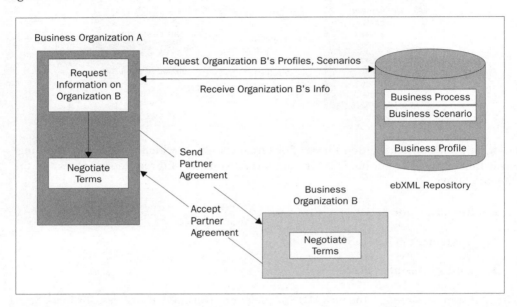

Just as Organization A published its profile, Organization B has done the same. The first step that Organization A takes is to retrieve Organization B's profile information from the ebXML Repository. Once it has the profile, it is in a better position to understand Organization B's capabilities; whether it supports the business processes that Organization A is interested in, the messages to be exchanged, transport mechanisms, security and reliability of the process, etc.

In the real world, businesses always negotiate terms and implement business contracts before conducting any business. ebXML is no different in that regard, so the next step for Organization A is to send a business contract called a **Collaborative Partner Agreement (CPA)**, in ebXML, to Organization B. The CPA will be a reflection of the profile (CPP) of both the organizations. Both organizations can now collaborate on the CPA and refine it to meet their business needs. Finally, both parties accept the agreement. During this phase, it is very likely that key personnel from both organizations will meet in person and make assessments before committing to an eBusiness relationship.

Transaction Phase

We are now ready to conduct transactions. A CPA was accepted in the previous phase and the transactions can now be conducted in a predefined fashion where each business organization plays a predetermined role in the transaction. The transactions consist of ebXML messages, which are sent over the standard *ebXML Messaging Service*.

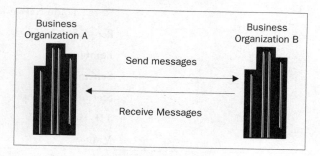

What ebXML Does Not Address

It is important to remember that though ebXML provides a common repository of business models, business scenarios, messages, etc., it **does not mandate how to implement** them in your system. As we saw in the previous section during the implementation phase, an organization is free to implement the ebXML standards on its own or using a variety of ebXML platforms/tools being provided by several vendors.

Current Industry Support

It is encouraging to note that ebXML has broad support not only from industry standard groups and bodies, but also from organizations that have decided to provide ebXML support in their systems. Several vendors are also actively involved in providing platforms and tools that organizations can use today in making their systems ebXML-compliant.

Take a look at the list below showing the organizations that have endorsed ebXML:

Standards Bodies and Industry Groups	Vendors and Users
EBES	Bind Systems
e centreUK	Care Data Systems
Korea Institute of Electronic Commerce	Commerce One
Open Applications Group	Data Access Technologies
Open Travel Alliance	Documentum
RosettaNet	Edifecs

Table continued on following page

Standards Bodies and Industry Groups	Vendors and Users
Tradegate ECA	Fujitsu
	Future Three/Synapz
	IPNet Solutions
	Korea Trade Network
	PeopleSoft
	Pointgain
	Schemantix
	Sterling Commerce
	TIE Holding NV
	Viquity

For a current list consult the following URL: http://www.ebxml.org/endorsements.htm.

Comments from Some organizations

The following quotes from vendors help to illustrate that support for ebXML is widespread in the industry. These quotes are reproduced from the following web site, where more quotes can be found:

http://www.ebxml.org/endorsements.htm#vendlist

RosettaNet

"RosettaNet plans to integrate support for the ebXML Messaging Services Specification in future releases of RosettaNet's Implementation Framework (RNIF). While RosettaNet remains committed to developing business process standards required to support the complex needs of the high-technology industry, we also want to ensure interoperability across all supply chains. To that end, we see tremendous value in ensuring our vertical supply chain standards are supported by a horizontal, universally accepted messaging service, such as the one from the ebXML initiative."

Jennifer Hamilton
CEO
http://www.rosettanet.org/

Bind Systems

"The ebXML initiative has delivered a comprehensive set of specifications that enable vendors such as ourselves to deliver solutions that meet the stringent demands necessary for secure, yet open, collaborative electronic computing. We see ebXML as a pivotal component enabling the delivery of 'business ready' Web Services, particularly through its support for electronically enforceable partner agreements.

These agreements define both business and technology critical parameters that can then be used to govern electronic interaction between partners. It is for these reasons, among many, that ebXML plays a central role in our BindPartner Business Collaboration Platform. Overall, an excellent achievement by the teams involved."

David Russell
CTO
http://www.bindsys.com/

Care Data Systems
"We see the ebXML standards as a sound basis for multi-entity integration that is fully dynamic, yet secure, manageable and flexible. Therefore as we develop our tool set for zero-coding massive-scale multi-entity integration of person-centric data, we consider ebXML support be way more than a 'cost of doing business' but rather a key enabler of excellent and responsible 'consumer-centric' B2B."

Jon Farme
Principal, LuoSys, Inc.
http://www.caredatasystems.com/

Accelerating ebXML – The Role of Web Services

Web Services are the new buzzword in programming circles. Almost everyday we hear of vendors announcing support for Web Services in their products. We'll briefly recap what Web Services are. A Web Service exposes software functionality, which can be accessed over the Internet from a service publisher, and seamlessly incorporated into an application residing on the service subscribers' computer. For example a Brokerage House (the service publisher) would write a StockQuote Web Service (the functionality) that would be accessible to people or organizations (the service subscriber) over the Internet.

In essence, then, a Web Service would help you expose certain functionality over the Internet so that other clients can consume it. But what is so unique about this approach? After all, haven't companies been doing business over the Internet for quite some time? Haven't they been exchanging information with each other to facilitate business transactions? Aren't there business exchanges, which bring buyers and sellers to a common Internet ground?

Yes, definitely! Before we answer how Web Services could be unique, let us first look at the programming model for Web Services and some of the specifications/technologies that Web Services work on.

Shown below is the Web Services programming model and the different players involved:

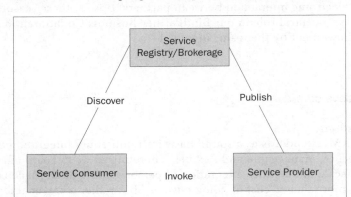

Let us try and understand the above diagram from the point of view of a sample organization Tect, which is interested in providing a Web Service.

Tect is the Service Provider in the diagram. Tect is a Foreign-Exchange agency and is interested in exposing certain functionality (foreign-exchange calculator service) in their existing application as a Web Service. The Web Service in common parlance is described by its Web Services Definition Language (WSDL) document. So the Service Provider, Tect, creates the WSDL document for others (potential Service Consumers) to analyze and determine how to invoke their service. Since Tect is keen that its service be publicized to a wide audience, it is important that they publish this information in some sort of a global registry.

This is where the third player in our diagram, the Service Registry/Brokerage, comes into play. Essentially, they hold a repository of Web Services that other organizations can query and determine if certain Web Services are of interest to them. One of the open standards to publishing and querying information from a global registry is UDDI (Universal Description, Discovery and Integration). The organization that is interested in using some of the external Web Services completes the picture in the above diagram. They are known as the Service Consumer, who scans brokerages/registries for Web Services that they may be interested in. Once they are interested in a particular Web Service, they retrieve the WSDL document for that Web Service. The WSDL provides them enough information in terms of endpoint URLs, operations, messages, etc., such that they can invoke the Web Service over the Internet using an open protocol like SOAP (Simple Object Access Protocol).

Thus, in essence, we use WSDL to **describe** a Web Service, we might use a UDDI API to **publish** and query information from a UDDI Registry, and finally we **invoke** the Web Service using SOAP.

Now, let us revisit the question of why Web Services are unique in their approach? In WSDL, SOAP, and UDDI, we have open standards that have been accepted by almost all organizations. Prior to these standards, vendors often propagated their own architectures that were proprietary and expensive. Moreover, connecting to a new organization with different systems needed integration work that was often time-consuming, difficult, and expensive. The advent of these open standards makes the task of an organization very simple. Subscriber organizations now have programmable access to the functionality, so that they can code it into the applications that they develop. These open standards also go a long way towards ensuring the platform independence that has plagued integration projects the world over.

Web Services – Benefits

From the discussion in the previous section, it should be easy to see how open standards like WSDL, SOAP, and UDDI would benefit an organization that has decided to go down the Web Services route.

❑ An organization can describe its services via WSDL and publish these to a global UDDI registry or a Web Services brokerage. By publishing information about their services to a global registry, organizations are able to reach a wider audience. This should result in an increase in business opportunities.

❑ Integration costs between an organization's applications and their trading partners can see a significant lowering. This is due to the fact that if both organizations have already accepted and implemented the Web Services standards, by default they would be able to communicate almost immediately with each other.

❑ For consumers of Web Services, it presents them with a large number of organizations providing similar kinds of services. Consumers can now compare Web Services of a similar kind, and in certain cases even try them out on a trial basis, all via a few clicks since all these systems are communicating via SOAP.

Web Services – Current issues

In spite of the several advantages that Web Services offer us today, we need to look at the current issues that early adopters are trying to address:

❑ Current tools from several vendors are focused more on the publish-lookup-invoke programming model. For organizations involved in deeply collaborative and long-running transactions, it is essential that we see better support from Web Services vendors in the areas of transactions, versioning, support for business processes, etc.

❑ Since the subscriber organization uses the Web Services provided by the service provider, it is important for the subscriber organization to pay attention to the response times of the Web Service, the support setup of the service provider, etc. After all, the Internet as a network has its deficiencies in terms of bandwidth, response time, security, reliability, etc. It is also important to make alternative plans if the service provider decides to close down its business or discontinue the particular Web Service.

❑ Despite the fact that vendors providing Web Services toolkits have accepted the open standards, interoperability across vendor toolkits and platforms is still an issue.

Current Landscape

Web Services, since their advent, have had tremendous support from vendors that have been introducing Web Services tools at a feverish pace. Several organizations with established products have also announced full support for exposing their current implementations as a Web Service. Organizations interested in implementing Web Services solutions in their products have a wide variety of choices. Some of the vendors supporting Web Services are listed below:

❑ Microsoft Corporation.

❑ IBM.

❑ BEA Systems.

❑ Sun Microsystems Inc.

❑ Oracle.

❑ Cape Clear.

❑ Shinka Technologies.

❑ Silverstream Software.

Relationship Between Web Services and ebXML (Implementation Phase)

In this section, we shall examine the functional architecture of ebXML, and see how the Web Services programming model fits in. This will help organizations to understand better where technologies like WSDL, UDDI, and SOAP fit within a standards specification like ebXML. Alternatively, it could also help them in designing their own framework if need be.

The following diagram shows the Functional Service view of an ebXML system, which is described in detail in the ebXML Technical Architecture Specification, available at http://www.ebxml.org/. The diagram has been modified to help us understand it better. We are interested in the functional service view because that is the view associated with implementation details and in our case the implementation technologies that we have at hand are WSDL, UDDI, and SOAP.

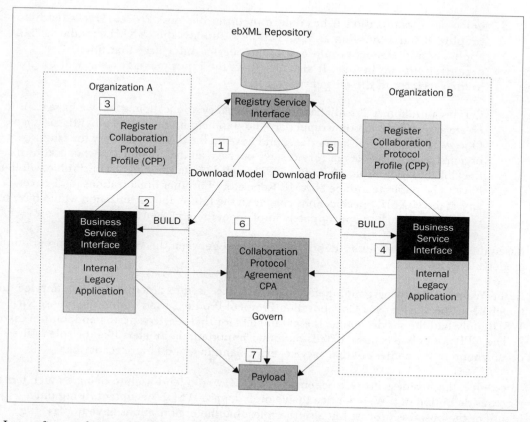

Let us first understand how the whole system functions, and at the right points we shall inject the key words WSDL, UDDI, and SOAP, to understand where those technologies fit in.

You should recollect that the ebXML Repository is a collection of Business Processes and Business Scenarios that apply to most businesses. Let us take our sample **Organization A** that is interested in enabling its existing legacy application to confirm to ebXML standards. By exposing this legacy application as a Web Service, it aims to be a provider of such a Web Service to other organizations. Here is how an organization would go about doing this (we will keep referring to the diagram):

1. Our Organization A downloads the ebXML Specifications (the Business Process models and Business Scenarios) and understands them.

2. After our Organization A has understood the specifications, it determines which Business Processes best fit the needs of its business. What this means is that an organization can implement only a subset of the business processes that it can engage in. At the same time, an organization can modify an existing Business Process if it does not find a perfect fit with the Business Process defined in the specifications.

3. Once our Organization A has determined the Business Processes it is ready to support, it starts building an application to support the ebXML standards. This application in essence would define the Service Interfaces that other organizations can invoke. It also describes the input messages that will be given to the service and the output messages.

Our organization A already has an internal legacy application, so all we have do is to create an implementation wrapper around it to help it understand ebXML messages. Once we have built these interfaces and have all the details necessary for other organizations to invoke our services, we package all that together in what is known as the Collaboration Protocol Profile (CPP) in ebXML terminology. This Profile will then have to be published to the ebXML Repository for other organizations to discover. If any of the ebXML Specifications change in the future, the organization would have to re-evaluate them and appropriately implement them in their application.

Based on the steps so far, let us identify the relations between the Web Services programming model and ebXML.

In the Web Services programming model, WSDL was used to describe the Web Service. In the ebXML specifications, a Collaboration Protocol Profile is used to describe the service. The WSDL only had the service name, the parameters for that service and the endpoint to invoke it. The CPP not only has those details but other important parameters like the role of the organization in the context of that service, error-handling, and failure scenarios.

In essence, the Business Process Schema of ebXML would lend itself to being a much more rigorous definition of a Web Service than simply a pure WSDL document. It not only identifies the business process but also the roles that the organizations have to play, the messages being exchanged, etc.

UDDI is used in the Web Services programming model to publish the services to a global UDDI Repository. In ebXML we use the Registry Service Interface to publish the CPP of the organization.

4. Now, along comes Organization B, who has followed exactly the same steps as us in enabling their legacy application for ebXML. At the same time they are in need of a particular service and are interested in discovering possible organizations providing that. Let's assume for the sake of the example that our Organization A does provide that service, and has published the details using their Collaboration Protocol Profile (CPP).

The discovery of a business and downloading its CPP will be done via the Registry Service in ebXML. One may be confused now whether to use UDDI to discover a service or to use the ebXML Registry Service to do the same. UDDI is used to publish and discover Web Services, while ebXML Registry Services provide not only that, but also information on business processes, business documents, business profiles, etc.

In fact, they are quite complementary. Organizations can continue to use UDDI to inquire about businesses in the global UDDI Registry. Those entries would then be used to refer to ebXML Services in the ebXML Registry.

5. Organization B looks in the ebXML Repository for possible organizations providing the service it wants, and downloads our CPP. The CPP gives them details on what our service provides, the messages that flow into and out of our service, and how to invoke the service.

6. The next step is for both organizations to come up with an agreement. This involves key personnel from both organizations meeting in person and working out the details. These details include the business process requirements of both organizations, the messaging protocols to use, etc. Once an agreement has been reached, the organizations come up with a Collaboration Protocol Agreement (CPA) between them, which captures all of the agreed terms. The CPA, as you see from the previous diagram, is really derived from the capabilities of both organizations (described by the CPP). The CPA is agreed upon by both organizations, and is then responsible for governing the transactions between the two organizations.

7. The final step, as you might expect, is the actual transaction between the two companies. The Payload (messages) is exchanged between the two organizations, and they are governed by the CPA defined above. The messages are transported in a standard manner using the secure and reliable ebXML Messaging Service.

In the Web Services programming model, once we have the WDSL for a particular Web Service, we can invoke that Web Service using SOAP and HTTP. On the other hand, in ebXML we need to use the ebXML Messaging service, which will provide a uniform way of sending messages. The ebXML Messaging Services utilizes SOAP and HTTP (in fact it allows for attachments too). The ebXML Messaging Service will thus provide a standard way to send messages to your trading partner; it not only provides a secure and reliable transport infrastructure based on SOAP and HTTP, but it also makes sure that the CPA governs the business transactions.

Conclusion

This paper has taken a look at the need for a global electronic business standard and how the ebXML standard is a step in the right direction. The ebXML standard as it stands today has received widespread endorsement from leading standards groups, industry consortiums, vendors and users. With the advent of Web Services and the open standards that they are based on (WSDL, UDDI, and SOAP), it is strongly believed that Web Services would provide the right kind of stimuli to help organizations take a big step towards implementing ebXML standards in their systems and thereby reaching new levels of interoperability with partner organizations.

Author: Judith M. Myerson

- WebServices.Org

- IBM

- W3C

- Microsoft

- Sun

Web Services Architectures

With Web Services, information sources become components that you can use, reuse, mix, and match to enhance Internet and intranet applications ranging from a simple currency converter, stock quotes, or dictionary to an integrated, portal-based travel planner, procurement workflow system, or consolidated purchase processes across multiple sites. Each is built upon an architecture that is presented in this paper as an illustrated stack of layers, or a narrative format.

Each vendor, standards organization, or marketing research firm defines Web Services in a slightly different way. Gartner, for instance, defines Web Services as "loosely coupled software components that interact with one another dynamically via standard Internet technologies". Forrester Research takes a more open approach to Web Services as "automated connections between people, systems, and applications that expose elements of business functionality as a software service and create new business value."

For these reasons, the architecture of a Web Services stack varies from one organization to another. The number and complexity of layers for the stack depend on the organization. Each stack requires Web Services interfaces to get a Web Services client to speak to an Application Server, or Middleware component, such as Common Object Request Broker Architecture (CORBA), Java 2 Enterprise Edition (J2EE), or .NET. To enable the interface, you need Simple Object Access Protocol (SOAP), SOAP with Attachments (SwA), and Java Remote Method Invocation (RMI) along with other Internet protocols, principally Hypertext Transfer Protocol (HTTP).

Although we have a variety of Web Services architectures, Web Services, at a basic level, can be considered a universal client/server architecture that allows disparate systems to communicate with each other without using proprietary client libraries, according to the WebMethods whitepaper, *Implementing Enterprise WebServices with the WebMethods Integration Platform* (March 2002, http://www.webmethods.com/content/1,1107,EnterpriseWebServices,FF.html). The whitepaper points out that "this [architecture] simplifies the development process typically associated with client/server applications by effectively eliminating code dependencies between client and server" and "the server interface information is disclosed to the client via a configuration file encoded in a standard format (WSDL.)" This approach allows the server to publish a single file for all target client platforms.

For the purposes of this paper, we present the architecture stacks starting with the most simple, proceed to the more complex ones, and then compare them.

More simple	WebServices.Org
	The Stencil Group
	IBM
More complex	W3C

After this, we will cover other architecture types from Microsoft, Sun Microsystems, Oracle, Hewlett-Packard, BEA Systems, and Borland.

Based on initial findings or the current state of implementations, IBM's architecture looks to be the most acceptable. All architectures will eventually come into one umbrella, as there is a risk that if companies go away and keep on building their own extensions to the basic architecture stack, the promise of Web Services could be lost. The IBM versions, current and future, could serve as an industry-wide Standard Stack model, after W3C accepts new standards resulting from, for example, the convergence of IBM's WSFL and Microsoft's XLANG on workflow processes.

WebServices.Org

The following is the Web Services stack from WebServices.Org.

Layer	Example
Service Negotiation	Trading Partner Agreement
Workflow, Discovery, Registries	UDDI, ebXML registries, IBM WSFL, MS XLANG
Service Description Language	WSDL/WSCL

Layer	Example
Messaging	SOAP/XML Protocol
Transport Protocols	HTTP, HTTPS, FTP, SMTP
Business Issues	Management, Quality of Service, Security, Open Standards

Service Negotiation

The business logic process starts at the Services Negotiation layer (the top) with, say, two trading partners negotiating and agreeing on the protocols used to aggregate Web Services. This layer is also referred to as the Process Definition layer, covering document, workflow, transactions, and process flow.

Workflow, Discovery, Registries

The stack then moves to the next layer to establish workflow processes using Web Services Flow Language (WSFL) and MS XLANG, which is an XML language to describe workflow processes and spawn them. Microsoft previously achieved recognition for WSDL by working with IBM. History may repeat itself since IBM now has a similar technology to XLANG. In April 2001, IBM published WSFL. Gartner expected IBM and Microsoft to jointly agree to submit a proposal to W3C to combine XLANG and WSFL by the end of 2001. Yet, the W3C web site has not indicated whether it has received the proposal for consideration. If it did, the proposal has not yet been posted on the web site (June 2002).

WSFL specifies how a Web Service is interfaced with another. With it, you can determine whether the Web Services should be treated as an activity in one workflow or as a series of activities. While WSFL complements WSDL (Web Services Definition Language) and is transition-based, XLANG is an extension of WSDL and block-structured based. WSFL supports two model types: **flow** and **global** models. The flow model describes business processes that a collection of Web Services needs to achieve. The global model describes how Web Services interact with one another. XLANG, on the other hand, allows orchestration of Web Services into business processes and composite Web Services. WSFL is strong on model presentation while XLANG does well with the long-running interaction of Web Services.

You may declare a Web Service as private, meaning that it cannot expose details of what it does to public applications. You can create Web Services with the WebMethod Attribute in Visual Basic.NET, or with EJB wrappers for existing J2EE applications in either the Internet (public) or intranet (private) environment. You may declare them as public or private methods when you code.

Among the software supporting WSFL is IBM WebSphere Process Manager (previously known as MQ Series Workflow) that automates business process flows, optimizes Enterprise Application Integration (EAI) with people workflow, provides scalability, and complies with the Workflow Coalition and multi-platform capabilities. MS XLANG is the language implemented in BizTalk Server 2000 from Microsoft.

239

Web Services that can be exposed may, for example, get information on credit validation activities from a public directory or registry, such as Universal Description, Discovery and Integration (UDDI). The ebXML, E-Services Village, BizTalk.org, and xml.org registries and Bowstreet's (a stock service brokerage) Java-based UDDI (jUDDI) are other directories that could be used with UDDI in conjunction with Web Services for business-to-business (B2B) transactions in a complex EAI infrastructure under certain conditions. Web Services is still primarily an interfacing architecture, and needs an integration platform to which it is connected. Such an integration platform would cover the issue of integrating an installed base of applications that cannot work as Web Services yet.

The first release of UDDI's Business Registry became fully operational in May 2001, enabling businesses to register and discover Web Services via the Internet. Its original intent was to enable electronic catalogues in which businesses and services could be listed. The UDDI specification defines a way to publish and discover information about services. In November 2001, the UDDI Business Registry v2 beta became publicly available.

Hewlett Packard Company, IBM, Microsoft, and SAP launched a beta implementation of their UDDI sites that have conformed to the latest specification, including enhanced support for deploying public and private Web Service registries, and the interface (SOAP/HTTP API) that the client could use to interact with the registry server. In addition to the public UDDI Business Registry sites, enterprises can also deploy private registries on their intranet to manage internal Web Services using the UDDI specification. Access to internal Web Service information may also be extended to a private network of business partners.

Service Description Language

As you move further down the stack, you need WSDL to connect to a Web Service. This language is an XML format for describing network services. With it, service requesters can search for and find the information on services via UDDI, which, in turn, returns the WSDL reference that can be used to bind to the service.

Web Service Conversational Language (WSCL) helps developers use the XML Schema to better describe the structure of data in a common format (say, with new data types) the customers, Web browsers, or indeed any XML-enabled software programs can recognize. This protocol can be used to specify a Web Service interface and to describe service interactions.

Messaging

Now, we get to the Messaging layer in the stack where SOAP acts as the envelope for XML-based messages, covering message packaging, routing, guaranteed delivery, and security. Messages are sent back and forth regarding the status of various Web Services as the work progresses (say, from customer order to shipping product out of the warehouse).

Transport Protocols

When a series of messages completes its rounds, the stack goes to its penultimate layer: the transport layer using Hypertext Transfer Protocol (HTTP), Secure HTTP (HTTPS), Reliable HTTP (HTTPR), File Transfer Protocol (FTP), or Standard Mail Transfer Protocol (SMTP). Then, each Web Service takes a ride over the Internet to provide a service requester with services or give a status report to a service provider or broker.

Business Issues

Finally, the Business Issues row in the table lists other key areas of importance to the use and growth of Web Services. Without consideration to these points, Web Services could quickly become objects of ridicule.

The Stencil Group

Now let's take a look at the Stencil Group's Web Services technology stack. It is similar to that of WebServices.Org with three exceptions:

1. The WebServices.Org stack does not divide the layers into emerging and core components. Not doing so could confuse the reader as to which standards are emerging. What is now an emerging standard could become a core standard at a future date.

2. The Stencil Group does not apply Management, Quality of Service, Open Standards, and Security to any layer. The reader could get the wrong impression that they are proprietary and treated as not important. When this happens, the reader will opt for another architecture stack that has these features.

3. The Stencil Group starts the stack with undefined business rules while WebServices.Org begins with a clearly defined business process such as service agreement. The reader could get confused on what undefined business rules are, and how many would eventually be defined.

Layer	Type
Other Business Rules (undefined)	Emerging Layers
Web Services Flow Language (WSFL)	
Universal Description, Discovery and Integration (UDDI)	
Web Services Description Language (WSDL)	
Simple Object Access Protocol (SOAP)	Core Layers
Extensible Markup Language (XML)	
Common Internet Protocols (TCP/IP, HTTP)	

IBM

The IBM Conceptual Web Services stack is part of their Web Services Conceptual Architecture (WSCA) 1.0 (http://www-4.ibm.com/software/solutions/Webservices/pdf/WSCA.pdf). It is presented in a slightly different way than that of the first two stacks, by starting with Web Services tools and then showing what each layer is used for.

Tools	Layer		
TPA (Trading Partner Agreement)	Service Negotiation		
WSFL	Service Flow		
UDDI+WSEL	Service Description	Service Publication (Dynamic UDDI) Service Directory (Static UDDI)	Endpoint Description
WSDL	Service Interface Service Implementation		
SOAP	XML-Based Messaging		
HTTP, FTP, email, MQ, IIOP	Network		
Quality of Service, Management, Security	Business Issues		

The IBM Web Services stack does not show WSCL and ebXML, included in the WebServices.Org stack. It associates the Network layer with WebSphere MQ (previously IBM MQSeries) messaging systems and the Internet Inter-ORB Protocol (IIOP) – a protocol CORBA uses to transmit data, information, and messages between applications. They do not appear in either that of WebServices.Org or The Stencil Group. IBM considers WSDL as a description of the service endpoints where individual business operations can be accessed. WSFL uses WSDL for the description of service interfaces and their protocol bindings. WSFL also relies on WSEL (Web Services Endpoint Language), an endpoint description language, to describe non-operational characteristics of service endpoints, such as quality-of-service properties.

Together, WSDL, WSEL, and WSFL provide the core of the Web Services computing stack. IBM perceives UDDI in two categories: **static** and **direct**. Static UDDI refers to the Service Directory established after applying WSFL to the Service Flow, while dynamic UDDI pertains to the Service Publication of directory items. Similar to the WebServices.Org stack, the IBM stack applies QoS, management, and security to all layers.

As of May 2001, IBM announced software and tools that enable businesses to create, publish, securely deploy, host, and manage Web Services applications, using the IBM Web Services stack as the framework. They include WebSphere Application Server Version 4.0, WebSphere Studio Technology Preview for Web Services, WebSphere Business Integrator, DB2 Version 7.2, Tivoli Web Services Manager (to monitor performance of all aspects of the Web Services environment), and Lotus software suite (to enable Web collaboration, knowledge management, and distance learning). WebSphere was originally the collective name of IBM's J2EE application server family. It has since been stretched to include most of their middleware and application development offerings, such as MQSeries Workflow (now known as WebSphere Process Manager). IBM currently offers a Web Services ToolKit (WSTK) to help in designing and executing Web Service applications, and enabling them to find one another and collaborate in business transactions without programming requirements or human intervention.

W3C

The W3C Web Services Workshop, led by IBM and Microsoft, has agreed that the architecture stack consists of three components: Wire, Description, and Discovery.

Wire Stack

The following table shows what layers constitute the Wire Stack.

Other "extensions"	
Attachments	Routing
Security	Reliability
SOAP	
XML	

As you will notice, this Wire Stack has extensions to two layers: SOAP and XML. This means whenever SOAP is used as the envelope for XML messages, they must be attached, secure, reliable, and routed to the intended service requester or provider. In the stacks of other organizations, SOAP and XML are not treated as "extensions." IBM, for instance, refers to SOAP as a tool for its stack layer, "XML-Based Messaging."

Description Stack

The Description Stack, the most important component, consists of five layers:

Business Process Orchestration		
Message Sequencing		
Service Capabilities Configuration		
Service Description (WSDL)	Service Interface	WSDL
	Service Description	
XML Schema		

This stack starts with orchestration of business processes from which the messages are sequenced, depending on how service capabilities are configured. Whatever comes out of the proposal on combining WSFL and MS XLANG that IBM and Microsoft submitted to the W3C last year, will be the tool for the Business Process Orchestration Layer. What needs to be resolved is to consider what parts of WSFL and MS XLANG are more open than the other: transition-based versus block-structured based control flow, and extending versus complementing WSDL among others.

The Service Capabilities Layer is similar to IBM's WSEL as mentioned in IBM WSCA 1.0 and WSFL 1.0 (http://www-4.ibm.com/software/solutions/Webservices/pdf/WSFL.pdf). Like IBM, the W3C uses WSDL to describe service interface and service implementation, neither of which is explicitly highlighted in other stacks. WSDL may use a hefty chuck of XML Schema and takes advantage of SOAP/HTTP bindings to WSDL. SMTP, Reliable HTTP (HTTPR), and HTTP GET are other possible bindings that could be used.

Discovery Stack

As the name implies, the Discovery Stack involves the use of UDDI, allowing businesses and trading partners to find, discover, and inspect one another in a directory over the Internet, as follows:

Directory (UDDI)
Inspection

The Inspection Layer refers to WSIL (Web Services Inspection Language) and WS-Inspection specifications. Please refer to the Microsoft section opposite for more information on WSIL.

Putting all three stack-components together, we have the Architecture Stack.

Wire Stack	Other "extensions"		
	Attachments	Routing	
	Security	Reliability	
	SOAP		
	XML		
Description Stack	Business Process Orchestration		
	Message Sequencing		
	Service Capabilities Configuration		
	Service Description (WSDL)	Service Interface	WSDL
		Service Description	
	XML Schema		
Discovery Stack	Directory (UDDI)		
	Inspection		

The remaining part of this paper covers Web Services architectures from Microsoft, Sun, Oracle, BEA Systems, Hewlett-Packard, and Borland.

Microsoft

On May 24, 2000, Microsoft announced it had posted three additional specifications on its XML Web Service Web site: XLANG, SOAP-Routing, and Direct Internet Message Encapsulation (DIME) protocol, a method of packaging up attachments in SOAP messages. SOAP-Routing along with DIME, however, were not included in .NET My Services (formerly codenamed "HailStorm"). This was because the Global XML Web Services Architecture (GXA) replaced SOAP-Routing with WS-Routing which supports one- and two-way messaging, including peer-to-peer conversation and long-running dialogs.

The global architecture builds upon the foundation of baseline specifications – SOAP, UDDI, and WSDL among others. In April 2001, Microsoft and IBM co-presented their vision of this architecture to the W3C Workshop on Web Services. Both vendors contributed to the development and implementation of the W3C Web Services Architecture Stack – more complex than their own versions.

Layer	Type
WS-Inspection, WS-License, WS-Referral, WS-Routing, WS-Security	Global Architecture
UDDI, WSDL, XML, SOAP	Baseline Architecture

The GXA is modular, meaning that you can use one specification with another to address a set of specific requirements. For example, **WS-Referral** does not explicitly specify security, but rather relies on other specifications in the architecture to enable the routing strategies used by the SOAP nodes in a message path.

Other specifications for the global architecture are:

❑ **WS-Inspection** assisting in the inspection of a site for available services. Due to the decentralized nature of Web Services, this specification doesn't work well if the communication partner is unknown. In such cases, you would be better off with UDDI. This specification (also known as WSIL) was announced by both IBM and Microsoft to the W3C in November 2001. It is another service discovery mechanism (http://www-106.ibm.com/developerworks/library/ws-wsilover/index.html) and is complementary to UDDI (http://www.webservicesarchitect.com/content/articles/modi01.asp).

❑ **WS-License** describing a set of commonly used license types and how they can be placed within the WS-Security "credential" tags, such as X.509 certificates and Kerberos tickets.

❑ **WS-Routing** referring to a simple, stateless, SOAP-based protocol for controlling the route of SOAP messages in an asynchronous manner over a variety of transports such as TCP, UDP, and HTTP.

❑ **WS-Security** describing enhancements to SOAP-messaging to provide three capabilities: credential exchange, message integrity, and message confidentiality, each of which you could use by itself or in combination with another as a way of contributing to a security model. For more details, see http://msdn.microsoft.com/ws/2002/04/Security/.

Additional specifications will become available as Microsoft releases them for public review.

To accommodate the architecture, Microsoft offers the .NET Framework as a platform for building, deploying, and running XML Web Services and applications. It allows a Web Service consumer to send and receive information in a loosely coupled manner, including a description of the Web Services that it and other consumers offer. SOAP is supported by XML Schema Data types (XSD), WSDL, XML, and HTTP.

As part of the Microsoft .NET initiative, Microsoft provided a user-centric architecture and a set of XML Web Services, collectively called Microsoft .NET My Services. Using .NET Passport as the basic user credential, the .NET My Services architecture defined identity, security, and data models that are common to all services and can help orchestrate a wide variety of applications, devices, and services – all in one basket. The initial set of .NET My Services included:

- **.NET Profile.** Name, nickname, special dates, picture, address.

- **.NET Contacts.** Electronic relationships/address book.

- **.NET Locations.** Electronic and geographical location and rendezvous.

- **.NET Alerts.** Alert subscription, management, and routing.

- **.NET Presence.** Online, offline, busy, free, which device(s) to send alerts to.

- **.NET Inbox.** Inbox for items like e-mail and voice mail, including existing mail systems.

- **.NET Calendar.** Time and task management.

- **.NET Documents.** Raw document storage.

- **.NET ApplicationSettings.** Application settings.

- **.NET FavoriteWebSites.** Favorite URLs and other web identifiers.

- **.NET Wallet.** Receipts, payment instruments, coupons, and other transaction records.

- **.NET Devices.** Device settings, capabilities.

- **.NET services.** Services provided for an identity.

- **.NET Lists.** General purpose lists.

- **.NET Categories.** A way to group lists.

Since the first publication of this paper, however, Microsoft has rethought its strategy. The move is away from providing .NET My Services as a global set of Web Services, and towards being a solution internal to a company.

Sun Microsystems

Sun Open Net Environment (Sun ONE) is an open framework to support "smart" Web Services, and in which the Java 2 Platform Enterprise Edition (J2EE) platform plays a fundamental role. The Sun ONE Web Services developer model shows how developers can build Web Services, using XML, servlets, JavaServer Pages, EJB architecture, and Java technologies as shown overleaf. Note that EJB wrappers allow existing applications to become Web Services.

Component	Purpose
Java API for XML Processing (JAXP)	Provides a Java interface to DOM, SAX, and XSLT.
Java API for XML Binding (JAXB)	Provides a way to bind XML data to Java code. A developer uses JAXB to compile XML schema information into Java objects. At runtime, JAXB automatically maps the XML document data to the Java object, and vice versa.
Java API for XML Messaging (JAXM)	Provides a Java interface to XML messaging systems, such as the ebXML Message Service, XMLP, and SOAP
Java API for XML Registries (JAXR)	Provides a Java interface to XML registries and repositories such as the ebXML Registry and Repository, and the UDDI Business Registry.
Java API for XML-based RPC (JAX-RPC)	Provides direct support for an RPC programming convention for XML messaging systems, such as SOAP and XMLP.

The Sun ONE architecture recommends four types of XML-messaging systems: SOAP, SwA (SOAP with Attachments), ebXML Message Service, and XML Protocol (XMLP). ebXML Message Service extends SwA by adding a QoS network that ensures reliable and secure message delivery. An ebXML message can transport any number of XML documents and non-XML attachments.

Layer	Type
JAXP, JAXB, JAXM, JAXR, JAX-RPC, servlets, JSP, and EJB	Java Technologies
UDDI, ebXML	Registries
WSDL	Service Description Language (may be automatically generated depending on a partner module)
SOAP, SwA, ebXML, XMLP	XML-Messaging Systems

A Web Service example is myServices.ONE that provides a shopping basket spanning multiple sites. Created using iNsight for Forte for Java, this Web Service allows Internet shoppers to view and update their purchases in one basket. Making up myServices.ONE are three basic services:

❑ **myIdentity** providing identification across the sites. This identifies the users uniquely across multiple sites, so they will not log in repeatedly as they go from one site (http://www.barnesandnoble.com/) to another (http://www.sears.com/).

❑ **myBasket** consolidating items from multiple sites. Users can add items to the basket from different sites and view the consolidated list of all items in a central, secure basket.

❑ **myJeeves** automating the purchase process across various domains. It handles the actual payment and shipping details.

Oracle

The core of the Oracle9*i* Web Services Framework is the Web Service Broker, a J2EE execution engine deployed in the Oracle9*i* Application Server. Application developers can access the engine using the Oracle Web Services Java client APIs that provide a level of abstraction over the communication protocol to connect to the execution engine (direct Java method calls, PL/SQL calls, HTTP, HTTPS, or JMS (Java Message Service) messages).

Oracle's Web Services framework is based on open industry standards, defining four requirements: description, discovery, request/response, and transport.

Requirement	Standard	Remarks
Description	WSDL	All service attributes, including input/output parameters, version, provider, and copyright/licensing information, are stored in registries. The Oracle9*i* Web Services framework supports two registries: ❑ Service Registry: stores service definitions (called service descriptors). ❑ Application Profile Registry: stores information about the consumer applications that are allowed to access services.

Table continued on following page

Requirement	Standard	Remarks
Discovery	UDDI LDAP	Search registries for services with the desired characteristics. ❑ Development-time: Service descriptors can be published in UDDI registries (natively or in WSDL). ❑ Run-time: Service descriptors can be stored in Oracle Internet Directory (OID) for security, centralized management, and lookup (via LDAP).
Request/ Response	XML	Request and response formats are defined per service in XML documents and XML Schema documents.
Transport	SOAP ICE (See Note 1)	Send requests to services and receive responses. Oracle9*i* Web Services framework includes adapters for common transport protocols and supports custom adapters.

*Note 1: **Information and Content Exchange**. A syndication protocol that standardizes interaction between information publishers and subscribers via the Web.*

The illustration opposite shows how various parts of the Oracle9*i* Web Services framework are related to one another. Starting in the upper-left, Consumer Applications send XML Service Requests to the Web Services Client Library, using SOAP and ICE. The Client Library provides Java and PL/SQL interfaces to the Web Services Broker. Interacting with the Broker for Web Services and Database Services is accomplished through SOAP, Java reflection, or JDBC via software components called adapters. When the Broker returns results to the Services, it dispatches them to the Consumer Applications for display to end users. Software components called transformers allow the framework to support several output formats, including HTML pages, and pages formatted for wireless and mobile devices:

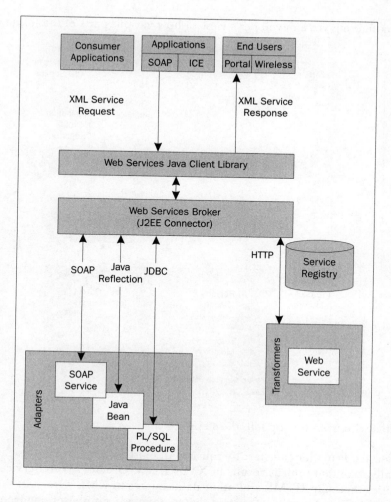

The Oracle9*i* Web Services framework insulates developers from the complexity of interacting with multiple information sources, protocols, and delivery channels. It is component-based to maximize reuse. It includes tools for creating, managing, and monitoring services.

The following figure gives a developer's view of how various parts of the framework interact:

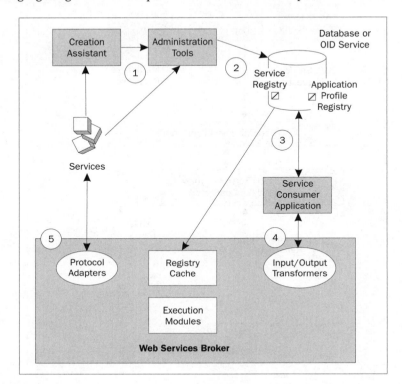

Working clockwise from the top left, the steps are:

1. A Service Provider can start by reusing an existing web or database application – ideally, one that returns results in XML. If not, Oracle9*i* Web Services includes utilities that map HTML and other data sources to XML. Oracle9*i* Web Services also includes a Creation Assistant that generates a simple service from a web page.

2. Next, a Service Administrator uses a tool of choice (command-line utility or graphical Oracle Enterprise Manager) to register the service, making it available to consumers.

3. Service Consumer Applications query the Service Registry to get the data required to find and invoke a service. Data about Service Consumer Applications, including access privileges, is stored and maintained in the Application Profile Registry.

4. Then, the Service Consumer Application interacts with the Web Services Broker, which uses an input transformer, if needed, to convert the Consumer's request to a format it can use internally. When the service returns a result, the Web Services Broker applies an output transformer, if needed, and dispatches the data to the Service Consumer application. The Service Consumer Application can display the data to end users, or use it in the flow of some business logic.

5. The Web Services Broker invokes the service via an adapter appropriate for the service's protocol (HTTP, SMTP, etc.).

Hewlett-Packard

In May 1999, HP was the first to develop a Web Services platform under the name E-speak. Hewlett-Packard kept quiet as Microsoft, Oracle, and IBM responded, until March 2001 when it put a large number of software products together in two groups. The first of these groups was the NetAction suite, which contained products for Web Services, with 25 new products, including Bluestone. Bluestone software, which runs transactions for e-commerce, took an important role. Also brought under NetAction were E-speak, Chai (HP's version of embedded Java), and Open Call, an API bundle for call centers, and HP Security. Analysts say HP has possibilities as a major player.

The Hewlett Packard Web Services Platform supports both Web Service interactions and Web Service implementation bindings via an architecture that addresses three key infrastructure services, as shown in the following illustration of the HP Web Services Platform. In addition, supporting functions that handle transactional semantics, security, availability, scalability, monitoring, and management are provided by the underlying HP Total-e-Server platform.

Application Processing (Workflow, servlet, EJB, JSP, Cocoon)	Security Transactions
Interaction Control (Envelope Processing, Dispatch to Application Components)	Availability Scalability
Messaging (Transports, Listeners, Content Format Handlers)	Monitoring Management Tools

BEA Systems

BEA Systems develop Web Services on the J2EE platform using the SOAP protocol. J2EE applications expose EJBs and JMS destinations as Web Services. Private registries (possibly based on UDDI) are used to integrate with partners by some applications. Typical enterprise application integration is based on the J2EE Connector Architecture (JCA). Shawn Willet, principal analyst at Sterling, commented, "The JCA technology is a bit immature and a lot of enterprise users may want to go with a ... more mature tool". BEA views their application platform as an integration platform.

Unlike other vendors, BEA (and Borland) uses Business Transaction Protocol (BTP) – an XML dialect for orchestrating inter-enterprise business transactions that address the unique business-to-business (B2B) requirements. This protocol is stack-agnostic, so it can be easily implemented in conjunction with other standards such as ebXML or SOAP. For example, a header can be added to the ebXML message envelope to carry the transaction context defined by BTP.

BEA offers two types of Web Services: remote procedure call (RPC)-style and message-style. The first type supports simple Web Services (like stock quotes), is synchronous, and is often given by vendors, while the second type is targeted toward a loosely coupled, asynchronous model and is a key requirement for enterprise-class Web Services.

RPC-Style Web Services

You use a stateless session EJB to implement an RPC-style Web Service. When clients, for example, invoke the Web Service specific to a service, they send parameter values to the Web Service, which executes the required methods, and then sends back the return values. RPC-style Web Services are synchronous, meaning that when a client sends a request, it waits for a response before doing anything else. This means that they are tightly coupled with a resemblance to traditional distributed object paradigms, such as RMI and DCOM. One example is a computer screen showing a stock quote ticker with an input block, with which the user can get current information on a list of stock during trading hours.

Message-Style Web Services

This type of Web Service is loosely coupled and document-driven rather than being associated with a service-specific interface. When a client invokes a message-style Web Service, the client typically sends it an entire document, such as a purchase order, rather than a discrete set of parameters. The Web Service accepts the entire document, processes it, and may or may not return a result message, such as a manager's acknowledgment of the order. This means the client does not wait for the response before it can do something else. It can wait for hours, days, or even weeks unless the system has some kind of mechanism to alert the manager to respond within a time frame.

You can also use a message-style Web Service to request a record with the information you need all at once in an XML message – last name, first name, social security number, and so on. This coarse-grained communication example is far better than making three or more separate calls to get the record.

Borland

Borland offers cross-platform development by, for example, using Delphi 6 to create Web Services running on IIS for Windows and then take that same code to Linux, recompile using Kylix 2, and deploy on Apache Web servers. The Internet protocols they use to expose internal Web Services and access external Web Services include: SOAP, WSDL, UDDI, BTP, and ebXML.

Both Delphi 6 and Kylix 2 provide three SNAP™ families you need to build and deploy Web Services. They are:

❑ *BizSnap* that simplifies e-business integration by creating and using XML/SOAP-based Web Services. It interacts with Microsoft's BizTalk.

❑ *WebSnap* a component-based web application development framework that supports leading Web Application Servers, including Apache, Netscape, and Microsoft Internet Information Services (IIS).

❑ *DataSnap* a Web Service-enabled database middleware component that enables any client application or service to easily connect with any major database over the Internet. It supports all major database servers such as Oracle, MS-SQL Server, Informix, IBM DB2, Sybase, and InterBase. Client applications connect to DataSnap servers through industry-standard SOAP/XML HTTP connections over the Internet without bulky database client drivers and complex configuration requirements; DCOM, CORBA, and TCP/IP connections are also supported.

Conclusion

The W3C Architecture Stack is complex as compared to the stacks presented by other organizations. While this stack is theoretically correct, it may be inconsistent from a customer or end user's perspective. The W3C's Wire Stack is at the top; however, the SOAP/XML protocols are usually found at the bottom stack layer, such as in the WebServices.Org Transport Protocols layer, the Stencil Group's Common Internet Protocols layer, and IBM Web Services Network. While the W3C's Discovery Stack is at the bottom, UDDI is at the second layer for WebServices.Org, The Stencil Groups third layer and IBMs third layer that combines with WSEL. While the WebServices.Org Business Processes and The Stencil Group's Other Business Rules are similar to the Business Process Orchestration in W3C's Description Stack, IBM's stack lacks a layer on business processes. IBM, a primary member of the W3C Web Services Workshop, presented its simpler version, and recently included TPA as its top layer.

Microsoft, another primary member of the workshop, presented the GXA apparently derived from the W3C Architecture Stack. Its global architecture is restricted to Microsoft operating systems, while in Sun's ONE Architecture Web Services run on a wider range of platforms. In the near future, we will see .NET on non-Microsoft operating systems as a result of the ongoing efforts to make .NET Web Services available to non-Microsoft users in all five categories: consumers, service providers, independent software vendors, managed service providers, and corporate application developers. When this happens, vendors' future market share of Web Services may change today's landscape. Around that time, an architecture stack (similar to IBM's) will rise on the horizon – as the industry-wide standard.

Authors: J. Jeffrey Hanson, with additional material by Chanoch Wiggers

- Description
- Implementation
- Publishing, Discovery, Binding
- Invocation and Execution
- Time to Choose

.NET and J2EE, a Comparison

Introduction

Web Services is the term being used to describe some of the technologies for solving the problems of integrating applications across the enterprise and between disparate companies over the Internet. Web Services are also being described as the concepts and technologies for delivering services and content to any Web-enabled client or device. A simplified attempt at defining Web Services generically might be as follows:

> **Web Services are URI-addressable resources that use existing Internet infrastructures and protocols to allow applications, services, and devices to discover them, connect to them, and execute their business logic using remote method calls.**

Sun is touting its Java Web Services Developer Pack (http://java.sun.com/webservices/webservicespack.html) as its Java 2 Platform, Enterprise Edition (J2EE) toolset for wrapping XML-based Web Services technologies such as SOAP, UDDI, ebXML, and WSDL with Java objects and interfaces. At the same time, Microsoft is working on its .NET platform. Among other things, .NET is designed to facilitate the development of interoperable Web Services. As usual, Microsoft is presenting a comprehensive set of development tools to accommodate this new technology. Among these is the SOAP 2.0 Toolkit (http://msdn.microsoft.com/library/default.asp?url=/library/en-us/soap/htm/kit_intro_19bj.asp). This toolkit provides a broad range of SOAP support tools such as a component that maps Web Service operations to COM-object method calls. Similar facilities have been built into the .NET Framework from the start, and these can be unleashed using Visual Studio .NET.

Offerings from other sources include the Apache SOAP project and IBM's Web Services Toolkit.

The Apache SOAP project (http://xml.apache.org/soap/) is an open-source, Java-based implementation of the SOAP v1.1 (http://www.w3.org/TR/SOAP) and SOAP Messages with Attachments (http://www.w3.org/TR/SOAP-attachments) specifications in Java. Apache SOAP can be used as a client library to invoke Web Services or as a server-side tool to implement Web Services.

IBM's Web Services Toolkit (http://alphaworks.ibm.com/tech/webservicestoolkit) provides a run-time environment and examples to design, implement, and execute Web Services on any operating system that supports Java 1.3 or above. The toolkit provides a Web Services architectural blueprint, a private UDDI registry, some sample programs, some utility services, and tools for developing and deploying Web Services. The toolkit also includes a Web Services client API that can be used to access a UDDI registry.

Web Services Overview

The Web Services model as it stands attempts to allow potentially unrelated services to be dynamically combined, in a loosely coupled manner over a distributed network. Web Services encourages developers to evolve to a services-based model.

Web Services are currently concerned with four basic challenges:

1. Service Description.

2. Service Implementation.

3. Service Publishing, Discovery, and Binding.

4. Service Invocation and Execution.

Current technologies are solving these challenges by:

5. Describing Web Services using the Web Services Description Language (WSDL).

6. Using XML as the common language for Web Service communication. XML is ubiquitous throughout all aspects of Web Services. Web Services can be implemented in any programming language that can read and write XML, and can be deployed on any Web-accessible platform.

7. Publishing Web Services in a registry to be discovered later by interested parties accessing the registry. One type of registry provides a directory service for Web Service providers and their services. This registry provides information categorized by industry-type, product-type, service-location, service binding, etc. Taxonomies are used to enable searches on this information. One implementation of this registry is based on the Universal Description, Discovery and Integration specification (UDDI). Another type of registry also acts as a repository where Web Services entities such as a business-process schema are stored. A current example of this type of registry is the electronic business XML (ebXML) Registry and Repository.

8. Invoking Web Services over an existing Internet protocol such as HTTP or SMTP using the Simple Object Access Protocol (SOAP).

Service Description

In order for Web Services to proliferate it is important to be able to describe them in some structured way. The Web Services Description Language (WSDL) (http://www.w3c.org/TR/wsdl) addresses this need by defining an XML grammar for describing Web Services as collections of message-enabled endpoints or ports.

In WSDL, the abstract definition of endpoints and messages is separated from their concrete deployment or bindings. The concrete protocol and data format specifications for a particular endpoint type constitute a binding. An endpoint is defined by associating a web address with a binding, and a collection of endpoints defines a service. A WSDL document uses the following elements in the definition of Web Services:

❑ **Types** – data type definitions used to describe the messages to be exchanged.

❑ **Message** – a typed definition of the data to be exchanged. Messages and operations are bound in order to form an endpoint or port.

❑ **Operation** – a description of an action exposed by the service. Operations can support input and/or output messages.

❑ **Port Type** – a named set of abstract operations and related messages supported by one or more ports.

❑ **Binding** – a concrete protocol and message format specification for operations and messages defined by a particular port type.

❑ **Port** – a single endpoint defined as a combination of a binding and a network address. In a WSDL document, services are defined as collections of ports or endpoints. The abstract definition of a port is separated from its concrete protocol and data format specification.

❑ **Service** – a collection of related ports. Multiple port definitions, sharing the same port type within a service, provide semantically equivalent alternatives to service consumers. This allows service consumers to choose the port or ports to communicate with.

The following example taken from W3C's WSDL (http://www.w3.org/TR/wsdl) site shows a simple stock-quote WSDL document:

```
<?xml version="1.0"?>
<definitions name="StockQuote"
             targetNamespace="http://example.com/stockquote/definitions"
             xmlns:tns="http://example.com/stockquote/definitions"
             xmlns:xsd1="http://example.com/stockquote/schemas"
             xmlns:soap="http://schemas.xmlsoap.org/wsdl/soap/"
             xmlns="http://schemas.xmlsoap.org/wsdl/">

    <message name="GetLastTradePriceInput">
      <part name="body" element="xsd1:TradePriceRequest"/>
    </message>

    <message name="GetLastTradePriceOutput">
      <part name="body" element="xsd1:TradePrice"/>
    </message>

    <portType name="StockQuotePortType">
      <operation name="GetLastTradePrice">
        <input message="tns:GetLastTradePriceInput"/>
        <output message="tns:GetLastTradePriceOutput"/>
      </operation>
    </portType>
</definitions>
```

This, simply put, describes a service that provides Stock Quotes. It accepts a Trade Price Request and returns a Last Trade Price as output. This description of the service is quite devoid of implementation details and yet provides sufficient information to use the services. Web Services can, in this way, provide a system for hiding the implementation specifics of systems making interoperability possible.

J2EE

J2EE-enabled Web Services are described by WSDL documents. Third parties who want to transact business with a J2EE-enabled Web Service company can look up information about the company's Web Services in a registry. There, they will find links to URLs containing the WSDL information needed to format XML documents correctly for integrating with the Web Services exposed by the company.

.NET

As with a J2EE Web Service, a .NET Web Service supports the WSDL 1.1 specification and uses a WSDL document to describe itself. An XML namespace, however, is used within the WSDL document to uniquely identify the Web Service's endpoints.

.NET provides a client-side component that allows an application to invoke Web Service operations described by a WSDL document and a server-side component that maps Web Service operations to COM-object method calls as described by a WSDL and a Web Services Meta Language (WSML) (http://msdn.microsoft.com/library/en-us/soap/htm/soap_overview_72r0.asp) file. This file is needed for Microsoft's implementation of SOAP.

Service Implementation

Implementing Web Services currently means structuring data and operations inside of an XML document that complies with the SOAP specification. Once a Web Service component is implemented, a client sends a message to the component as an XML document and the component sends an XML document back to the client as the response.

J2EE

Existing Java classes and applications can be wrapped using the Java API for XML-based RPC (JAX-RPC) and exposed as Web Services. JAX-RPC uses XML to make remote procedure calls (RPC) and exposes an API for marshaling (packing parameters and return values to be distributed) and unmarshaling arguments and for transmitting and receiving procedure calls.

With J2EE, business services written as Enterprise JavaBeans are wrapped and exposed as Web Services. The resulting wrapper is a SOAP-enabled Web Service that conforms to a WSDL interface based on the original EJB's methods.

The J2EE Web Service architecture is a set of XML-based frameworks, which provide infrastructures that allow companies to integrate business-service logic that was previously exposed as proprietary interfaces. Currently, J2EE supports Web Services via the Java API for XML Processing (JAXP). This API allows developers to perform any Web Service operation by manually parsing XML documents. For example, you can use JAXP to perform parsing operations with SOAP, UDDI, WSDL, and ebXML.

J2EE also uses the Java API for XML Messaging (JAXM) to integrate one back-end system with other back-end systems via the following five document-centric message exchanges:

1. A synchronous update whose response is an acknowledgment that the update was received.

2. An asynchronous update whose response is an acknowledgment that the update was received.

3. A synchronous inquiry whose response is data requested in the original message.

4. An asynchronous inquiry whose response is data requested in the original message.

5. An exchange where the sender sends a message and does not expect a reply.

When a JAXM client sends a message, the message first goes to a JAXM provider, which then handles the actual transmission of the message to its destination. A JAXM client receives a message from a JAXM provider that has received the message on behalf of the client and then forwarded the message. A more likely scenario is that a JAXM client will receive an XML message from another platform, and because it is in XML it will understand it.

.NET

.NET applications are no longer directly executed in native machine code. All programs are compiled to an intermediate binary code called the Microsoft Intermediate Language (MSIL). This portable, binary code is then compiled to native code using a Just In Time compiler (JIT) at run-time and run in a virtual machine called the Common Language Runtime (CLR). This is similar to the way that Java works, except .NET encompasses several languages; each is translated to MSIL, which is executed in the CLR using the JIT – simple, really.

With the .NET platform, Microsoft provides several languages based on the Common Language Infrastructure (CLI), such as Managed C++, JScript.NET, VB.NET, and C#. On December 13, 2001, ECMA (formerly the European Computer Manufacturers Association) ratified specifications for C# and the CLI making them official industry standards.

For existing Microsoft technologies like VB6, the Microsoft SOAP Toolkit offers components that construct, transmit, read, and process SOAP messages. The toolkit also includes an alternative to using the XML DOM API to process XML documents in SOAP messages called the SOAP Messaging Object (SMO) framework (http://msdn.microsoft.com/library/en-us/soap/htm/soap_adv_2wdv.asp). The toolkit provides a component that maps Web Service operations to COM-object method calls as described by the WSDL and WSML files of the service. Conversely, the toolkit provides a generator that will generate WSDL files from COM typelib descriptions.

Microsoft has merged its InterDev and Visual Studio products into a new development environment, Visual Studio .NET. Together with the .NET framework, practically all of the details of SOAP, XML, and Web Services discovery and binding are hidden from the user.

To create a Web Service with the .NET Framework outside of the Visual Studio.NET environment, you simply create a file with an ASMX extension. The ASP.NET run-time, part of the .NET Framework, recognizes this file as a Web Service and uses a built-in HTTP handler to process requests on it. The run-time then forwards the requests to a .NET class that's either included in the ASMX file or implemented separately. The following code shows a simple Web Service written in C#:

```
<%@ WebServices Language="C#" class="Hello" %>
using System.Web.Services;
class Hello
{
    [WebMethod]
    public string SayHello(string userName)
    {
        return "Hello " + userName;
    }
}
```

This example demonstrates the WebServices directive, the directive for referencing the System.Web.Services namespace, and a public method with the WebMethod attribute. The WebMethod attribute makes a method accessible from a Web Services client. To deploy a .NET Web Service, the implementation code is saved to a file with the ASMX extension, in an IIS virtual directory.

Service Publishing, Discovery, and Binding

Once a Web Service has been implemented, it must be published somewhere that allows interested parties to find it. Information about how a client would connect to a Web Service and interact with it must also be exposed somewhere accessible to them. This connection and interaction information is referred to as *binding* information.

Registries are currently the primary means to publish, discover, and bind Web Services. Registries contain the data structures and taxonomies used to describe Web Services and Web Service providers. A registry can be hosted either by private organizations or by neutral third parties. Currently two types of registries, UDDI and ebXML, are being addressed by the Web Services community.

At the time of this writing, IBM and Microsoft have announced the Web Services Inspection Language (WSIL) specification to allow applications to browse Web servers for XML Web Services. WSIL promises to complement UDDI by making it easier to discover available services on web sites not listed in the UDDI registries.

J2EE

Sun Microsystems is positioning its Java API for XML Registries (JAXR) as a single general-purpose API for interoperating with multiple registry types. The Java API for XML Registries (JAXR) provides a uniform and standard API for accessing disparate registries within the Java platform. A registry provider is an implementation of a Web Services registry conforming to a registry specification. A JAXR provider provides an implementation of the JAXR specification typically as a façade around an existing registry provider such as a UDDI or ebXML registry. A JAXR client uses the JAXR API to access a registry via a JAXR provider.

There are three types of JAXR providers:

❑ The JAXR Pluggable Provider.

❑ The Registry-specific JAXR Provider.

❑ The JAXR Bridge Provider.

The Pluggable Provider implements features of the JAXR specification, which are independent of any specific registry type. The Registry-specific JAXR Provider implements the JAXR specification in a registry-specific manner. The JAXR Bridge Provider is not specific to any particular registry. It serves as a bridge to a class of registries such as ebXML or UDDI.

Sun provides a freely downloadable (http://www.sun.com/software/xml/developers/regrep/) ebXML implementation based on the J2EE platform and implements the ebXML Registry Information Model 1.0 and the ebXML Registry Services Specification 1.0. This registry/repository implementation uses EJB technology and includes the following components: a registry information model, registry services, a security model, a data access API, Java objects binding classes, and a JSP tag library.

.NET

At first, Microsoft had the discovery of Web Services with DISCO in the form of a discovery (DISCO) file. A published DISCO file is an XML document that contains links to other resources that describe the Web Service. Since the widespread adoption of UDDI, however, Microsoft has supported it in order to maximize interoperability between solutions in what is, after all, a set of specifications for interoperability.

In addition to providing a .NET UDDI server, the UDDI SDK provides support for Visual Studio .NET and depends on the .NET framework. Products such as Microsoft Office XP offer support for service discovery through UDDI.

Service Invocation and Execution

The Simple Object Access Protocol (SOAP) is a simple, lightweight XML-based protocol that defines a messaging framework for exchanging structured data and type information across the Web.

The SOAP specification consists of four main parts:

- ❑ A mandatory envelope for encapsulating data. The envelope contains an optional header element (`<SOAP-ENV:Header>`) and a mandatory body (`<SOAP-ENV:Body>`).
- ❑ Optional data encoding rules for representing application-defined data types, and a model for serializing non-syntactic data models (such as object).
- ❑ A request/response message exchange pattern.
- ❑ An optional binding between SOAP and HTTP.

SOAP can be used in combination with any transport protocol or mechanism that is able to transport the SOAP message.

Web Service recipients operate as SOAP listeners and can notify interested parties (other Web Services, applications, etc.) when a Web Service request is received. The SOAP listener validates a SOAP message against corresponding XML schemas as defined in a WSDL file. The SOAP listener then unmarshals the SOAP message, turning it into a format understandable by the Web Service implementation. Within the SOAP listener, message dispatchers can invoke the corresponding Web Service code implementation. Finally, business logic is performed to get the reply. The result of the business logic is transformed into a SOAP response and returned to the Web Service caller. This process is shown in the following diagram:

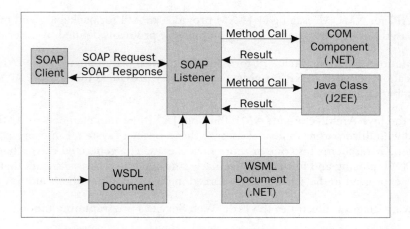

J2EE

J2EE uses the Java API for XML-based RPC (JAX-RPC) to send SOAP method calls to remote parties and receive the results. JAX-RPC enables Java technology developers to build Web Services incorporating XML-based RPC functionality according to the SOAP 1.1 specification.

Once a JAX-RPC service has been defined and implemented, the service is deployed on a server-side JAX-RPC run-time system. The deployment step depends on the type of component that has been used to implement the JAX-RPC service. For example, an EJB service that is implemented as a stateless session bean is deployed in an EJB container. A container-provided deployment tool provides support for the deployment of a JAX-RPC service.

During the deployment of a JAX-RPC service, the deployment tool configures one or more protocol bindings for this JAX-RPC service. A *binding* ties an abstract service definition to a specific XML-based protocol and transport. An example of a binding is SOAP 1.1 over HTTP.

A Web Service client uses a JAX-RPC service by invoking remote methods on a service port described by a WSDL document. A WSDL-to-Java compiler generates the client-side stub class, service definition interface, and additional classes for the service and its ports.

There are three different modes of interaction between clients and JAX-RPC services:

- **Synchronous Request-Response**: The client invokes a JAX-RPC procedure and blocks until it receives a return or an exception.

- **One-Way RPC**: The client invokes a JAX-RPC procedure but it does not block or wait until it receives a return.

- **Non-Blocking RPC Invocation**: The client invokes a JAX-RPC procedure and continues processing in the same thread then, later, blocks or polls for the return.

The Java API for XML Messaging or JAXM provides an API for packaging and transporting of message-based business transactions using on-the-wire protocols defined by emerging standards.

Implementations of JAXR (Java API for XML Registries) providers may use JAXM for communication between JAXR providers and registry providers that export an XML Messaging-based interface.

J2EE uses the Java Architecture for XML Binding (JAXB) to map elements in XML documents exchanged with third parties to Java classes, so that a business system can process them. JAXB compiles an XML schema into one or more Java classes. The generated classes handle the details of XML parsing and formatting. Similarly, the generated classes ensure that the constraints expressed in the schema are enforced in the resulting methods and Java data types.

The following diagram illustrates the J2EE Web Services programming model:

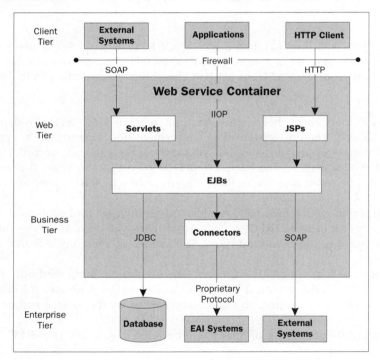

.NET

In Microsoft's .NET framework, interested parties can gain access to a Web Service by implementing a Web Service listener. In order to implement a Web Service listener, a system needs to understand SOAP messages, generate SOAP responses, provide a WSDL contract for the Web Service, and advertise the Service via UDDI. If the Web Service is hosted within IIS as an ASMX file, there is no need to implement a SOAP Listener, since IIS does that job for you. Also .NET has built-in classes that understand SOAP messages.

Microsoft Developers creating SOAP-based Web Service listeners and consumers currently have three choices:

1. Construct a Web Service listener manually, using MSXML, ASP, ISAPI, etc.

2. Use the Microsoft Soap Toolkit version 2 to build a Web Service listener that connects to a business facade, implemented using COM.

3. Use the built-in .NET SOAP message classes.

The Microsoft SOAP Toolkit 2.0 offers a client-side component that lets an application invoke Web Service operations described by a WSDL document.

The following diagram illustrates the .NET Web Services programming model:

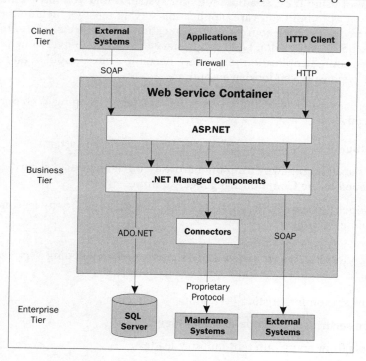

Time To Choose

Having looked from a high level at how J2EE and .NET handle Web Services, we are faced with a choice – which version do we implement? From a purely technical standpoint, each method has advantages and disadvantages: .NET code often runs faster than J2EE systems, but only works on Microsoft operating systems; it is often easier to turn existing J2EE code into a Web Service due to the object-oriented nature of Java, whereas .NET code will have to be written from scratch, particularly where the original code was Visual Basic; the list continues.

It is worth noting that there is a project underway to create an open-source implementation of the .NET Framework, so non-Microsoft operating systems will soon be able to support .NET. See http://www.go-mono.com/ for more details. As standardization continues, the availability of .NET on non-Microsoft platforms will become easier. Although much existing Microsoft code is not object oriented, .NET is entirely object oriented, including VB.NET. Writing wrappers for VB components is no harder than doing the same for a Java component – the difficulty arises when the VB code provides functionality that isn't exposed as a component.

The key advantage, perhaps, of using the .NET approach to Web Services is that it has been designed for that purpose, whereas J2EE is being retrofitted by the addition of a number of APIs. Despite this, J2EE is an inherently modular platform, so the problem here is one of maturity of technology; .NET has only just reached final release.

One advantage of using J2EE as a base for your system is that you have a much wider choice of vendor for your pre-built software (application servers mostly), including many open source projects. In many ways, open-source J2EE application servers are closer to the standards laid down for Java, because they don't add proprietary extensions to overcome problems. As time creeps on, open-source application servers are becoming more popular, and more competitive than the more expensive vendor-driven options.

Microsoft offers several compelling business reasons for developing Web Services using its .NET architecture:

❑ Easy migration for existing COM and Windows-based systems.

❑ .NET's abstraction away from the hardware offers increased security for applications developed to the Common Language Runtime.

❑ Developer tools are, as usual, world-class and greatly ease the learning curve and ease of development.

J2EE, as well, offers several enticing business reasons for developing Web Services using its technologies:

❑ Easy migration for existing Java shops.

❑ Proven security at the code-execution level.

❑ Support from many different industry leaders.

Ultimately, unless you are starting your system from the bottom up, your choice of Web Services implementation is more than likely going to be influenced by your present system. If you have a team of skilled Java programmers, with a J2EE business system, realistically you'll want to continue with J2EE. Similarly with .NET, there is no sense in wasting your investments in Microsoft products (both time and money) by switching to J2EE – you're going to want to keep on with what your team knows best. As Integrated Development Environments (IDE) for Java become more powerful, the ease of development with Visual Studio (.NET) may no longer be the deciding factor it may once have been.

From an adoption point of view, while Microsoft has provided systems for wrapping pre-.NET code so that it can work in the .NET framework and vice versa, the nature of the MS languages before this change means that many will probably be unsuitable for this purpose. The reverse – the ability to wrap .NET services so that they can work in a COM environment – means instant interoperability with legacy systems while allowing a migration to the .NET framework.

Existing Microsoft shops are unlikely to move to J2EE, due to the current investment in Microsoft technologies (skills base, hardware, software, and business relationships). In addition, the perceived cost of Microsoft-based solutions is lower, although there is room for clarification on the total cost of ownership. A primary problem in J2EE systems appears to be over-engineering at the cost of development time, performance, and the hardware needed to run these systems. On the other hand, Microsoft systems are PC-based, and these systems are inherently less scalable and powerful, and the cost for scaling is high.

It may be worth noting that Microsoft has a conflict of interest in the area of Web Services. Since Microsoft wish to be the providers of Web Services in addition to providing the tools and specifications for implementing Web Services, it appears to have a first option advantage in providing services such as single sign-on authentication and authorization, and referral services that will make competing with them strictly for the biggest companies if at all.

J2EE is a mature, proven platform with architecture and operating system-independence – this independence so resembles the principle of Web Services that it is no wonder it is a natural fit. The ability to move from Intel-based machines to more powerful servers makes applications written on this platform very scalable with an excellent Cost of Change curve. Assuming that the business case for the application is sound, the system should work equally well on a 486 PC with Windows (intranet application/small Internet user base) or an IBM server farm with thousands of users (Internet enabled – customer and client system), and will scale in cost as well as in performance according to the business needs at hand.

Perhaps one way of expressing the difference between the two is that the Microsoft camp advocates buying more computers whereas Sun/IBM would support buying bigger computers.

In addition, Java has proven to be a language that makes it easy to architect and implement maintainable systems. The fact that patterns are core to Java and the Java platform makes it easy to communicate architectural semantics. The specification system that is in place for Java means that industry leaders are responsible for making sure that the available APIs for application development are relevant to the needs of existing and future systems.

Existing J2EE software houses will no doubt appreciate these benefits, in addition to the flexibility that well-architected Java systems offer and the existing base of supporting packages and open-source initiatives that can be a starting point for the creation of servers. In addition, there is a wealth of information available on the subject.

The primary difficulty with J2EE is Sun's apparent conflicting tendencies as far as Web Services are concerned. While strongly pushing a proprietary platform for Web Services in the form of the iPlanet server, the work of creating usable specifications for development appears to be lagging behind Microsoft in effort. In this way, Sun's strategy of both offering products for the creation and hosting of Web Services, and providing Web Services strongly resembles that of Microsoft, only in this case it appears to be interfering with their ability to provide the systems for Web Services creation and deployment.

The upside to this is that there are several other proponents of Web Services, such as IBM, BEA, and others, that are strongly supporting the creation of Web Services on the Java platform, with the additional support of open-source initiatives such as the Apache Software Foundation. As well as this, several companies are offering products that automatically expose Java applications as services through a process known as introspection. This means that developers are able to create software in the usual way, and make it available for use by in-process non-distributed systems and distributed systems using technologies such as RMI that resemble Web Services but that involve Java-only protocols or heavyweight protocols such as CORBA as is currently the case. Additionally, they can be made available as Web Services using XML as the communication and data encoding mechanism. This makes Web Services a glue or façade to the existing Java infrastructure.

In any case, Java programmers are not used to the Point and Click support for software development that Microsoft developers receive and so the lack of these systems will not hold them back.

Conclusion

Web Services promise to revolutionize not only the way we develop software systems, but how we do business. Some aspects of Web Services development, such as security and transaction handling, are yet to be completely solved, and they must be in order to make the Web Services dream a reality.

WDSL, SOAP, UDDI, XML, Microsoft's .NET, and Sun's J2EE provide the technologies and tools needed to get Web Services off to a running start. Are these technologies and tools enough to make Web Services a reality and fulfill all of their promises? Time will tell.

For the sake of simplicity, we have assumed the world of software development in the business world in neatly divided into two camps – Microsoft vs. Java. In any case, this view is sufficiently accurate to validate the analysis of the competing standards. It is apparent that Microsoft-based development will, on the whole, continue to be based on Microsoft technologies, while Java-based development will continue to use Java technologies after the introduction of the Web Services model. No surprises there.

A final nod must be made to those entities for which the above considerations do not apply. In companies where systems are contracted, there is more flexibility in choosing between the two since there is less risk in terms of current investment in one technology or the other. In absolute terms, the two platforms are suitable for somewhat different needs. Microsoft-based solutions are generally more suitable for smaller companies (up to SME), which need simpler lighter systems with less need for scalability. This is both in terms of the type of hardware supported, and in the level of flexibility available to modify low-level aspects of the platform for specific needs. The .NET platform is ideal for the creation of new systems due to the rapid development offered through Visual Studio .NET and as it naturally benefits from the last few years of distributed application research by virtue of being new.

It is, however, not especially suitable for integration, even with existing Microsoft-based solutions. Legacy applications are usually run on legacy systems, and it is therefore a considerable advantage for J2EE that the Java platform is hardware and OS independent. Integration on .NET is more a matter of controlled migration.

J2EE is also architected for enterprise systems and so is currently more scalable. The fact that a Microsoft solution is PC-based means that scalability comes through clustering and with this comes the increased complexity and cost of data management, synchronization (especially relating to transactions), and session management. While J2EE is often also clustered, this has been factored in at its inception, so it is generally less necessary to cluster J2EE servers, and when it is used each machine can handle more load so fewer machines can serve the same load as a cluster of Microsoft servers, thus simplifying the clustering process.

Finally, J2EE systems are more secure. This comes partly through Microsoft's focus on ease of use over security, and partly through their dependence on vast amounts of existing and ancient code. The recent drive for reducing bugs and improving security by overhauling the code base may help, which will go some way to revising the existing record of Microsoft with security problems.

The choice between the two systems should be based on business needs. This will certainly include considerations such as the prevalence of the systems with one or the other of the platforms. Companies with existing relationships with Microsoft and Microsoft-based software houses will no doubt find that it is more convenient and less costly to stay with this technology and it may be that the inconvenience of a completely new platform (that .NET represents) will be outweighed by the benefits of the countless improvements in software engineering that .NET also represents in addition to the close customer relationships that Microsoft keeps.

On the other hand, the flexibility that J2EE offers means that a company's systems will be more readily sensitive to meet changing business needs. Current investment in J2EE products (which may be as much as $15,000/processor) may also prohibit changing systems, even if there is a perceived need for it since many companies find that J2EE already meets most of their needs.

The choice will of course ultimately be dependent on the prevalent conditions in the company. The considerations above, however, should give you a number of pointers as to how each of these conditions should be weighted in making your decision.

Authors: Gunjan Samtani and Dimple Sadhwani

- Application Frameworks Fundamentals
- Application Frameworks and Web Services
- .NET
- J2EE
- How to Choose

Web Services and Application Frameworks (.NET and J2EE)

Application frameworks are a holistic set of guidelines and specifications that provide platforms, tools, and programming environments for addressing the design, integration, performance, security, and reliability of distributed and multi-tiered applications. An application framework includes presentation services, server-side processing, session management, a business logic framework, application data caching, application logic, and support for persistence, transactions, and security, as well as logging services for applications.

Thus, an application framework provides the following:

- Transaction Management.
- Scalability.
- Security.
- State Management.
- Application Integration Services.
- Administration Services.
- Run-time Services.
- Connection Services.
- Messaging Services.
- Application Development, Deployment, and Execution Platform.
- Web Services.
- Business Process Management Services.
- Support for various graphical user interfaces including web browsers and Wireless devices.

The following diagram illustrates how an application framework fits into the rest of the system world:

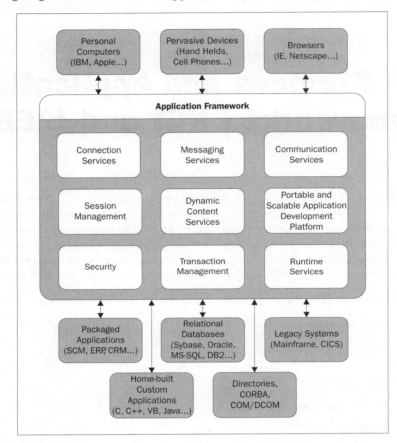

The application development tools and application servers are built on top of application frameworks. The application framework aims to provide a single and unified software infrastructure that reduces the number of enterprise software products to be supported, maintained, and integrated. The unified software infrastructure should provide a fully integrated application environment, reaching from the need to include and integrate a wide variety of legacy applications through to the need to create and deploy Web Services.

Flavors Of Application Frameworks

Application frameworks for client-server and Web-based applications can broadly be classified into two distinct fundamental physical architectures and technologies – Microsoft .NET and Java 2 Enterprise Edition (J2EE) .

Let's have a brief look at these two frameworks.

Microsoft .NET Framework

Microsoft .NET is a platform that comprises of servers, clients, and services. The .NET framework includes everything from basic run-time libraries to user-interface libraries – the common language run-time (CLR), the C#, Managed C++, VB.NET, and JScript.NET languages and the .NET Framework APIs. It comprises the following:

1. **.NET Platform**: This includes the tools and infrastructure to build .NET services and .NET device software.

2. **.NET Product and Services**: This includes Microsoft .NET-based enterprise servers, which provide support for the .NET framework, such as BizTalk Server 2002 and SQL Server 2000, Windows .NET, Visual Studio .NET, and Office .NET.

3. **Third-party (Vendor) .NET Services**: Third-party (vendor) services built on the .NET platform.

The following diagram illustrates how the elements of the .NET Framework, including some of the APIs, fit together:

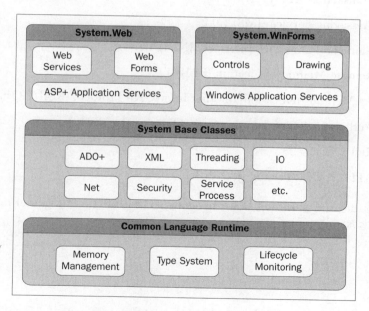

For more details about Microsoft .NET Framework, visit Microsoft's web site http://www.microsoft.com/net.

Java 2 Platform, Enterprise Edition (J2EE) Framework

J2EE is a set of specifications, which define the standard for developing multi-tier enterprise applications with Java. J2EE provides a complete framework for design, development, assembly, and deployment of Java applications built on a multi-tiered distributed application model. The J2EE specification defines numerous API services and multiple application programming models for developing applications and integrating them with the enterprise systems.

The latest J2EE 1.3 APIs include the following:

- ❑ Enterprise JavaBeans (EJB) 2.0.
- ❑ J2EE Connector Architecture 1.0.
- ❑ JDBC 2.0 (for database connectivity).
- ❑ JavaServer Pages (JSP) 1.2.
- ❑ Servlet 2.3.
- ❑ Java Transaction API (JTA) 1.0.1.
- ❑ Java Messaging Service (JMS) 1.0.2.
- ❑ Java Name and Directory Interface (JNDI) 1.2.
- ❑ Java Remote Method Invocation (RMI) 1.0.
- ❑ Remote Method Invocation/Internet Inter-ORB Protocol (RMI/IIOP) 1.0.
- ❑ Java Authentication and Authorization Service (JAAS) 1.0.
- ❑ JavaMail 1.1.
- ❑ Java API for XML Parsing (JAXP) 1.1.

The following diagram illustrates how the elements of J2EE 1.3 fit together to provide support for Web Services:

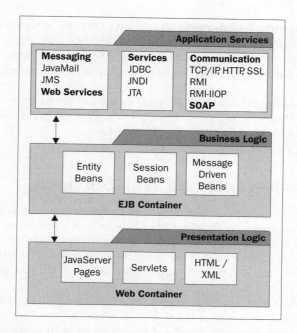

For more details about J2EE Framework, visit Sun's web site http:/java.sun.com/j2ee.

Web Services: All About Interoperability

Web Services are self-contained, modular applications that can be described, published, located, and invoked over a network. They are an emerging technology that is based on service-oriented architecture (SOA) and enable new and existing applications to be integrated using XML as the data format and standard network protocols such as HTTP for transportation.

Web Services are based on an "open" environment and standards, which ensures that a Web Service can be located and used, no matter where it is, what platform it runs on, or who developed it.

Classification of Web Services

Web Services can be classified as follows:

❑ **User-centric Web Services:** User-centric Web Services are used to provide user personalization, interface customization, and support for multiple languages, thereby greatly enhancing user experience. They logically separate the layout (presentation) in formats such as HyperText Markup Language (HTML) from the actual data in Extensible Markup Language (XML).

277

❏ **Application-centric Web Services:** Application-centric Web Services are used to integrate enterprise and business-to-business applications. Application-centric Web Services enable companies to integrate applications and business processes without the constraints of a proprietary infrastructure, platforms, and operating systems.

Both user- and application-centric Web Services make full use of open standards, including HyperText Transfer Protocol (HTTP), Extensible Markup Language (XML), Simple Object Access Protocol (SOAP), Web Services Description Language (WSDL), and Universal Discovery, Description, and Integration (UDDI).

Application Frameworks and Web Services

As we saw in the previous section, XML-based Web Services architecture allows programs written in different languages on different platforms to communicate with each other in a standards-based way. It is the application frameworks that provide guidelines and infrastructure for the deployment, management, and execution of Web Services. The application frameworks have to provide support for all the Web Services standards.

The tools and servers built on top of the application frameworks provide a programming model with a development and run-time environment for building both user- and application-centric Web Services. Furthermore, they have to implement all the Web Services standards as supported by the underlying framework. The following diagram shows the relationship between application frameworks, Web Services servers, and Web Services standards:

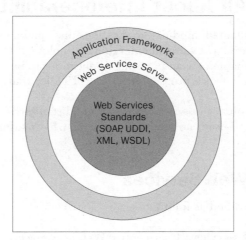

Let's discuss how Microsoft .NET and J2EE frameworks are providing support for Web Services:

Microsoft .NET

Microsoft .NET is the Microsoft XML Web Services platform. It provides built-in support for building and consuming standards-based Web Services. It enables the creation and use of XML-based applications, processes, and web sites as Web Services. Through just a single line of code or setting a value of an attribute, it is possible to turn an application into a Web Service in the .NET environment. Furthermore, by default all inter-process communication is done using the SOAP standard. According to the president of Microsoft Mr. Steve Balmer, "to the .NET framework, all components can be Web Services, and Web Services are just a kind of component".

As shown in the following diagram, Microsoft .NET provides:

❑   A programming model to build XML Web Services and applications.

❑   Web Services development tools such as Visual Studio .NET to define and develop application functionality and architecture for XML Web Services and applications.

❑   Web Services-enabled servers such as BizTalk Server 2002 and SQL Server 2000. BizTalk Server Toolkit for Microsoft .NET enables Web Services orchestration through its integration with Visual Studio .NET. Further, the SQL Server 2000 Web Services Toolkit enables the usage of Visual Studio .NET to extend the capabilities of applications built on SQL Server 2000.

❑   A set of pre-built user-centric XML Web Services such as Microsoft .NET My Services.

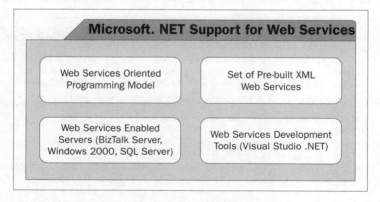

Java 2 Platform, Enterprise Edition (J2EE)

The new APIs released by Sun, as part of J2EE 1.3, provide a top-to-bottom, end-to-end solution for a Web Services-based architecture. J2EE 1.3 simplifies integration with new technologies for Web Services, such as Java Message Service (JMS) and the J2EE Connector Architecture (JCA).

J2EE server products are already providing basic Web Services support such as accessing J2EE components using the SOAP 1.1 protocol. Furthermore, J2EE-based application servers, such as iPlanet, WebSphere, and WebLogic, are also supporting the automatic generation of Web Services interfaces, including the WSDL file that describes the service, and the facilities for marshaling and un-marshaling the SOAP request to back-end EJB components.

Recently released, Sun Microsystems' Java Web Services Developer Pack (WSDP) and Java XML Pack contains:

- ❑ JAXP (Java API for XML Processing) – to support the creation, receipt, and manipulation of XML data, including XML Schema.
- ❑ JAX-RPC (Java API for XML-based Remote Procedure Calls) – to enable the creation of Web Services using SOAP and WSDL.
- ❑ JAXM (Java API for XML Messaging) to support XML messaging via SOAP.
- ❑ JAXR (Java API for XML Registries) to support access to UDDI registries.

Lastly, as far as Web Services security is concerned, apart from the security package that is already a part of the Java Developers Kit 1.3, Sun has released the JSSE (Java Secure Socket Extension) API as part of the Java 2 SDK, Standard edition 1.4. This API supports data encryption, authentication on the server side (and optionally on the client side), message integrity, SSL (Secure Sockets Layer), and transport layer security across any TCP/IP connection.

The following diagram illustrates the range of support for Web Services now available with J2EE:

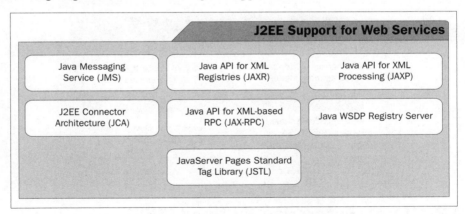

Differences Between J2EE and .NET Frameworks for Web Services Support

J2EE and the Microsoft .NET frameworks both hold the promise of being the predominant Web Services framework. In this section, we compare and contrast between the two frameworks, ignoring all the hype associated with their marketing campaigns.

Criteria	J2EE Framework	.NET Framework
Fundamental Design and Support for Web Services	J2EE is supporting Web Services through a pack of APIs such as JAXM, JAXP, JAXR, and JAX-RPC.	Web Services are built right into the platform, and Microsoft's .NET framework provides ready support for Web Services standards such as SOAP, WSDL, and UDDI.
Implementation	The implementation of Web Services in J2EE will typically be done through Enterprise JavaBeans. You can, however, also have standalone Java applications providing a Web Services implementation. It all depends on how the business processing and data logic layer of an application is designed and built.	The implementation of Web Services in the .NET framework will typically be done in .NET-managed components, including managed classes and COM/COM+ components.
Pricing	Expensive compared to .NET. If a company already has a J2EE-based application server platform, however, it makes much more sense to use the existing infrastructure and assets.

On average (as a ballpark estimate), if J2EE-based application servers are run on UNIX platforms, it would cost a company five times more to have a Web Services implementation on the J2EE platform compared with the .NET platform. This factor of five includes the hardware and the software cost. It is worth stressing that the actual price would also include the cost of development and maintenance. | Much cheaper compared to the J2EE-based application servers. J2EE, however, is still a better choice for industry-strength server-side applications. |

Table continued on following page

Criteria	J2EE Framework	.NET Framework
Portability	Java code can be ported across multiple platforms including Windows, UNIX, OS390, and AS400. Thus, Java-driven Web Services may be developed on one platform, but deployed and executed on another.	.NET ties primarily to Microsoft's operating systems. The .NET framework, however, includes the Common Language Runtime (CLR), which is analogous to the Java Runtime Environment (JRE). The CLR acts as an intermediary between .NET sourcecode and the underlying hardware. The .NET code runs within the CLR. Once the CLR is ported to another platform, .NET software should run as on the platform where it was written.
Tools and Servers	There are several companies that have built Integrated Development Tools (IDEs) and application servers based on the J2EE framework. A majority of these companies have already started supporting Web Services creation, deployment, and execution within their products. The support for Web Services standards differs from product to product.	Microsoft's cornerstone IDE for Web Services is Visual Studio .NET. As of this writing, there is no doubt that Microsoft's tool Visual Studio .NET is ahead of its competition in terms of its support for Web Services. Web Services-enabled servers from Microsoft include BizTalk 2002 and SQL Server 2000.
Promoting Companies	Several (independent) companies including IBM, BEA Systems, Oracle, HP, and Sun Microsystems. All these companies will be providing support for Web Services in their J2EE-based development tools and application servers. This is a comforting factor, as there are competing products in this technology, which means that there is no monopoly.	All the tools, servers, and technology are controlled by a single company – Microsoft. Although there is no question about Microsoft's stability and commitment towards Web Services, without competition the technology promoted and offered may not be best one.

Criteria	J2EE Framework	.NET Framework
Maturity of Platform	J2EE has proven to be a robust, scalable, and mature platform over the last four years. The addition of support for Web Services is just another feature for this platform.	Although .NET inherits a lot of features from the Windows DNA architecture, it is still relatively new and has to prove itself to be able to offer an enterprise-wide framework.

On a final comparison note on popularity, according to a poll (conducted in December 2001) of enterprise IT professionals run by ZDNet UK's Tech Update channel, a majority of implementations of Web Services will be based on Java (79%) rather than Microsoft's .NET (21%) alternative. It is, however, worth mentioning that this poll was taken before the release of the key Microsoft products that provides Web Services development tools and servers, which were launched in February 2002. It will be interesting to see what the actual position will be in December 2002, once J2EE and .NET-based products have been out in the marketplace for a while.

How To Choose an Application Framework for Web Services

If your company is debating how to choose between such architecturally different frameworks for Web Services implementation, you are not alone. This debate within IT groups in several companies is going on at every level – right from developers, through mid-level managers, to senior executives. It is not an easy choice if a company is not already totally committed to either framework.

The Ten Most Important Deciding Factors

Here are the ten most important factors that should be carefully considered before making a conclusive decision on J2EE and/or Microsoft .NET as a framework for Web Services within your company:

1. What is the existing framework within your company? Is it J2EE or Microsoft/.NET or a mix of both?

2. Which framework's implementation will yield a higher return on investment (ROI)? Which framework's products fit within your budget?

3. Which framework fits both the short-term and long-term IT and business strategies of your company?

4. Which framework can be easily supported within your IT infrastructure, eventually leading to lower total cost of ownership?

5. What technologies are your developers experts in?

6. Which framework's products are evolving more rapidly and closely to the Web Services standards, which are still being defined?

7. Which framework's products are more robust, scalable, and most importantly meet your integration needs with less complexity?

8. Which framework's products offer greater security so that you feel comfortable in using Web Services for business-to-business integration?

9. Which framework's products offer greater flexibility for integrating third-party (vendor) services?

10. Which framework offers greater support for aggregation and personalization of user preferences?

Now that we have discussed the questions, here are the answers, in the same order. It is very important to mention at this juncture that these answers are not the ONLY correct answers and that there may be several answers to these questions. It is in fact quite possible that these questions may not **have** a single answer. In such cases, companies have to keep their long-term goals in mind when making decisions. The decision may very well be to implement both frameworks within the company, and that may be perfectly right for a specific organization. After all, Web Services address connectivity needs by enabling open interaction between systems implemented on disparate platforms such as Microsoft's .NET and Java 2 Enterprise Edition (J2EE).

1. Evaluate the existing infrastructure (applications, development tools, and application servers) within your company. If the answer is J2EE, then use J2EE to implement Web Services within the firm. If the answer is Microsoft-based technology, then use .NET. Try to make the best use of your existing infrastructure as much as possible.

If there is a mix of both platforms within your company, then decide on a project-by-project basis. In some cases J2EE would make more sense and in others .NET.

2. Try to apply the following formula when deciding which platform to use for Web Services implementation:

> **Increased Revenue + Decreased Cost + Improved Efficiency = Higher Profitability**

Obviously, you have to consider your budget as well when deciding between the two frameworks. As mentioned in the comparison table between J2EE and .NET frameworks, J2EE is much more expensive as a new proposition when compared to .NET.

3. There is no definite answer to this question. You have to do the homework yourself in evaluating the short-term and long-term goals of your company. Choose a platform that fits them. See answer 7 for more details.

4. The total cost of ownership is defined as follows:

> **Cost of Ownership = Cost to implement + Cost to maintain**

The framework that has a lower cost of ownership, however, may not be suitable for your company – based on the existing infrastructure, goals, etc.

5. This is one of the most important deciding factors. If the in-house developers are experts in Microsoft-based technology, introducing and implementing J2EE is a very tough (not to mention strange) call. No matter how good the technology is, only correct usage makes it useful for a company. If you're not using in-house developers, you should pick a company who offer a Web Services solution that best fits with the answers to the other issues.

6. After the Visual Studio .NET and .NET-based enterprise server release in February 2002, Microsoft has indeed taken a lead over any of the J2EE framework-based products, such as BEA's WebLogic and IBM's WebSphere, as far as support for Web Services is concerned. This may, however, very well be a short-term lead as several J2EE product vendors (BEA, IBM) have already or are about to release new versions of their products that would provide complete support for Web Services and their standards.

7. As far as scalability and robustness are concerned, there is no question that J2EE beats Microsoft technology hands down. But if you are a small-to-medium size organization where these are secondary issues, then Microsoft's .NET may fit your organizational needs. The complexity of development, deployment, and maintenance is much less in Microsoft technology-based products. Visual Studio .NET is a marvelous example of how Microsoft eases the development work required for Web Services.

8. As of now, both the frameworks appear to be at par as far as their security features are concerned. The role-based security model of .NET may have an edge over J2EE, as it will be widely used in Web Services.

9. As far as open architecture goes, J2EE is far superior to .NET. Whether this is a deciding factor for your company is something that can only be determined by the need for using third-party vendor services within your company. One point worth mentioning here is that all the major packaged application providers have announced support for both J2EE and .NET. So, check with your packaged application vendor companies as well.

10. Microsoft .NET offers a much wider support for personalization of user preferences through .NET My Services.

> The answers to these questions should be sought both from top (senior management) and bottom (developers) within an IT organization.

Application Servers and Packaged Application Providers

Most of the application server vendors have already started providing at least partial support for Web Services and their standards. Based on the industry trend and press releases by these vendors, it appears that full and complete support for Web Services by all the major application server vendors is now a matter of dotting the i's and crossing the t's. Thus, the probability that you will be able to utilize your current EAI and B2B integration infrastructure in deploying and using Web Services is very high.

Furthermore, all the major packaged application software vendors are racing to embrace Web Services. These include the enterprise resource planning (ERP), the supply chain management (SCM), and the customer relationship management (CRM) software providers. The trend among these packaged application providers is to stay on the sidelines of this emerging battle between J2EE and .NET – which by the way is the correct approach too. They are doing so by supporting both these frameworks. For example, SAP – the biggest ERP vendor – has recently announced that its implementation of Web Services would include support for both J2EE and .NET. SAP's Web Application Server (which is being touted as the next-generation Web Application Development Platform) will allow application components to be provided as Web Services.

A Word of Caution

Everything mentioned above is good, but companies are looking for answers about where the support for Web Services by different application server vendors stands today. The fact of the matter is that Web Services standards don't yet define security, operational management, workflow, business rules, transactional integrity, and other elements necessary for an enterprise-ready computing platform.

An Example of Application Servers and Web Services

In this example, the retail clients and in-house clients of a financial company use a portfolio management portal to monitor their investments. The front-end of the portal is built using Microsoft technology (Active Server Pages .NET (ASP.NET), Internet Information Services (IIS) Web Server, VB Script, etc.) One of the features provided within the portal application is quote information. Using this feature, the clients can retrieve real-time quotation for any stock. When a client requests a quote for any stock, the request is sent from the browser to the Web Server.

As may potentially happen within any mid-to-large size company, we are assuming that the quote service is provided to multiple clients as a Web Service by a middleware application, with our portfolio management portal being just one of those clients. Another client, as shown in the figure, is a VB application.

The information about Web Services offered by this middleware application (which may be published by some other group within the company) is obtained from the private internal UDDI registry and invoked over the intranet. The implementation of the business methods exposed by the Web Service is provided by EJBs contained in another application server.

This is a typical example of .NET-to-J2EE Application server integration using Web Services. The binding information for frequently used Web Services, such as those for requesting quotes, can be cached by the client application, to avoid the resource-intensive and time-consuming dynamic binding. In this example, Web Services loosely integrate the Microsoft technology-based portfolio management application with the J2EE-based middleware application that interfaces with the mainframe to receive the quote:

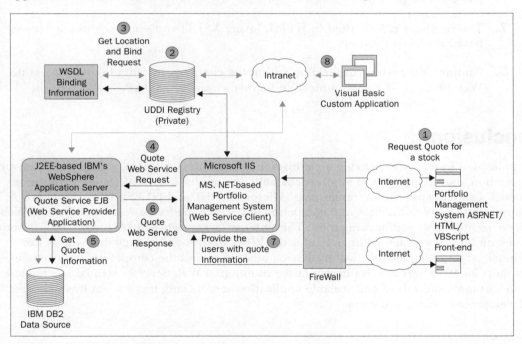

The sequence of steps is as follows:

1. The user requests quotes for a specific company on an ASP.NET/VBScript/HTML frontend that is passed over to the portfolio management portal running within Microsoft IIS. Here for the sake of simplicity it is assumed that the user has already successfully logged in to the application and has a valid session established.

2. The .NET-based portal application gets information about Web Services made available by the J2EE-based middleware application by performing a look-up in the private UDDI registry.

3. The location of and WSDL binding information for the Web Services is sent to the portal application as a SOAP-based message.

4. The portal application invokes the Web Service published by the middleware application, passing a stock symbol as a part of a SOAP-based message.

5. The actual implementation of the appropriate Web Service is provided by EJBs running within a J2EE-based application server. The EJBs use the JDBC API to get information from the data source, which in this case is IBM's DB2.

6. The EJBs send the Web Services response to the portal application as a SOAP-based message.

7. The response is formatted in HTML (using XSLT) and sent back to the browser-based client application.

8. Another VB custom application within the company intranet invokes the same Web Service. The communication happens based on SOAP.

Conclusion

Application frameworks provide a platform for design, development, assembly, deployment, execution, and monitoring of applications built on a multi-tiered distributed application model. Leading application frameworks (Microsoft .NET and J2EE) are providing full support for the Web Services and competing to become the framework of choice for Web Services initiatives within companies. This enterprise war between J2EE and .NET is bound to go on for a few years. Ultimately, it is the Web Services technology that will be the winner, as these frameworks will push each other to outbid the competition in providing support for Web Services, leading to faster adoption of Web Services standards, creation of efficient tools and robust and scalable application servers and, last but not least, cheaper development tools and servers.

Author: Eduardo B. Fernandez

- Communications Level
- Framework Providers
- Web Services Providers
- Security Products
- Supporting Levels

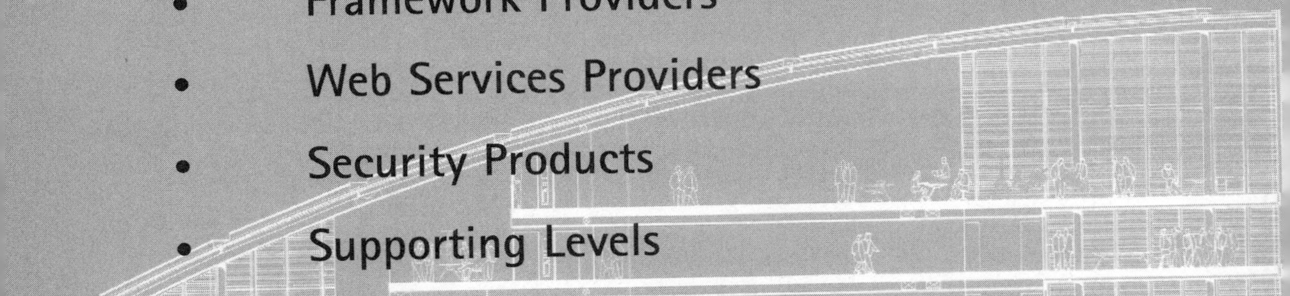

Web Services Security

At the InfoWorld Next Gen Web Services conference in January 2002, 51% of the attendants considered security the single largest obstacle to general acceptance of Web Services. Are these fears warranted, or are these people just scared of something they don't fully understand? Is the security of Web Services so precarious? Can we overcome these problems so that businesses and the general public will trust these services? We'll take a look at these issues trying to evaluate the situation. We don't pretend to be comprehensive but instead touch on the most important issues.

First we should take a look at the participants in this game. We can distinguish four basic roles related to Web Services (some institutions could support combinations of them):

- ❑ *Provider* – This is a person or business that creates a Web Service and places it in a public repository. They only want authorized customers to access their services.

- ❑ *Keeper of repositories of Web Services* – These are the institutions that provide public catalogs of services. They must assure authorized access to these catalogs.

- ❑ *Keeper of Web Services* – These store the Web Services code and data. They may be the same as the keepers of repositories or the Web Services providers, but could also be specialized institutions.

- ❑ *Consumer of Web Services* – They expect high quality services without malicious software. If they send their data to a Web Service, this data should be used in the proper way and protected from leakage or corruption.

The expectations of these roles imply in turn the following security requirements:

- ❑ Secure authentication between principals. This is a precondition for applying authorization to access Web Services.

- ❏ Secure communication between principals. Their message should not be intercepted or corrupted.

- ❏ Certification of the origin of a Web Service.

- ❏ Secure storage of repositories and Web Services. There may be different types of access to a Web Service, different users should have authorization to add, delete, or modify entries from a repository.

- ❏ Secure transit and residence of Web Services through different domains.

By security we mean the protection against unauthorized reading, modification, or destruction of information. Obviously, there are many degrees of security; we consider here the level required for e-commerce, where a system penetration could mean the loss of large amounts of money and of business prestige. There are two basic security models that apply to Internet systems: the access matrix, and Role-Based Access Control (RBAC, see *R. C. Summers, Secure Computing: Threats and Safeguards, McGraw-Hill, 1997, ISBN 0070694192*). The most common model now is RBAC and most of the new systems support this model. Another concern is privacy, the right of individuals to have control of their personal information.

The possible attackers can be external (hackers) or internal (insiders). Some security mechanisms such as firewalls are mostly intended to control external attacks, while others such as audit trails are useful to control internal attacks. The security features of the operating system should control both internal and external attacks. The design principles needed to build secure systems apply to both types of attack.

To provide a complete perspective, we consider the architectural levels involved in satisfying these security requirements. This is what some call the Web Services stack, although it is not really a stack. A basic principle of security is the need to secure all these levels; any weak level will permit attackers to penetrate the system. These levels include (some of these levels could be further refined but for our purposes this is enough detail):

- ❏ Workflow or business process level.

- ❏ Cataloging and description of Web Services.

- ❏ Communications level (typically SOAP).

- ❏ Storage of XML documents.

We will call these levels the Web Service levels and we discuss them first. It should be noted that they require supporting layers that we discuss later. The following diagram shows one of these supporting layers, the HTTP layer:

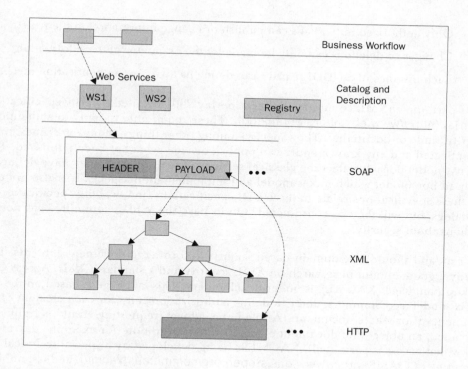

The Web Service Levels

These levels consider the definition and storage of Web Services and their incorporation into business processes.

The Workflow level is defined by languages such as ebXML (http://www.ebxml.org/), RosettaNet (http://www.rosettanet.org/), and BizTalk (http://www.biztalk.org/). There is also an Oasis Committee specification for this level: XLANG (http://xml.coverpages.org/xlang.html). These languages specify business processes, activities, coordination of tasks, and the flow of tasks or documents to perform these activities. The idea is to encourage business interaction by making known the processes they can provide to each other. To my knowledge none of the organizations responsible for these languages has defined security standards or recommendations for security specifications (ebXML has recommendations for the catalog and description level). They are also overlapping and competing languages, which makes it harder to evaluate their effect on the security of future systems.

The next Web Services level is concerned with the cataloging and description of Web Services. The Universal Description, Discovery, and Integration (UDDI) committee has defined some general security guidelines with few details (http://www.uddi.org/specification.html). These policies include:

❑   Only authorized individuals can publish or change information in the registry

❑   Changes or deletions can only be made by the originator of the information

❑   Each instance of a UDDI registry can define its own user authentication mechanism

On its part, the ebXML committee defined in May 2001 detailed security specifications for registries (http://www.ebxml/org/ebrim2.pdf). These requirements apply to authentication, integrity, and confidentiality. They specify, among other things, that each request must be authenticated and any known entity can publish or view what has been published. Their security model doesn't reflect the classical security models; instead they have defined a rather ad hoc model which mixes model and implementation aspects. It is also not clear how these specifications relate to the UDDI specifications; that is, both specifications refer to catalogs, but will they be coordinated? On its part, the WSDL committee has not said anything about security.

One can (and should) use domain-based security according to document contents. There is already a good amount of research on XML security and a standard, XML Access Control Markup Language (XACML), is under development. This language is based on the access matrix model (see Summers) and can define authorization rules for each element of an XML document or for whole documents. A rule has a subject (requesting entity), a right (read, write, etc.), an object (the document element), and a condition (for example, day of the week when access is permitted). XACML is being developed by a special technical committee of OASIS (http://www.oasis-open.org/committees/xacml/), and it combines work of the IBM Tokyo Research Lab and the University of Milano, Italy. This is a well-thought out standard based on sound principles and should be used for the security of repositories and storage of Web Services.

Similarly as for transmission, each element of a document can be encrypted according to the XML Encryption standards mentioned later. Finally, the document schemas, DTDs, and DOMs can also be used to provide security. Because documents may contain links to other documents, the security constraints applied to a document must consider also the security of these links. These aspects, however, are mostly at the research stage and just starting to be considered in products.

Because Web Services are used in distributed environments, their data, code, or descriptions must move across different security domains. If a Web Service moves to another security domain, it must carry its security restrictions so that the other domain can properly handle the Web Service. This propagation is done through the Security Assertion Markup Language (SAML, see http://www.saml.org/ and http://www.oasis-open.org/committees/security/). SAML defines authentication and authorization assertions encoded in XML. Similarly to the ebXML registry model, this security model appears rather ad hoc and does not follow standard security models, which may result in inconsistencies. Nevertheless, SAML has already been incorporated into several security products.

The Communications Level

The following level is defined by the Simple Object Access Protocol (SOAP). There are other protocols proposed for this level, but they have not gained general acceptance. SOAP itself has no security; all of its security comes from the SOAP Security Extensions. These extensions have been defined by the W3C XML Encryption Working Group (http://www.w3.org/Encryption/2001/). One of these standards, XML Encryption, defines a process for encrypting and decrypting messages considering the granularity of the message contents. This can be as small as one element (including start/end tags) or apply to the element content (between the start/end tags). Super-encryption is possible, where the whole message with parts encrypted can be encrypted again, as is done when SSL is used for secure transmission over HTTP. A variety of encryption algorithms can be used, including the Advanced Encryption Standard (AES, see http://csrc.nist.gov/encryption/). There is a related standard for digital signatures, also from the W3C.

A SOAP message includes a header and a payload. As shown in the following diagram, SAML assertions can be included in the header or in the payload:

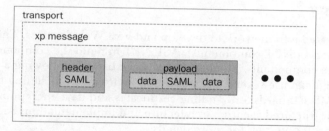

XML encryption protects the secrecy of the message. A Public Key Infrastructure (PKI) can be used to provide authentication, digital signatures, and key distribution. This PKI is based on XML Key Management Specification (XKMS), intended for the integration of PKI and digital certificates. For example, digital signature processing can be delegated to a Web Service in order to simplify the PKI structure. XKMS is an open standard that applies to any vendor PKI approach. The XKMS uses two specialized standards:

❑ *XML Key Registration Service* (X-KRSS), for the registration of key pairs and location of keys for later use.

❑ *XML Key Information Service* (X-KISS), that defines validation and location information associated with a key. This standard can be complemented or replaced by XML Trust Assertion Service Specification (XTASS, see http://www.oasis-open.org/committees/security/docs/draft-xtass-v09.pdf), which provides some higher-level functions, such as validation using SAML.

Web Services Framework Providers

There are a few companies that have developed frameworks to host Web Services. These are companies that sell operating systems, web servers, component lines, tools, and other structures to support the development and deployment of Web Services. Some of these are:

IBM Web Services

There is a new version of WebSphere Application Server, the Web Services Business Integrator that will allow the MQ Series to deliver SOAP messages. IBM's DB2 Version 7.2 has a new XML Extender, where Web Services can access a DBMS and can store SOAP and UDDI data.

The security of WebSphere is considered to be good. WebSphere has several levels of security and uses Role-Based Access Control (RBAC) . It was developed by Tivoli. See http://www-106.ibm.com/developerworks/webservices/ for more.

Microsoft .NET

Microsoft has created a framework to develop and host Web Services. This framework includes components (.NET components), ASP.NET to build the components, and a series of servers to host the components. The components can be built following a Role-Based Access Control model and can use several authentication approaches, including Kerberos. They have adopted the XKMS standards for handling certificates and data encryption. Overall, this appears as a well-structured security architecture and implementation. See http://www.microsoft.com/net/ for more details.

Sun Microsystems

Sun's Open Net Environment (Sun ONE) architecture is based on Java components (J2EE). Notice that this is only an architecture, to be adopted by other vendors, although Sun has its own implementation based on its iPlanet server.

A Web Service can use a policy engine to dynamically adapt processing and/or results according to rules based on user identity, authorization levels, and other contextual information. The user and policy information is stored in the Lightweight Directory Access Protocol system. Sun uses PKI and Kerberos for authentication and message protection, and SAML for exchanging security information. The Web Services reside in Sun's iPlanet server. This uses Role-Based authorization with role hierarchies, administrative privileges, and domains for segmentation of roles. Each domain has one administrator. A "superuser" administrator controls all domains. It also has several authentication options. This security architecture is close to that of .NET, and at this level there is no clear advantage for either approach. See http://www.sun.com/sunone/ for more details.

Hewlett Packard

HP will be one of the hosts for repositories and Web Services. HP has a secure version of the Unix operating system, the Virtual Vault, and a secure Web structure, the Praesidium. Most likely these will be the basis of their security. This is a strong supporting structure, but they have not defined any specific approach at the Web Services level. See http://www.hp.com/ for more details.

BEA Systems

BEA uses their WebLogic application server to host Web Services. This is based on Java J2EE components and shares their good security properties. They use security products such as Netegrity or Oblix to provide security to Web Services. See http://www.bea.com/ for more details.

webMethods

This is a Web Services integration platform that supports XML, SOAP, and WSDL. They claim to have good security but show no details of how is this accomplished. See http://www.webmethods.com/ for more details.

Web Services Providers

Several companies that specialize in component development are converting these into Web Services. They are responsible for the contents of the Web Services they provide. Web Services can be implemented in any language that can process XML, and may include a variety of functions. They may be quite complex and hide Trojan Horses or be infected with viruses or worms.

Certifying that a program doesn't contain malicious software is what computer scientists call an undecidable problem; there is no method to guarantee that a given program is free of malicious code. Web Services will be trusted based on their origin and general fame, but there is no guarantee for the consumer. Certified software only proves the origin of the software and can guarantee a given functionality; there is no guarantee of the security of its contents. Naturally, vendors who develop their services carefully will be more trusted. As David Guinan said in his Software Development East 2001 keynote speech, Web Services are about trust. Some of the current providers include the following.

Microsoft's .NET My Services (Formerly code-named HailStorm)

This was initially a set of Web Services from Microsoft that provides a centralized way to store and access user data, reachable from anywhere through the Internet. Services were to include calendar, wallet, and notification, among others. Users would be owners of their data and can check who has had access to it. Users must log in through Microsoft's Passport authentication service. Services and data were to be kept on Microsoft's servers. Recently, however, this plan has been withdrawn due to a number of contributory factors. Principally, at this stage in the development of Web Services people do not feel comfortable with trusting all their personal data to a third party. Microsoft is said to be taking steps to provide .NET My Services as an internal authentication and authorization solution for companies with disparate, distributed systems.

.NET My Services security partially depends on the strength of their authentication system, Passport. Passport uses a centralized repository of authorized subscribers but it can also use more sophisticated approaches, including Kerberos, an approach considered quite strong. The problem is in Microsoft IIS Web server, a system that has rather poor security and has been hacked many times. .NET My Services doesn't use SOAP's security, another negative aspect, because by not following its security standards it is harder to ascertain their level of security. Microsoft is well aware of their low security image, and is working to improve the situation by tightening up security in all their products.

Bowstreet

Provides a methodology to build Web Services embodied in the Business Web Factory product. This uses Java components and can use BEA, IBM, and Sun ONE platforms. See http://www.bowstreet.com/ for more details.

SAP

Provides a variety of business solutions components that are available for enterprise e-business requirements. See http://www.sap.com/ for more details.

Security products

Several companies provide products to provide security for Web Services. We enumerate below a few of them.

Netegrity

The TransactionMinder is a product for management and security of Web Services. It follows SAML and XKMS. It can support Sun ONE, MS .NET, Oracle 9i, and BEA Web Services. This product is an extension of their earlier product SiteMinder for the security of web sites.

The facilities in the Delegated Management Services (DMS) of Netegrity follow closely the proposals we made in 1979 (C. Wood and E. B. Fernandez, "Authorization in a Decentralized Database System," *Proceedings of the 5th International Conference on Very Large Databases*, 352-359, Rio de Janeiro, 1979). In that paper we proposed to separate administrative roles from operational roles; administrators had a special set of rights and we presented policies for delegation of those rights. It was also possible to assign users to roles; create, modify, and delete users; create, modify, and delete organizations (domains) and their administrators. Most of these functions are present in DMS. See http://www.netegrity.com/ for more details.

Securant

This is an access control system where we can define users, groups, and realms (domains). It can apply security constraints dynamically. There is transaction authorization and delegated administration. Other features include Single Sign-on (SSO), policy evaluation, auditing, and reporting. It was recently acquired by RSA to complement their PKI systems. See http://www.rsasecurity.com/ for more details.

Oblix

Oblix includes facilities for user profiles (Identity service), authorization (Access), and administration (Presentation). Their new product, NetPoint 5.0, includes AccessXML, IdentityXML, and PresentationXML. AccessXML uses SAML. They also support security for LDAP, and have recently announced the integration of their product with .NET Passport. See http://www.oblix.com/ for more details.

Grand Central

Grand Central provides a specialized network to securely interconnect enterprises and manage the use of Web Services. The network interfaces apply authentication and Role-Based Access Control at the message-or document-level of granularity. See http://www.grandcentral.com/ for more details.

Quadrasis

Quadrasis emphasizes the need for unified security across the layers and units of an organization. Policies should be uniformly applied across domains and should be simple to use and administer. This system uses SSO, SAML, centralized audit, and an administrative structure to accomplish these goals. These are embodied in their Enterprise Application Security Integration (EASI) Framework that centralizes the control of authentication and authorization. See http://www.quadrasis.com/ for more details.

WSBANG (Web Services Broker and Network Gateway)

This is a Web Services broker marketed by Primordial, a proxy server to manage the Web Services consumed by a given company. It performs activities such as monitoring behavior, metering, caching, and others. It can be used for authentication; storing passwords, certificates, and authorization information. WSBANG can also be used to enrich and transform SOAP messages. It complements the work of a secure network such as Grand Central's. See http://www.primordial.com/ for more details.

The Supporting Levels

All this considers the Web Service levels only. But how about the infrastructure needed to support them? There are several more levels to consider here: web server and application server levels, database level, operating systems level, and communication levels (not present in the following diagram). All these levels have been studied in the classical security literature (Summers). We consider the most important, one by one.

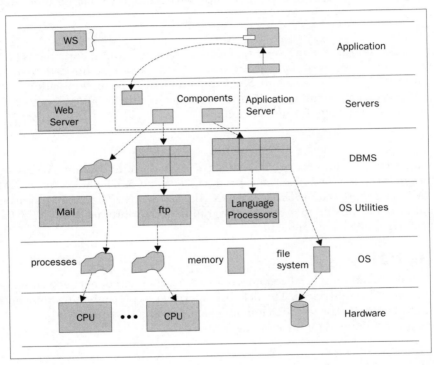

The web server and the application server define a presentation and business model level, respectively. For web servers, Apache has shown to be quite strong, due to its open design and simple structure. On the other hand, Microsoft's IIS is quite weak, although hopefully their new servers should be better. IBM's WebSphere and Sun's iPlanet use role-based access control and appear to provide a good basis for security. Application servers implement their business models using components. The market here has narrowed down to two component architectures: Microsoft .NET and Sun ONE. Both architectures provide a standard set of authentication services and authorization based on Role-Based Access Control. Both architectures appear to have a good level of security; in fact, the component level is the strongest in both systems, the weaknesses appear in the web server side.

The Database Management System (DBMS) level is also very important because the Web Services and their descriptions must be stored in some type of database. DBMSs usually have good authorization systems but these can be bypassed from web servers that run with high privilege; for example, in Unix systems the web server programs run with root privileges. DBMSs are supported by operating systems and use their file systems for data storage. There are only three varieties of operating systems in general use and they all have had serious security problems, having been hacked many times. In particular, their mail servers have appeared to be quite vulnerable, both Unix Sendmail and Microsoft's Exchange have been attacked many times. From these, the whole operating system can be compromised because of poor isolation design. A few hardened operating systems exist, such as HP's Virtual Vault and Sun's Trusted Solaris, and should be used in applications requiring high security. The new Microsoft operating system, Windows XP appears much better in this sense than its predecessors.

The communications level of current systems is quite strong with respect to security. Message transmission can be protected using symmetric encryption algorithms, such as the new Advanced Encryption Standard (AES). These algorithms have been shown to be quite robust. Digital signatures, authentication, message secrecy, and non-repudiation can be obtained through PKI systems. The corresponding aspects of Web Services are based on this accumulated knowledge and appear to be equally strong. Web Services can use SSL for end-to-end encryption, which should assure the confidentiality of messages, although there are concerns about the performance overhead incurred. Firewalls are important for general-purpose security, and they will have a role in Web Services security by controlling the source of requests. A serious problem in networks is the Distributed Denial of Service (DDoS) problem. This problem occurs when multiple unprotected systems are penetrated and used as slaves to send large numbers of messages to a target. Web Services are vulnerable to new forms of these types of attacks (see http://www.webservicesarchitect.com/content/articles/deJesus01.asp), and firewalls can be useful to stop them.

Conclusions

We have looked at most of the issues that have an effect on the security of Web Services. Web Services are indeed a very promising technology, and their use will continue to increase. We need, however, to be aware of the potential security problems that may occur. We have history as reference but undoubtedly there will be new problems. Currently, the Internet is not a safe place. The problem with many of the existing systems is that their software is of poor quality, written without regard for sound software engineering and security principles. There are two types of software errors that may lead to security problems: design errors and implementation errors. Design errors come from lack of awareness of security principles during development; they are the hardest to correct. Implementation errors come from coding errors and can be fixed through patches, although this is not viable in some cases. Many systems are too complex and they are hard to configure, which brings new exposures.

This situation is slowly changing, as companies are realizing that systems should be developed considering security as an integral part of their design and implementation. A good security model is basic to producing a consistent and complete security specification that can be realized in the language used to implement the system. The access matrix and Role-Based Access Control models appear as obvious choices for authorization models that can guide the design of a secure system. Object-oriented approaches using modeling languages, such as the Unified Modeling Language (UML, see http://www.omg.org/uml/), are necessary to develop secure software (see E. B. Fernandez, "*Patterns for secure system design*", http://www.cse.fau.edu/~ed); the code-only approach for building systems is one of the reasons of the poor quality of some systems. On the positive side, we already have some promising security products and the basic frameworks for Web Services have a sound security architecture. Further, cryptographic measures have solved some of the important security problems, such as authentication, message confidentiality, signatures, and non-repudiation, and all their power can be applied to Web Services as well.

When we try to predict the future we have a rather confusing state to consider: it is not yet clear how all the security levels fit together and there is much change with new products and evolving standards. New sets of development tools are appearing, and their use will have a direct effect on the security of the products developed with them. Another aspect that has an effect on security is the way reliability is provided; security and reliability affect each other. Finally, privacy is another concern that will become important when more personal information is stored in Web Services; the Platform for Privacy Preferences is concerned with this issue (see http://www.w3.org/TR/P3P/#introduction). Although we have pointed out many possible problems, overall we see things improving, many companies and users realize the importance of security, and what is more encouraging, are starting to do something about putting security in their products or requesting security from vendors.

Author: Whitney Hankison

- Strategy Overview
- Guidelines
- Components
- Configuration Alternatives
- Business Strategies

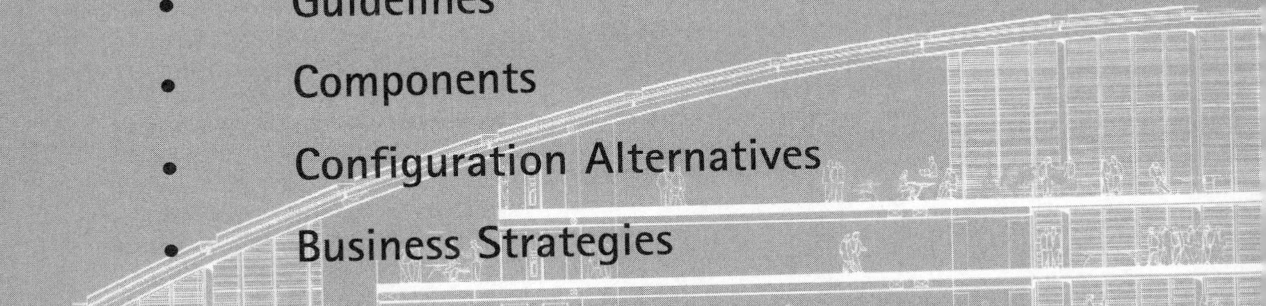

Network Security for Web Services

Security is a broad and important topic that needs to be considered when configuring a network to support the Web Services infrastructure. In this paper we will attempt to outline what the concerns are, some steps to remediation, and some further sources of information. In addition we will approach security from a programmatic standpoint and discuss measures developers need to take to add to the security of a Web Services application.

To begin, we will look at some overall network security problems and remediation independent of what core operating system is used. We will then be featuring details from a Microsoft Windows 2000 and Internet Explorer perspective regarding configuration of software and permissions for users. After this, we will identify some hardware solutions that assist in securing the network. We'll transition into programmatic security by discussing some of the new Microsoft .NET infrastructure strategies and the section finishes with a discussion of the uses of certificates. At the end of the article we'll look at the overall business issues to consider when looking at security and what the costs are to implement the environment we will be outlining. Let's begin by looking at an overall strategy for security within a network.

Strategy Overview

The purpose of this section is to provide an overview of the physical security and identity security aspects of utilizing a network-based computer system. We will discuss how physical security is important to consider in protecting a network from unwelcome users and how identity security can play an important role in determining who accesses important corporate files. Independent of what the core operating system is within the network environment, there are some common rules to network organization and authentication which are worth identifying. One of the first of these topics is that of physical security.

Physical Security

If a malicious user gains physical access to a machine, that machine is compromised. There are many tools available that we will cover in the next section that can assist users in compromising the security of the network. Once an intruder has gained access to the network, they can set up programs that can be either malicious in nature or intrusive in nature. Some programs that gather and send confidential information over the Web to other locations can go relatively undetected. Other programs can corrupt or altogether delete information from your network. These programs are really related to viruses due to their malicious nature, but are different in their purpose being specific to a goal that the intruder is aiming to accomplish. Without physical security, no other security measures are good enough to stop intruders from doing what they want.

Physical security is maintained by ensuring that only authorized personnel gain access to critical network resources. This can be accomplished in a number of ways. Many large organizations house their servers in a central, secure location. This is a good idea also because a central location is easy to control environmentally to ensure dependability of the equipment. Organizations that require more of a decentralized configuration of their servers need to ensure each site that requires a hardware resource provides an adequate location to house it. The location should be secured and adequately maintained so that the equipment will last the longest and not get compromised. Some of these disparate locations can employ methods like locking, well-ventilated computer cages or storage room facilities. The key is to control the physical access to the computer resource.

In addition to being concerned over server resources, we need to be aware of the physical access to machines that hook into our network. If a machine is given access to log in to a network, it needs to be physically located within a trusted area in order to prevent an intruder from using it as a staging ground for gathering information and transmitting it from within the enterprise. If a real concern is present and a computer must be housed in an insecure location, there are additional hardware devices that can be used to authenticate users and lock out intruders. These devices include card readers, fingerprint readers, and key readers. All of them require the user to possess one additional piece of information, other than their user information, usually in the form of hardware, to log in to the machine.

Identity Security

It is as important to protect the user identity inside a business, as it is to protect our credit cards from being compromised over the Internet. Why? Because there are endless ways to compromise an entire network by compromising a single user logon. We must keep in mind that the people who want to gain access to a system by going around its security. Such programs seldom do so without causing problems for the company along the way. We should seek to implement a balanced security policy that ensures adequate security without overburdening the user with compliance requirements.

Each and every operating system environment has a form of identity security that needs to be configured appropriately to secure the enterprise against the security-based attacks that virtually all Internet sites go through. Again, each enterprise has users on the inside of the corporation as well as users from the Internet accessing the web site. It is important to develop integrity for identity security on the inside of the corporation that can flow to users which we allow in from the outside of the corporation. User ID and password security are important issues that always need to be addressed. Some common guidelines are:

1. Protect the user ID and password information by never writing it down, and not sharing it with other users for any reason.

2. Passwords should be at least 8 characters in length, include capital and smaller case letters, include numbers and special characters such as *&^%$#@ or !.

3. Passwords should not be left the same, but be changed either on a regular basis, which would be at least once a quarter, or on an irregular but frequent basis. The latter would present an intruder with the challenge of not having changes occur on a predictable schedule.

4. Passwords should never include a word that can be found in a dictionary nor end in an S.

5. Passwords should not simply be changed back and forth between two primary passwords, but be unique.

The guidelines above are some ways to slow down people who are trying to "crack" the password in order to use it for their own purposes. There are several tools freely available and easily found on the Internet that can crack passwords. These tools look for simple passwords to crack first and can often crack a password that is less than 8 characters in a matter of seconds. Longer passwords that include the recommendations listed above can take more time depending on the computer resources the hacker is using to crack a password. It should be kept in mind that if the system-level password is insecure then that makes the rest of the passwords just as insecure as well due to the administrative privileges often associated with the system level user IDs.

When it comes to identity security within an application, it is just as important for the outside users to realize the importance of keeping their identity secure. When issuing user credentials to people outside the corporation for use with a web application, it is recommended that information that only that user would know is gathered for second-level authentication. Gathering the secondary information can be accomplished when the user initially requests user credentials for the web site and further ensures that someone is not trying to imitate the user and gain access for other purposes. Information such as mother's maiden names, social security numbers, and birth dates are commonly used. These, however, are publicly available, so it is recommended the person also supply a keyword of their choosing that can be prompted for as a "surprise" question every once in a while.

These surprise questions can deter unwanted users by creating an element of inconsistency and unpredictability.

In addition to the above suggestions, there is hardware available that can assist in verifying identity. The hardware includes devices such as retinal scanners, fingerprint and handprint devices, and card readers. These devices hook up to a machine and become a required step in the user authentication process.

Patches and Security Guidelines

This section will outline some useful web sites that give information about security, virus, and patch information.

Microsoft-Specific Information

In the past year it has become quite apparent that some of the Microsoft products may have security weaknesses. As viruses continue to exploit these weaknesses, Microsoft has come up with both commitment and a stronger approach to dealing with the weaknesses in their products. While they are working on these it is still important that people keep up to date with the weaknesses and deal with them promptly as they are exposed. Microsoft has a few sites that assist administrators in dealing with these, such as the http://www.microsoft.com/security and http://windowsupdate.microsoft.com/ sites.

There is a Tools and Checklists section to the Microsoft site that deals with the most common practices for securing a Microsoft product. They also have an e-mail service that administrators can subscribe to in order to keep abreast of the latest news on security within the various Microsoft products.

The Windows update site is the simplest way to have a machine analyzed for update needs. The site checks the machine that accesses the site and then makes recommendations on patches needed based on what is loaded already. This site is also an easy way to retrieve product updates for applications network-wide.

Other Helpful Web Sites for Security and Virus Information

There are several web sites that specialize in security, computer crime, and virus hoax information that administrators need to be aware of. The following screenshot is of the Computer Security Institute site, which details information about computer crime and has resources for intruder detection. They also give seminars on this topic. The address is http://www.gocsi.com/.

There is also a U.S. Government organization which has a good website that lists more security guidelines for Information Technology systems in general. This is the Computer Security Resource Center under the National Institute of Standards and Technology. The address is http://csrc.nist.gov/.

One more site that is invaluable is from the SANS Institute (System Administration, Networking, and Security). The site has the FBI top 20 list of vulnerabilities and lists the top 10 security loopholes in Windows and Unix systems. The site is located at http://www.sans.org/.

The other issue that administrators should be able to deal with is virus hoaxes. Many times e-mails that list a critical virus, such as the Budweiser Dog Screen Saver, are simply a hoax sent out to waste time and money of large corporations. Having said that, they are often forwarded in good faith, so informing the workforce how to deal with virus alerts is a must; rather than forwarding it to everyone they know, the details should be checked. Along with the common virus software company sites such as McAfee and Symantec, a good hoax site is the F-Secure site, located at http://www.europe.f-secure.com/virus-info/hoax/. The site gives lists of hoaxes as well as other good information regarding the latest virus news.

Additional Security Software

Additional security that should be considered is software that functions with the corporate firewall to monitor both incoming and outgoing requests and data for destination addressing or questionable content. This software is called **patrolling** software and it can assist in monitoring both incoming and outgoing traffic and create logs or even alarm administrators when a potential for a problem is noticed. It can act as an Internet filter, as well as monitor the Windows Security Log and create information useful for alerting administrators to problems. One such piece of software can be found at http://www.gfisoftware.com/languard for more information.

In addition to server-based patrolling software there is software that works in conjunction with local firewalls that monitor and alarm the DSL Internet users of situations occurring, such as incoming viruses that are blocked at the DSL router. One such piece of software can be found at http://www.networkice.com/products/blackice_defender.html.

Security Infrastructure Components

In addition to what we've already spoken about regarding the software aspects to security, there are additional steps needed from an infrastructure perspective that form the critical gauntlet that stops intruders from getting where they want to be. Fundamentally, securing a Web Service is very similar to securing any web site. At a network level, the topics that we grapple with relate to the types of users who we want to gain access, what level of authentication we find necessary to protect our resources yet allow our users access, and securing the data that the Web Service needs to access itself so that users can't directly get at that data.

Network Configuration

We've already spoken previously of many ways to provide software authentication to secure the web site and ensure users must have valid credentials to gain access. One goal for creating our network infrastructure is to prevent any intruder from getting to any destination. Getting through many layers of security is always more challenging to a potential intruder than if just one layer is presented.

Another goal is for the firewall to be configured so as to prevent some common ways of bringing down a web site so that it can't respond to user requests. Such attempts by hackers to accomplish this are termed Denial of Service attacks.

The Web server that contains the Web Service Site usually lives in an area of the network called the DMZ, or demilitarized zone. This area is called this because it is open to the Internet and has less security enforced than an internal portion of a network usually would. The DMZ sits between the Internet and the internal corporate network, surrounded by firewalls to shield against users who might try to gain access from the Internet to internal network resources. The firewall usually filters traffic from the Internet and directs the traffic coming from the web site machine directly to any internal resources, such as data servers, and prevents any other resources from being accessed by traffic coming from the web site machine. The DMZ and firewall concepts are illustrated in the diagram below.

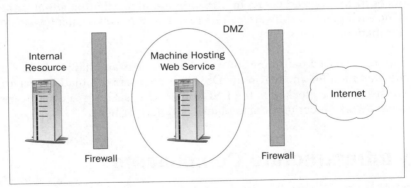

The firewall mechanism can do two things for us: it can limit the traffic coming from the web site to a specific IP address within our internal structure, and it can limit the type of traffic. Traffic travels through areas of the firewall called **ports**. Different types of traffic get routed through different ports. If a corporation opens up these ports for too many types of traffic to get through it can become like there isn't a firewall at all, so care should be taken when making these decisions. A good example would be where the firewall would limit the traffic to data requests, refusing to respond to a request for another type of file.

In addition to this methodology, internal servers generally have an authentication that is necessary for any user to get to them. There are often special accounts on these servers that the Web Server utilizes, which are additionally limited, so if that account gets compromised it doesn't have as much power as an internal user would. It is most important to remember that incorporating the firewalls and DMZ concepts into the network infrastructure is a critical step to protecting the enterprise data. Without these the corporation is open to attack as soon as a web server is installed and linked up to the Internet.

As well as these critical components there are other steps that need to be considered. If there are subscribers to a Web Service that are frequently connected to your server, or if there are vendors that work with the corporation but are located off-site it is wise to invest in VPN (Virtual Private Networking) technology to enhance the security of the communications between such clients. VPN rides on top of the current Internet system of communication to provide secure, encrypted communications between two points in the Internet. It is often termed a "secure pipeline" through the internet because the data riding through the pipe cannot be accessed, but just in case it were, it is encrypted and therefore would have to be decrypted to be readable. The diagram below illustrates this concept.

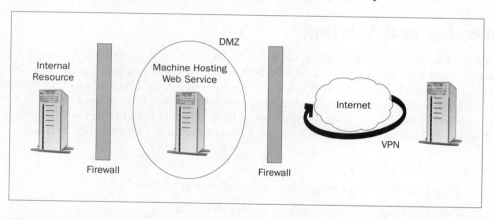

In addition to firewalls and VPN security, the internal network infrastructure that supports day-to-day communications within the corporation should have protection from any malicious user sending data to a specific destination. The internal network components are called routers, and they serve the function of routing network traffic, called packets, from one destination to another. The routers can read the information regarding the content, source, and destination and can filter out packets that should not be going into the network. Leaving network router devices too open can be dangerous should a program get through the VPN or firewall security we have in place surrounding our web servers.

Program Deployment Infrastructure

With Web Services deployment we are working with web servers that share their resources between multiple web sites and Web Services. When this is the case it is very important to keep in mind that any one program can bring the Web Server down, thus disabling many services and sites at once. Since this is the case, there is a need for a program deployment infrastructure to be in place within the organization.

Beyond the standard of having a separate development server, there needs to be a test lab or test server where developers can test their code pre-deployment. This lab should be configured as close to the production environment as possible to catch any conflicts. Between the lab and production areas of the network should be a staging area where programs are placed before rolling out directly into the production environment. The staging area produces a controlled environment where code changes and new code can be placed into the production environment in a coordinated and timely fashion. This also gives us an area to provide rollback measures in case the newly implemented production code needs to be rolled back to the previous version.

Monitoring and Auditing

Once the hardware infrastructure is in place, it is by no means a completed project. Operating systems come with tools, as well as the addition of firewalls, VPN, and routers that need to be used on a regular basis to monitor the activity on the network. There are additional tools that can span all of the layers of the network that can help us troubleshoot areas of our applications by analyzing the traffic generated from them. A list of things we should audit includes, but is certainly not limited to, the following areas in our operating system:

- Failed logon attempts.
- Failed attempts at gaining access to a resource (such as a file).
- Failed attempts at using administrative privileges.

Within our network, from our firewalls and routers we should monitor:

- Types of data coming through, and which ports are being used.
- Traffic level at given times during the day, determining a normal level for a given time.
- Types of traffic generated by various computers, determining a normal level and type.

In addition to a day-to-day effort in monitoring and auditing, once the network is configured and the technical staff have implemented their plan, a security audit from an external agency is truly a must. There are several agencies that perform these audits, and they can evaluate the current configurations, list problems, and even recommend remediation procedures.

Security Configuration Alternatives

Security configuration, separate from hardware and programmatic solutions presented above, includes Certificate security, encryption, and global user cache alternatives such as the Microsoft Passport type of security. Currently the tools in the industry are specific to the hosting platform chosen for the Web Service, and there needs to be a revolution in this area to provide an approach that is hardware, operating system, and development tool independent. This "next step" is something that is on many minds, so I'm sure we'll see a revolution in this area soon. Until that point, we still need to review what we have today to make an intelligent decision on supporting the most versatile yet secure answer that meets the needs of our specific Web Service implementation.

Certificate Security

Certificate security is a standard for providing the highest level of software-based security for a web site. Certificates are based on a standard called Public Key Cryptography, and are used through implementing SSL (Secured Sockets Layer) for a web site.

You can tell a web site is using SSL because the address will be preceded with **https://** instead of **http://**. A notification box will often appear that informs you the site is using SSL.

On Internet Explorer, a padlock will appear in the right-hand part of the status bar on the bottom of the screen as well. The SSL implementation ensures that all data going between the web site and the user's computer is encrypted and secure. You will generally see this occur when you are on a site that is dedicated to sales of merchandise and asks for confidential information such as credit card numbers and expiration dates.

Certificates are issued by a very few companies and are issued uniquely on a site-by-site basis. The publisher signs a certificate so that it can be verified. When a certificate is issued by the web site to a client who is signing up for the service that the web site provides, the certificate comes across with Public Key Cryptography information attached.

In Internet Explorer, you can see the certificate that is attached to a web site by going to File | Properties.

If you then click the Certificates button on the properties screen you will see the certificate information screen.

Public Key Cryptography is a standard by which there is an exchange of information between two individual computers that only can be known by those two computers. The information that is exchanged is in the form of keys, one being a public key and one being a private key. As we said above, when a site issues a certificate to a user the key information is established. There is a public key, which is widely distributed by the web site to all users of the site, and a private key through which the secured messages that are sent between the two machines can be decrypted.

For instance, if I were to buy a ticket on Expedia, I would need to transmit my credit card information across the Internet in order to guarantee my purchase.

First I send a message that would relate to "I want to buy a ticket, here is your public key." The server would use the private key to verify that my certificate identity is valid, and then send a message back asking me for my credit card information. I would use my private key to ensure that I received the request from the appropriate computer, and then I could reply with my information. Communication would continue in this manner until the purchase was complete.

Essentially, secure communication is established between the two computers by a series of encryption and decryption steps that are performed based on verification of identity by issuing a certificate. Using certificates does slow the transaction, but it is currently the highest guarantee that we have to ensure secure communications.

Global Cache Security

Global Cache Security uses a cache of login information that lives at a central location on the Internet. The Microsoft Passport site is one example of this type of authentication. There are more sites subscribing to this type of security, which uses personal information to establish a user ID and password, then sends the information to an e-mail address. Once the user receives the e-mail they can use their user ID and password to get onto the site. The sites that are using this methodology do not generally need the level of security of certificates, but do want authentication credentials to be able to access their site. Sites with sensitive or restricted information would find this useful.

The thought behind this type of security is to form a consortium between web sites that accept the identity of a user based on that user establishing the credentials on one site. For instance, if I go to http://www.microsoft.com and want to access their MCP site I need a Passport. Once I establish the credentials I can then go to any site that will accept that Passport credential without having to re-establish it for each site I go to.

Custom Security

Custom Security is really the grouping that encompasses security done in a programmatic fashion. There are many web sites that have an authentication page, where the user provides a password or other information. This type of authentication generally utilizes a repository of user accounts that are internal to the corporation that hosts the web site. For instance if I hit my company web site and access a secure area as an employee, the site authenticates my credentials against an internal database server and grants me access based on the credentials I typed in.

Custom security can include custom encryption strategies. There are many publicly available encryption algorithms that programmers can use to encrypt transmission, all of which add overhead to the web site. Remember that encryption can be as fundamental as scrambling a message based on a certain set of rules, and unscrambling it at the other end based on the same set of rules. If the set of rules is too easy to break, then the encryption is not very useful.

Business Strategies

A business that is using Web Services architecture immediately assumes risks and costs; it needs long-term commitment and has to be able to commit resources to the infrastructure implementation. As we've seen, there is a lot to consider from both the programming and the infrastructure sides to a Web Service implementation. From a business strategy point of view, it is most important to take all aspects into consideration and plan for the implementation.

Many businesses take on implementations after the fact as a result of other business decisions, and the implementation ends up being rushed or incomplete. The business decision to be able to support Web Services and utilize them as a revenue-producing agent, or simply as an internal business tool needs a lot of consideration and planning. The risks involved in exposing a corporate infrastructure to the Internet have been outlined above, and can have a detrimental effect on the business should the implementation be incomplete. Potential questions are many, and just a few that need to be assessed regarding risk include:

❑ How dependent on this revenue is the company, and what level of downtime are we willing to put up with from the infrastructure supporting it?

❑ To what extent is the company willing to expose its assets to potential intruders?

❑ What level of financial commitment is there toward guarding against intrusion?

As with all projects, implementing Web Services has a cost. There is hardware to buy, personnel to pay, ongoing maintenance for the equipment and software. Some of the questions that should be answered in the cost area would be:

❑ What is the budget for the project, and is it enough to do it right?

❑ Are the ongoing costs going to be covered by the revenue generation of the implementation?

❑ What is the return on investment of the implementation?

❑ Does the company currently have the people to handle the additional security requirements, or is there need to budget for additional personnel?

As far as long-term commitment goes, there is hardware and software maintenance, and the dedication of personnel to the ongoing task of security changes on the Internet. Server hardware has a limited lifetime similar to that of desktop workstations, and so there needs to be a plan of replacement and upgrades. When a corporation has an Internet site, response time can be a major factor in revenue generation, so the hardware and software on the server needs to be maintained.

Keeping up to date with the security of servers and applications that are exposed to the Internet is a daily task when done correctly. It can truly take a full-time position within a corporation to keep up with it.

There is the daily monitoring and review of reports that should be undertaken to guard against intruders and detect new ways they might attempt to get through. There is also an ongoing task of monitoring authentication credentials to make sure old, unused credentials aren't available for use in the wrong manner. Every week new viruses come out that need the servers to have patches installed so that the they can guard against a new strain.

The last, but perhaps most important, area to talk about in terms of business strategy is regarding disaster recovery. Many businesses see disasters as just natural events that could interrupt the business flow, but disaster planning is really a day-to-day plan on alternative ways to do business should it get interrupted for any period of time.

For instance, if a primary revenue source is a sales Web Service that links to many other dealers of a product and a major telephone outage occurs, that revenue source could be interrupted for a fairly long period of time. In addition, say the outage occurs on a day where payroll is being transmitted to the banks for automatic deposit into the employees accounts, and there is a deadline for that transmission. All of a sudden, not only is the business revenue interrupted, but perhaps the revenue is interrupted for employees as well. There need to be plans in place for even minor emergencies, so that day-to-day critical business processes can be continued. Having each department within the corporation prepare an alternative plan in case these processes get interrupted is critical.

A good example of this type of planning was when the world was planning for the potential of Y2K interrupting computer usage for an extended period of time. It is wonderful that there was no need for such plans in the end during that period of time, but the fact that plans were generated and in place was a very good outcome to the possibility of something going wrong. We really should be just as diligent when there is not a predictable potential for such problems, because you never know when such plans could save the entire business from financial disaster. Some of the questions to consider when formulating a disaster plan for computer system recovery are:

- What is the maximum downtime that the corporation could sustain in case of outage?
- Are there daily backups available in an offsite location should they be needed?
- Is there adequate documentation for the server configuration that supports the Web Service should it need to be replicated to another machine?
- Are the operating system software and other software required to restore the backup tapes available to be reinstalled if necessary?
- Is there more than one person on the staff who understands the configuration of the Server and Service in case the primary support person is unavailable?
- Are hardware available for substitution and timely repair contracts in place in case of hardware failure? Or if critical enough, is there redundancy currently in place to take care of such failure?
- Is there business process documentation available should an automated procedure need to be completed manually?

These are just some questions that should be included, and as each gets answered many more questions will be generated by the answer. There are tools available and sold with most backup software that facilitates disaster recovery. Offsite backup storage and configuration documentation truly play a critical role in disaster recovery. It is always a good plan to go through a disaster recovery scenario during the implementation phase of a server so that the configuration documentation can be as accurate as possible.

Conclusion

This paper has attempted to cover some critical areas of security within the organization's network infrastructure, programming, and Web Service development. We covered the following areas:

- ❑ Security within the network servers, workstations and hardware.
- ❑ Identity security through logins and authentication mechanisms.
- ❑ Windows 2000 approaches to security within the operating system.
- ❑ Internet Explorer security strategies.
- ❑ Internet sites which help with patches and security solutions.
- ❑ Infrastructure design solutions for security including firewalls, routers and VPNs.
- ❑ Programmatic concepts to consider about security.
- ❑ Highlights of programmatic security within the Microsoft .NET environment.
- ❑ Security configurations including certificates, global cache, and custom security.
- ❑ Highlights of business strategies dealing with security issues.

It is important to create a heightened awareness in both infrastructure and programming personnel so that security loopholes continue to be guarded against. There are many security concerns evolving today, and as the Internet is more accessible to everyday computer subscribers these concerns will continue to mount. There is an ever-growing resource targeting security, and many companies are building alliances with the security experts and leading anti-virus software manufacturers to provide integrated solutions to ongoing security problems. We have a way to go, and it is an ever-changing problem we are facing in this area, so vigilance will be the only answer.

Author: Jørgen Thelin

- Remote References in Existing Middleware
- Uses of Remote References
- Remote References and Web Services
- Interoperability
- Minimizing Problems

Remote References and XML Web Services

What are "remote references", and how do they relate to distributed object technology? Are the concepts of a remote object reference still applicable for Web Services technology? This paper describes the software architecture concept of remote references and shows why they are best avoided when using XML Web Services due to the fundamental mismatch between the service-oriented middleware approach of Web Services and the object-oriented middleware required to support a remote reference architecture. It assesses the impact of remote references on interoperability between different Web Service infrastructure products and applications, and examines some ways architects and developers can minimize the problems in this area. It also examines the problem of exposing as a Web Service an existing system that already uses remote references extensively as remote factory objects (which is a very common approach in mature CORBA systems), and how a simple "façade application" can be used in this context.

What Are "Remote References"?

A number of different technologies exist for building distributed client/server applications, but the most common and popular approach today is to use some type of "distributed objects", although this may well be replaced shortly by the "service-oriented" approach of XML Web Services.

Distributed Object Technology

Distributed object technology allows object-oriented software components running on one machine to be accessed from client programs running on different computers. It also allows calls between processes on the same machine where the "local" and "remote" hosts are actually the same computer. This allows distributed applications to be written without having to worry about the ultimate location of the server process – whether that is on the same computer, the same local network, or halfway across the world in the Internet. This is the important concept of "location transparency". This allows such things as testing an application in a development environment with both client and server on the same machine then, for production deployment, running each on different, bigger machines to maximize throughput of the system.

Distributed object technology is an amalgamation of the earlier concepts of remote procedure call (RPC) technology plus object-oriented programming approaches. Examples of distributed object technology include Java RMI, CORBA, and Microsoft DCOM.

For a distributed object system to work, there are five parts in the total end-to-end communication picture that are common to all different implementations of this technology:

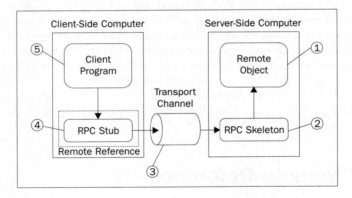

1. **The application logic itself, running on the remote computer.**
    This is the actual implementation of the remote object, written by the user.

2. **A server-side RPC skeleton, running on the remote machine.**
    This is a piece of middleware code that handles un-marshaling the parameter data for the call from its on-the-wire format used by the transport medium. The skeleton places the call invocation to the appropriate object instance, collects the return value plus any "output" parameters, and marshals all this data back into the transport format for return to the client. A return value is just a special output parameter that the middleware recognizes and treats specially. There can only be one "return value", but there may be zero or several output parameters.

Some middleware technologies (such as EJB) only allow return values, while others such as CORBA support output parameters too. In general the only real distinction between a return value and an output parameter is how they are defined in the appropriate interface description mechanism used by the middleware (such as IDL for CORBA), and the programming model used to access the values. The middleware handles all the complexities of how many values are expected, and what to do with them at each end.

3. **A transport channel.**
Some form of communication channel is required between client and server. This may take the form of a TCP socket, or some more structured channel such as message-oriented middleware or a CORBA ORB. Ultimately, this will equate to some form of physical network connection between the RPC skeleton and stub over which the call request and response data can be exchanged.

4. **A client-side RPC stub, running on the local client machine.**
This is the piece of middleware code that marshals the input parameters, passes the call to the transport medium for sending to the server-side skeleton, then collects the response data if any, and unmarshals that data back to the client program. With synchronous calls, the middleware waits for the response before returning control back to the client program; with an asynchronous call, control returns to the client program as soon as the request has been sent, and the middleware will make a call back to the client program with the response data at a later point in time once the data is returned from the server. Asynchronous calls allow the client program to perform other actions while waiting for the response. Typically RPC is equated with a synchronous call, although this is not actually a strict requirement.

5. **The client application itself, running on the local machine.**
This is the user's program, and usually provides the presentation and user interaction functions of the distributed system.

For the sake of brevity, we will not discuss the numerous differences between the different types of distributed object technology systems.

Definition of the Term Remote Reference

The phrase "Remote Reference", which is more accurately called a **remote object reference**, is used to refer to the client view of the distributed object, which is primarily the client-side stub for the distributed object running on the remote machine, but ultimately encompasses all the other parts of the picture right through to the remote server implementation if viewed at a sufficient degree of detail.

In contrast, a local object reference is the normal reference or pointer to an object in the current program execution environment, although the results are similar – they provide a separation and decoupling of the user (client) of the object component from the details and mechanics of where that object was created and where it is stored.

"Remote References" are therefore a way for object-oriented software components to interact across process or machine boundaries, but with "location transparency" from the point of view of the client program.

Examples of Remote References from Existing Middleware

There are several common middleware technologies that use remote references, although sometimes using slightly different phrases to describe the concept:

CORBA

The CORBA standard (Common Object Request Broker Architecture, see http://www.omg.org/technology/documents/corba_spec_catalog.htm) from the OMG (Object Management Group) is based exclusively around remote references – all remote CORBA objects are accessed by an objref (object reference), and the IOR (Interoperable Object Reference) format is a standardized way to represent and store these object references in a serialized binary form defined by the CORBA specifications. It is possible to pass an objref as a parameter on a call to a CORBA object, or return an objref from a call as either a return value or an output parameter. CORBA objrefs can either be transient (the object references become invalid when the server implementation program stops) or permanent (server implementation instances created on demand if necessary), and object references can last longer than lifetime of a particular object.

CORBA objrefs are usually found through a look-up of a name in a CORBA Naming service (CosNaming), by calling a CORBA Trader service (CosTrading), by calling a suitable factory object, or by using a "stringified IOR" stored in a file on disk. CosNaming is the CORBA specification for a "white pages" look-up system where a server can be looked up by its name, while CosTrading is the CORBA specification for a "yellow pages" look-up system where a server can be found based on the capabilities and attributes it has previously registered with the CosTrading service. See the OMG web site http://www.omg.org/ for more details.

Interestingly, the ORBs (Object Request Brokers) implementing the CORBA standard have mechanisms for converting object references into calls to server implementations in non object-oriented languages. They do this by employing various activation policies and request queuing mechanisms – see the CORBA specifications and language bindings for a non-OO language such as C for details of how this can be achieved.

RMI – Java Remote Method Invocation

All RMI objects are remote objects, and calls to these use their remote references obtained through some form of registry look-up – usually either the RMI Registry process, or a JNDI naming context. Normally RMI objects are transient, but the RMI Activation system provides a means for "permanent" remote object references where an instance of the server object implementation is created on demand to service the request if necessary.

EJB – Enterprise JavaBeans

The Enterprise JavaBeans framework builds on top of the RMI or CORBA distributed object technology by adding the elements of managed object life cycles, managed transaction semantics, and declarative security policies to the basic RPC mechanism.

EJB objects can either be for Stateless Session Beans, Stateful Session Beans, Entity Beans, or Message Driven Beans, but all provide a similar pattern for creating the object reference and accessing the ultimate target object:

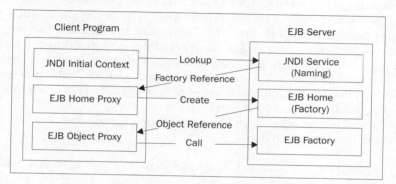

1. Get a reference to the JNDI root context through the **InitialContext** factory object.

2. Obtain a handle object to the EJB Home interface for the EJB by performing a look-up by name in the root JNDI context.

3. Narrow the handle returned to give a local proxy object for the remote EJB Home object.

4. Call a suitable "create" method on the home proxy, which will perform a remote method call to the EJB Home object on the server and return a remote reference for the actual EJB Object we wish to use.

EJB object references are mostly remote references, although EJB 2.0 has added support for "local interfaces". These "local interfaces" are a way of accessing EJBs directly inside the same process, through local object references while still maintaining the same parameter-passing semantics and programming style used for a remote call. This results in reduced invocation times since the usual remote transport and network layers can be bypassed.

DCOM

DCOM is Microsoft's RPC technology for making COM (Component Object Model) objects available across process and machine boundaries. Originally, it provided the basic RPC and object activation and life cycle facilities of RMI or CORBA, but over time it evolved to also cover the higher-level framework functions of transaction and security management through the combination of DCOM and MTS (Microsoft Transaction Server).

In DCOM programming, the remote references are typically registered with a local service manager, which acts as a registry for look-up of references to remote components based on a GUID (Globally Unique Identifier) for the target interface of the COM component.

DCOM has now been replaced by .NET Remoting as the easiest way to make a component accessible as a distributed object in a Microsoft execution environment.

.NET Remoting

Microsoft's new .NET Framework provides a standardized execution environment for component-based applications. This framework operates across any programming language and operating system that supports the .NET Framework Intermediate Language (MSIL). The .NET Framework includes as standard extensive facilities for supporting the making and receiving of remote method calls, including full control of object activation policies, declarative security, and transaction attributes. Microsoft provides extensive technical documentation on the .NET Remoting framework through the MSDN web site. For more details, see http://msdn.microsoft.com/ and http://www.msdn.microsoft.com/library/default.asp?url=/library/en-us/dndotnet/html/hawkremoting.asp.

Remote object references are obtained from an object URL specific to that remote object type – providing a form of registry look-up.

Typical Uses of Remote References

There are several common architectural design patterns where remote references are used, as outlined below.

Remote Procedure Calls

Now that the majority of new application development is done using object-oriented languages such as Java or C#, the vast majority of remote procedure calls are now done using remote references.

The typical usage pattern is for the client program to:

1. Perform some type of look-up operation to obtain a suitable remote reference.

2. Perform an operation to create a local proxy object based on this remote reference data – for example a narrow operation when using CORBA or EJB, or transparently as part of some data serialization process.

3. Then use the local proxy for all calls to the remote object.

One of the key challenges with this approach comes when using a strongly typed language such as Java or C#. Unless the appropriate interface class is available to the client program both at design time and at run-time, it is impossible to write a program that uses that remote object reference directly, and all method calls must be done through low-level reflection or DII (CORBA Dynamic Invocation Interface) framework calls. This is what is known as the **Interface distribution problem**, and can create many program packaging problems when using Java and to a large extent C# too.

The combination of remote references and an object-oriented programming language, however, greatly simplifies the task of developing distributed client/server applications.

Remote Factory Objects

This involves an interaction style typified by the approaches to connecting to an EJB object:

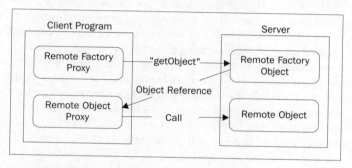

A remote reference is obtained to a "factory object" such as the EJB Home object in our example. This is a true factory in the sense of the Factory design pattern from the Gang-of-Four *"Design Patterns"* book (Addison-Wesley, ISBN 0201633612), even though it is a remote server in this case. A method call is then made to that factory object, which returns another remote reference to the "real" remote object itself (the EJB Object in this example). This second remote reference is then used for the intended operations.

There is a rather subtle assumption in play here – the assumption that the programming languages in use on both the client and server have an equivalent level of support for remote method calls and object orientation. We further assume that suitable client-side transport and RPC libraries exist to match the communication format and transport channel the server is using, and that suitable classes and interfaces already exist in the language used by the client-side program to create a semantic match with the interface used by the server-side. Obviously the easiest way to deal with this problem is to use the same programming language on both sides (for example Java-to-Java). It is equally feasible to use a clearly defined transport format (often binary) plus an abstract interface definition language and the appropriate language mapping specifications (the approach taken by CORBA or DCOM). A final approach would be to use a standardized RPC framework built on top of a standardized binary intermediate language, which is the approach taken by .NET.

Client Callback

The other major usage of remote references is for the distributed architectural pattern known as "client callback". This is where a client program creates a remote reference for a callback interface in its own process, and then passes that remote reference to a different remote server object running on a different machine to register to receive callback notifications from the server to the client process.

One of the biggest challenges when using any form of client callback system occurs in a situation where the client and server machines are separated by complex network topology. This is especially true where a client-side firewall exists between the client and server, which is the situation in almost all large corporations nowadays.

Any time a remote reference passes through a firewall or network bridge / router, it is quite likely that it will become invalidated due to network address translation or TCP port access security policies built into the firewall. For example a remote reference that contains an endpoint IP address of 192.168.0.2 will not work beyond the local network at all because this address is in the "non-routable" address range. Similarly very few firewalls in large organizations are configured to allow any incoming traffic into the corporate network at all (even on well-known ports such as 80), and all incoming calls are generally routed to segregated computers in a DMZ (Demilitarized Zone) where they can be closely monitored and controlled. Various types of application- or middleware-specific solutions have been tried in the past to solve this problem, but generally without much widespread success. The only generally accepted way around the firewall problem is to use a form of client-pull-based notification system, which ultimately boils down to the client polling for updates with a usual request-response style interaction that can easily pass through firewalls.

Remote References and Web Services

Having examined the general concept of remote references, and how they have been handled to date in existing distributed communications technology, it is now time to turn our focus on to the emerging area of XML Web Services technology, and look at how remote references fit into the new picture.

Applying Remote Reference Principles to Web Services

The concept of remote references can be mapped fairly cleanly into Web Service technology. The data required to represent a remote reference can be encoded into an XML format using the approach of a composite data type with the appropriate fields. A schema definition can be created for this representation, so that a remote object reference can be serialized into a recognizable form on the wire. When the remote reference data arrives on the client, the data can be stored in an appropriate internal storage object created by the middleware library ready for a suitable interface to be applied to make it usable to the client program.

There is the obvious question of who creates and controls the schema definition for the remote references, and the possibility that multiple competing formats may exist, up to one per possible implementation language that exists in the works. All of these are concerns for Web Services infrastructure vendors, but are likely to be resolved over time as the technology matures. The XML Protocol working group at W3C (http://www.w3.org/2000/xp/Group/) is looking at the related areas of the Asynchronous Messaging and Event Notification usage patterns, although they are not yet looking at the standardization of remote references specifically at the moment.

Remote Object Factory

The situation of a Web Service that acts as a "factory" for another service instance is much harder to deal with using general purpose Web Service software. This factory service will attempt to return the remote reference data for the client to construct a client-side proxy for the second service, and then use that newly constructed proxy for further communications. This requires a language capable of dynamically creating local proxy instances and the necessary SOAP libraries for the client-side programming language that can recognize this data as the representation for a remote reference and act accordingly. Finally, there needs to be a suitable pre-existing interface to provide a wrapper for the local proxy and make it usable in a strongly typed language such as Java.

The easiest way around this is to create a "composite service" that executes on the server but encapsulates the factory-based usage that would have to be done on the client side when remote references are being used. This has several advantages – it keeps the controlling logic on the server where it arguably should be for maximum scalability, it minimizes network communications traffic, and keeps all technology-specific constructs in the same technology domain.

Client Callback

All the previous discussion of the problem of factory objects applies equally to the client callback situation, just obviously in the reverse direction of course. As a simple example, how would a Visual Basic client program create a suitable remote reference to pass to a Java Web Service? Even though a VB.NET program may be able to create a callback reference compatible with .NET Remoting without too much trouble, it is not likely to be in the form that is directly usable with a Java Web Service. If the client and server use different middleware, a user may well have to implement a SOAP listener to receive request messages for the exported remote reference interface required by the server in order to be able to receive client callbacks, rather than this being handled automatically by the middleware libraries.

In addition, all the problems with client-side firewalls and network topology that were present in the non-Web Service situation are also present here. This will typically prevent the server talking directly back to the client, even through a well-known port such as HTTP port 80.

The WSDL specification has constructs for describing such client callbacks in a standard manner (the "Solicit-response" or "Notification" transmission types in a *PortType* definition), but this does not particularly help solve any of the above problems. Although WSDL allows the message formats and interaction style to be specified, there is currently no way to specify the additional configuration information needed to make this actually work in practice. As an example, there is no standardized way to specify a "client endpoint address" (such as a hostname and port number where a HTTP server will be listening for SOAP messages in the client program). Some form of "register" operation would need to be performed to inform the server of the client endpoint addressing and routing information before a client callback can work, and this is currently completely proprietary.

To be able to handle server-to-client communication in a standard manner across any network topology, Web Services infrastructure vendors need to use a client-pull style notification system, rather than through the use of remote references.

Interoperability Considerations

Having looked at how remote references can fit in with Web Services, it is now time to look at some of the interoperability considerations that face prospective projects in this area.

Language Interoperability

One of the main problems with the use of remote references, whether Web Service-based or not, is where different programming languages are being used on the client and server sides. It can be extremely hard to bridge this technology gap when remote references are involved, purely through the differences in the execution environment and run-time framework class libraries.

When Web Services are involved though, this is especially problematic as one of the main purposes of using XML-based Web Service communications is precisely to enable the easy communicating between different technologies.

Web Service Interoperability

The question of which schema definition is used for the remote reference data on the wire is an immediate problem, as there are currently at least three different formats in widespread use including Microsoft (.NET Remoting), Systinet (WASP), and the Indiana University SoapTeam group (XSOAP/SoapRMI).

In theory it would be possible for Web Service tools and SOAP libraries to recognize and support several different formats, but in practice this tends not to happen for various commercial and philosophical reasons. Because of this, deploying Web Services that use remote references almost always restricts use of that service to clients using exactly the same SOAP libraries as were used on the server.

Given that one of the fundamental purposes of using Web Services is to maximize interoperability, there are very few situations where this implementation choice could be viewed as anything other than highly limiting. There are only a few companies or organizations that have the dominant position to be able to dictate communications infrastructure to their suppliers and customers, and after all this is precisely the sort of tight coupling that Web Services technology is trying to avoid. It is not enough to agree to use the same schema definitions, because remote references require additional semantic interpretation of the remote reference data construct in the schema to create the local proxies for the remote reference to be usable. There is a big difference between just SOAP interoperability (where SOAP is just the transport medium) and true Web Services interoperability.

WSDL Interoperability

In general, the use of remote references does not create any interoperability problems at the WSDL level. All remote reference formats have type definitions based on the XML Schema standard, which can be read by tools from all the different vendors. The appropriate remote reference schema definition will be imported into the WSDL file for the Web Service, and can be syntactically decoded correctly by any Web Service development tools or run-time libraries. The only problem then becomes that additional semantic interpretation of that remote reference schema definition has to occur, and there is currently no way of specifying this fact in a WSDL definition.

Minimizing Problems with Remote References

By far the easiest way to minimize problems with remote references is simply not to use them at all! There are very few scenarios, if any, where what we are trying to achieve by using remote references cannot be achieved by other more "service-oriented" mechanisms.

For the situation of exposing as a Web Service an existing system that already uses remote references extensively as factory objects (which is a very common approach in mature CORBA systems), it is usually easier to create a simple "façade application" that mirrors the interface of the underlying service, but uses opaque handle values or tokens to ensure all reference objects remain in the same technology domain. Thus we avoid the problem of programming language semantic mismatch or technology translation gaps. This task can be done transparently by suitable infrastructure tools, so is not as big a challenge as it may at first appear. This is also an approach widely used for creating stateless façades to handle the mapping of stateful service instances, to keep the control in the right place (on the server, not on the client), and is where lessons from designing stateless DCOM systems are particularly relevant. This "re-purposing" of interfaces is an entirely desirable state of affairs, as one of the main reasons for using Web Services is to maintain low dependency and high interoperability between applications through the use of loosely coupled interfaces and loosely coupled interactions. A more detailed examination of this topic is beyond the scope of this paper.

Where the decision is taken that remote references are going to be used by a Web Service, then it is better to restrict that service to internal use inside the corporate firewall. It will be extremely hard unless you are a large company (Ford- or General Electric-sized, say) to get all your trading partners to change to using the same SOAP library as you have chosen just so they can use that one particular Web Service from your company, but it is considerably easier to adopt an in-house technology standard. By definition, remote references create a much tighter coupling between the client and server because of the additional semantic interpretation of the returned data to make remote references work – certain parts of the return data need to be extracted from the message and translated into a local proxy for the remote object reference.

Finally remember that, as soon as remote references are used in an application, the problems of "distributed garbage collection" need to be borne in mind so as not to restrict server scalability. When the server has full control of remote object lifecycles, it can take steps to intelligently optimize the number of object instances in existence at any point in time to match the current demand from clients.

Without distributed garbage collection features built into the distributed object technology, the client program has the responsibility to explicitly perform a "disconnect" or "close" operation so that the server middleware knows it is then safe to clean up and recycle the object instance and connection in use by that client. Whether through programming errors in the client program, or network communication problems, it is quite easy for this "disconnect" notification to not occur in a timely manner, meaning that server resources have to be tied up for longer than they need be. A distributed garbage collection system can detect when client programs have disconnected, even if they have not performed the normal "clean" disconnection. In a heavily used server environment, the difference between running with and without distributed garbage collection can be highly significant, although not all distributed object technologies have this facility, and currently SOAP falls into the latter group.

Conclusions

One of the hardest parts of a software architect's job is making decisions about the implementation technology and approach to use to solve a particular business requirement. All the new XML Web Services technology is making many fashionable sounding things possible now that were previously impossible or very hard. It is still the software architects' responsibility to consider the long-term implications of the decisions they make at the early stages of the technology adoption cycle, and there are a number of problem areas that need very careful decisions.

This paper has explored some of the mismatch between the service-oriented middleware approach of Web Services and the object-oriented middleware approach required to support a remote reference architecture. We have looked in detail at the effect of using remote references in conjunction with XML Web Services technology on application interoperability, to allow you to make more informed decisions for your organization.

Index

A Guide to the Index

The index is arranged in word-by-word order (so that New York would appear before Newark). Unmodified headings represent the principal treatment of a topic and acronyms have been preferred to their expansions as main entries.

B

E

R

rating Web Services, 209
RBAC (Role Based Access Control)
   Internet security model, 292, 302
   use by Grand Central, 299
   use by Web servers, 300
   use by Web Services framework providers, 296
RDBMS (Relational Database Management Systems) and
   Web Services security, 301
real estate industry
   benefits of Web Services, 146
   parties involved, 144
   use of Web Services, 143
      business drivers, 147
      case study, 150
      case study imlementation, 154
      technical drivers, 147
   web sites for end-users, 145
real-time B2Bi, 62
refacing, EAI, 43
registries
   see also ebXML; UDDI.
   Web Services publishing technology, 259
registry interface, UDDI, 125
Registry Service Interface, ebXML, 234
regulatory requirements and STP implementation, 177
remote factory objects
   use of remote references, 325
   Web Services as, 327
remote references
   definition, 321
   distributed garbage collection problem, 330
   interoperability considerations, 328
   middleware technologies using, 322
      CORBA, 322
      DCOM, 323
      EJBs, 323
      .NET Remoting, 324
      RMI, 322
   minimizing problems with, 329
   restricting to internal use, 330
   typical uses, 324
   Web Services and, 326
   XML Web Services and, 319
repositories, advantages of centralizing, 53
Repository, ebXML, 224
research on Web Services suppliers, 210
reusablilty of code and ROI calculations, 17
revenue streams
   Web Services industry roles and, 35
   Web Services revenue generation, 2, 4
RFQ (Request For Quotes)
   e-logistics process, 103
   UPS, deployed service information screenshot, 110
   Web Service provided by ELPIF, 107
   XML templates, 109
risk assessment
   quantifying risks as potential expenses, 21
   Web Services introduction, 315
risk management and ROI, 19
RMI (Remote Method Invocation), 237
   distributed object technology example, 320
   technology using remote references, 322
robustness advantage of J2EE, 285
ROI (Return On Investment), 9
   diversity of models, 13, 22
   example calculation, 10
   formula for calculating, 9, 284
      steps in applying, 20
   methodologies introduced, 10
   necessity of, for technology projects, 12
   risk management and, 19
   Web Services and, 12
      business benefits, 18
      costs and expenses, 14
      factors to include, 14
      models, tangible and intangible benefits, 13
      non-technical factors, 13
      technical benefits, 16
   Web Services used for EAI, 53
role-based security advantage of .NET, 285
roles in Web Services development, 213
roles, Web Services
   security requirements of, 291
RosettaNet
   BPSS precursor, 163
   e-commerce standards and, 64
   PIPs (Partner Interface Processes), 80, 91
   quoted on ebXML, 228
   Web Services workflow level language, 293
routing between specificed Web Services
   Intermediaries, 206
RPC (Remote Procedure Calls)
   see also JAX-RPC.
   DCOM as Microsoft's RPC technology, 323
   differences between Web Services and, 52
   distributed object technology and, 320
   superiority of Web Services for synchronous
      integration, 188
   use of remote references, 324
RPC-style Web Services, BEA Systems, 254
RTTM (Real-Time Trade Matching), GSCC, 179
   use of Web Services, 192
      advantages over current implementation, 195
rules component, Web Services Intermediaries, 205

S

SAML (Security Assertion Markup Language), 294, 299
SANS (System Administration, Networking and Security)
   Institute, 309
SAP
   MySAP uses broker hubs, 92
   Service Oriented Architecture, 93
   use of UDDI, 93
   Web Application Server, 286
   Web Services providers, 298
Save Binding UDDI publishing API call, 135
Save Business UDDI publishing API call, 135
Save Service UDDI publishing API call, 135
Save Technical Model UDDI publishing API call, 136
scalability
   integration broker open architectures and, 75
   integration broker required support, 77
   J2EE advantage over .NET, 269, 271, 285
   multi-hub integration broker architecture, 74
   requirement of B2Bi solutions, 60
schema definitions and interoperability, 328
SCM (Supply Chain Management)
   effect of defining UDDI fingerprints, 138
   ERP specialization for, 86
   ERP vendors' encroachment into, 98
   Product Shipment Status example, 80
   special case of e-commerce, 119

Notes

Notes

EXPERT

Registration Code: | 4132R4W5AYRVMH01 |

Expert writes books for you. Any suggestions, or ideas about how you want information given in your ideal book will be studied by our team. Your comments are always valued at Expert.

Free phone in USA 800-873 9769
Fax (312) 893 8001

UK Tel.: (0121) 687 4100   Fax: (0121) 687 4101

Web Services Business Strategies and Architectures – Registration Card

Name _____

Address _____

_____

_____

_____

City _____ State/Region _____

Country _____ Postcode/Zip _____

E-Mail _____

Occupation _____

How did you hear about this book?

☐ Book review (name) _____

☐ Advertisement (name) _____

☐ Recommendation _____

☐ Catalog _____

☐ Other _____

Where did you buy this book?

☐ Bookstore (name) _____ City _____

☐ Computer store (name) _____

☐ Mail order _____

☐ Other _____

What influenced you in the purchase of this book?

☐ Cover Design   ☐ Contents   ☐ Other (please specify):

How did you rate the overall content of this book?

☐ Excellent   ☐ Good   ☐ Average   ☐ Poor

What did you find most useful about this book? _____

What did you find least useful about this book? _____

_____

Please add any additional comments. _____

_____

What other subjects will you buy a computer book on soon?

_____

What is the best computer book you have used this year?

_____

Note: This information will only be used to keep you updated about new Wrox Press titles and will not be used for any other purpose or passed to any other third party.

EXPERT

Note: If you post the bounce back card below in the UK, please send it to:

Expert, Arden House, 1102 Warwick Road,
Acocks Green, Birmingham B27 6HB. UK.

Computer Book Publishers

BUSINESS REPLY MAIL

FIRST CLASS MAIL   PERMIT#64   CHICAGO, IL

POSTAGE WILL BE PAID BY ADDRESSEE

**Expert.,
29 S. LA SALLE ST.,
SUITE 520
CHICAGO IL 60603-USA**